A Journey in Translation

A Journey in Translation

Anne Hébert's Poetry in English

by

LEE SKALLERUP BESSETTE

University of Ottawa Press | OTTAWA

uOttawa

EDITING MODERNISM *in Canada*

The University of Ottawa Press gratefully acknowledges the support extended to its publishing list by the Government of Canada, the Canada Council for the Arts, and the Ontario Arts Council. This book has been published with the help of a grant from the Federation for the Humanities and Social Sciences, through the Awards to Scholarly Publications Program, using funds provided by the Social Sciences and Humanities Research Council of Canada.

Copy editing: Robbie McCaw
Proofreading: Helen Guri
Typesetting: CS
Cover design: Édiscript enr.
Cover image: Elizabeth Schwaiger

Library and Archives Canada Cataloguing in Publication

Skallerup, Lee, 1977-, author
A journey in translation : Anne Hébert's poetry in English / by Lee Skallerup Bessette.

(Canadian literature collection)
Includes bibliographical references and index.
Issued in print and electronic formats.
ISBN 978-0-7766-2376-4 (paperback).--ISBN 978-0-7766-2377-1 (pdf).--
ISBN 978-0-7766-2378-8 (epub).--ISBN 978-0-7766-2379-5 (mobi)

1. Hébert, Anne, 1916-2000--Translations into English--History and criticism. 2. Canadian poetry (French)--20th century--Translations into English--History and criticism. I. Title. II. Title: Anne Hébert's poetry in English. III. Series: Canadian literature collection

PS8515.E16Z887 2016 C841'.54 C2016-904881-0
C2016-904882-9

Printed in Canada by Gauvin Press

Contents

Acknowledgements

This book, which started out as my PhD dissertation, has been almost fifteen years in the making, and thus has fifteen years of people to acknowledge and thank. First and foremost, I would like to thank the University of Alberta's comparative literature program and Faculty of Graduate Studies. I was able to teach for four years, travel to many conferences, perform research on various travel grants, and take a year off to complete my dissertation. The financial support was truly appreciated. I would also like to thank my supervisor, Dr. Lynn Penrod. She supported my research, my administrative aspirations, and let me do the project I had envisioned. I would also like to thank Dr. Albert Braz for his support, patience, and a place to stay while I attended Trent University, in Peterborough; Dr. E. D. Blodgett for his thoughts on translation and Canadian literature; Dr. Anne Malena for her thorough editing job and useful suggestions; and my external reader, Dr. Sherry Simon. I would also like to thank Dr. Carl Amrhein for his sound advice and sympathetic ear.

The idea for this dissertation came while I was still an undergraduate student at the Université de Sherbrooke. Dr. Richard Giguère introduced me to the poetry of Anne Hébert and *Dialogue sur la traduction*, an exchange between a writer, Hebert, and a translator, F. R. Scott. He also allowed me to begin comparing translations of Hébert's "The Tomb of Kings" for a paper in his class. I will be eternally grateful for the wonderful journey he unknowingly sent me on. I would also like to thank Dr. Gregory J. Reid for his supervision of a long MA thesis. If I hadn't ever completed that, I would never have arrived here.

My research would have been impossible without the help of countless reference librarians, both in Canada and the United States. Here is a list of some of the people who helped me along the way (there are countless other librarians and staff members who undoubtedly spent hours fulfilling my photocopying requests who shall remain nameless, but no less appreciated). I would like to thank Bernadine Dodge and Jodi Aoki from Trent University; Stephen C. Jones and Ellen Cordes of the Beinecke Rare Book and Manuscript Library at Yale; Richard Virr and Mary Houde at McGill; Christiane Bisson and Natalie Watteyne from the Centre Anne-Hébert at the Université de Sherbrooke; Patti Auld Johnson at the University of New Brunswick, Saint John; Jennifer Toews and Sandra Alston at the University of Toronto; Apollonia Steele at the University of Calgary; Jessica Coffey at Oxford University Press; Catherine Bernier at Université de Montréal; Rebecca C. Cape, B. Breon Mitchell, Erika Dowell, and Michael Taylor at Indiana University, Bloomington; and finally, Anne Goddard, Alex McEwan, Sophie Tellier, Alain Lamarche, and Janet Murray at the National Archives in Ottawa. More recently, thank you to June Can at the Beinecke Library, Penny R. Ramon at the Lilly Library, Allison Wagner at the University of Calgary, Lauren Williams at the University of Toronto, and Sara Viinalass-Smith at the Library of Canada; I am grateful because they were able to provide for me the reference information I had neglected to save all those years ago in order to complete this manuscript.

There were others who were invaluable to me in navigating the archives. I would like to thank William Toye for granting me permission to visit the F. R. Scott and John Glassco archives. Brian Busby, who has written a biography of John Glassco and happened to be at the Glassco archives the same time I was, provided me with letters from Glassco regarding his views on translation later in his life, for which I am grateful. Patricia Godbout, whose theoretical approach became the centrepiece for my dissertation, not only provided me with the courage to continue on in my research, knowing there were others out there doing similar work, but also introduced me to a number of letters I never even knew existed. And Jo-Anne Elder, for whom my project became more personal, graciously shared with me stories and memories on her long-time colleague and collaborator Fred Cogswell, and her father, David Elder. She was also very supportive of my overall approach and project. I benefited from friends who lived close to some of the archives and were able to make last-minute visits and get me needed documentation, so thank you to Chris Doody and Trip Kirkpatrick for indulging me and sending me much-appreciated gems from the archives.

Some of the authors and translators discussed in my book were kind enough to answer my questions and share their insight with me. Daniel Slote granted me an interview at his home in Montreal, and it was a wonderful conversation. Graham Dunstan Martin wrote letters to me, answering my questions, and he sent me his press clipping as well as some of the original drafts of his translations. Willis Barnstone was also kind enough to chat with me about translation. Janis L. Pallister sent some of her drafts and correspondences electronically, which were invaluable as well. I would also like to thank P. K. Page, John Robert Colombo, Leslie Monkman, Morton Weinfeld, Bernard Pozier, Lola Lemire Tostevin, Wanda Campbell, and Evan Jones for their e-mail correspondences with me.

No dissertation or manuscript is without a few bumps in the road. A few well-timed conferences as I went through the process of writing helped me get out of slumps. So to Denise Merkle, who organized the conference "Translating from the Margins" at Université de Moncton, and Suzanne Jill Levine, who organized "Translation in a Non-Literary Age" at UC Santa Barbara, I say "thank you." At both conferences, I met and was able to speak with a number of translators and scholars who offered me their feedback and support, notably Sherry Simon and Lawrence Venuti. Their words of encouragement and feedback were timed perfectly and pushed me forward in my writing and my thinking. I would also like to thank Moira Killoran and Amy Benson Brown for the help and support to make the final push to polish this study into the book it is today. I have also benefited from the assistance and support of Dean Irvine and the Editing Modernism in Canada project. His enthusiasm for the project was invaluable, and I'm glad that the archival research I did will have a new life and a new home with EMiC. I wouldn't have been put in touch with him if not for Melissa Dalgleish, whom I met at the CWRC2 Canadian Women Writers: Space/Place/Play conference. All of these events and interactions reminded me that my work is a part of a larger dialogue and that I am a part of a larger community of scholars. I am also grateful for the patience and support Dominike Thomas at the University of Ottawa Press brought to shepherding this publication into existence, alongside Elizabeth Schwaiger, who, among other things, designed the cover, and copy editor Robbie McCaw, whose eye for detail greatly improved the scholarship herein.

To my friends and family who supported me throughout this journey, you will forever have my love and gratitude. Over the fifteen-plus years it took to prepare this book, I've lived in two countries, four American states, worked at seven different universities, gotten married, and had two kids. Every step along the way added another layer to this work. I would also be remiss not to mention how important my large and eclectic networked community was in supporting me during this long process. But my husband has been there from the beginning of this book, when I excitedly described my dissertation project to him on the night we first met.

This book, however, is dedicated to my Nanny and Granddad, who did not live to see it published. They are always in my heart.

A NOTE ON DOCUMENTATION AND THE ARCHIVES IN THE TEXT

The archives cited herein are varied and inconsistent in their documentation format. Every effort has been made to give as much information to the reader as possible in order to allow for further research and consultation of the primary sources used here. Below is a key to the abbreviations used in the parentheticals throughtout the book.

Alan Brown fonds—ABF

Barnstone MSS

Blackfish Press fonds—BPF

Contact Press records—CPR

Fiddlehead/Cogswell Papers—FCP

Fonds Anne-Hébert—FAH

Francis Reginald Scott fonds—FRSF

Gael Turnbull fonds—GTF

John Glassco fonds—JGF

Louis Dudek fonds—LDF

Mordecai Richler fonds—MRF

P. K. Page fonds—PKPF

A. Poulin papers and BOA Editions records—AP-BOA

Raymond Souster Papers—RSP

A NOTE ON TRANSLATION

All translations in the text, unless otherwise noted, are by the author herself. Thank you to Elizabeth Schwaiger for her feedback and advice.

Introduction

In 2013, Les Presses de l'Université de Montréal published, as part of their now-defunct Bibliothèque du Nouveau Monde collection, the first volume of the *Œuvres complètes d'Anne Hébert*, which focused on the author's complete works of poetry. Edited by Nathalie Watteyne, the book is an exhaustive critical edition, complete with annotations, versions, and introductory essays. Rare for a scholarly work of this nature, it received glowing reviews in both major French-language Montreal daily newspapers, *Le Devoir* and *La Presse*. In her review for *La Presse*, Chantal Guy calls Hébert "l'un de nos plus importants écrivains," while Marie-Andrée Lamontagne in *Le Devoir* says that Hébert's poetry has reached "le statut de classique." And Anne Hébert's poetry remains central to understanding her larger body of work; as Watteyne said in Lamontagne's review, "Chaque fois qu'elle terminait un roman, elle retournait à la forme brève. J'ai l'impression qu'on ne peut plus maintenant parler de sa poésie de la même manière." As put by Mary Lewis Shaw in her book, *The Cambridge Introduction to French Poetry*, Hébert is the "preeminent woman poet from Québec" (136).

But Hébert's poetry isn't just celebrated in Quebec. She is one of the best-known twentieth-century Québécoise authors; her death, in 2000, was noted in extensive obituaries in both the *Los Angeles Times* and *New York Times*. Her poetry and prose have transcended formidable regional and linguistic barriers to become part of the canon of world literature. Her case is unique in Canadian literary history. Hébert is considered one of Canada's foremost poets, and in both of the county's official languages. But she is also considered an important voice in French-language poetry more generally. Moreover, her inclusion in the larger French canon eventually facilitated her translation into the English-language version of the French canon as well, paving the way for her inclusion in the "world" literary canon.

Exactly how did this one woman's work travel so much further than the vast majority of that by Québécois[1] authors? Though the haunting quality of her art partly explains her wide appeal, her work would have never travelled so far without the effort of scores of passionately committed translators, editors, and archivists. Textual-studies pioneer Jerome McGann[2] highlights how all texts are in fact "social texts," with many different hands shaping the text before, during, and after publication. The amazing journey of Hébert's work was charted by people that critic André Lefevere describes as "in the middle" of the process of editing, publishing, distributing, and preservation. Though the work of such "middle men" is seldom recognized, much less scrutinized as a factor in shaping the meaning and reach of an artist, in Herbert's case a fascinating and extensive record of paratextual documents provides evidence of their influence. This study will interrogate the "socialization" (to use McGann's term) that led to pieces of Anne Hébert's œuvre's journey into a larger literary world.

This book traces the remarkable journey of Hébert's shifting authorial identity as versions of her work travelled through complex and contested linguistic and national terrain from the late 1950s until today. Though the impact of translation, editions, and archival work has been largely ignored in studies of Canadian literary history, the treasure trove of such paratextual records in Hébert's case allows us to better understand the reach of her work. More importantly, it provides insight into and raises critical questions about the textually mediated process of nation-building and literary-canon formation. Thus, the question this study seeks to answer is who made these texts in English? This is a question Martha Nell Smith explores in her own groundbreaking archival research on Emily Dickinson.[3] Pushing past the cult of personality that surrounds Dickinson, Smith focuses instead on the socially mediated textuality of Dickinson's published and unpublished writings. Like Smith, I am interested in socially mediated elements of Hébert's translations into and publication in English. The "who" at the centre of my exploration of Hébert's work are the people who were inspired by her poetry to translate and more widely disseminate her poems to a wider audience.

Certainly, these kinds of critical analyses of translation and anthologization have taken place in Canada, particularly in regards to the development of national identity that took place in the 1960s, but they rarely cross both linguistic *and* national lines. In looking at the specific journey of Anne Hébert, I will be taking an approach described by Kathy Mezei as looking at "the particular system of the text, the system of the culture out of which the text has sprung, and the cultural system in which the [translation has been] created" (Mezei, "Speak" 15) to see how these shaped the image of the author in English. More commonly known as a polysystem approach, it is an effort to consider the multitude of influences on the translation, translator, editor, and anthologizer, as well as the critical reception of the work.[4] Much like McGann, the polysystem approach seeks to answer the question who made this text, or what process of socialization was involved in the making of the text? As feminist translator and scholar Barbara Godard argues:

> Criticism and translation are two important modalities of textual 'manipulation' which, along with literary history, anthologizing, and many types of paritextual apparatus (prefaces, advertising, book jackets, etc.) engage in mediation and negotiation between different fields or different positions in a field, and so realign borders. Such rewriting functions metatextually to determine its reception in the process of forming an audience by means of specific textual regularities and performativity of discourse. Forms of 'rewriting' propose a certain ideology and a certain poetics in function of a given socioeconomic power by means of which one culture intervenes on another. ("A Literature in the Making" 58)

How was Hébert re-written into various canons and contexts, and how did she dynamically influence that process?

Vital to this study is the inclusion of archival research in order to more fully understand the systems Godard describes above. Unfortunately, this type of archival research is not very common in Canadian literature. Outside of two recent studies by Patricia Godbout[5] and Jane Everett,[6] there is little research on how archival research can inform our understanding of issues of translations, canon formation, and nation-building. Clearly, this type of archival research, as applied to translations studies, needs to be expanded. Not only does it provide a greater understanding, as Godbout points out in her work, of the formation of nation and national identity, but it brings the translator into a central and visible position. With the rise of globalization, archival research on translations and translators promises to shed new light on the process of cultural exportation. James S. Holmes defines the translator of poetry as a metapoet, and the archive provides invaluable insight into what he calls the "activity of confrontation and resolution," or

> the activity of organizing and resolving a confrontation between the norms and conventions of one linguistic system, literary tradition, and poetic sensibility, as embodied in the original poem as he has analysed it, and the norms and conventions of another linguistic system, literary tradition, and poetic sensibility to be drawn on for the metapoem he hopes to create (11)

In the case of Hébert, and indeed as regards her translators and anthologizers, the archives are invaluable in understanding her shaping and evolution as an author in the English-speaking world. Diaz-Diocaretz looks at the translator ("translator-function," as she calls it) as both an omniscient reader and an active writer. She points to the lack of analysis of the translator as reader (16), and one of the ways we may be able to close that gap is through archival resources. Many of the letters by the translators of Hébert's poetry focus on their initial readings of her poetry. As an active writer, the translator must make choices

> which are motivated by the will to solve translation problems, [while] the translator's own cultural and ideological presuppositions are a major factor, besides specific interests and objectives, and in addition to the restrictions imposed by language use and aesthetic norms in a given system. (27)

This insight into the process of translators further evidences how they perform as metapoets, in a sense, and again illustrates ways in which the archives can be useful in understanding the translator's decisions, influences, and so on. Many of Hébert's translators are open about their political, aesthetic, and cultural biases in their letters discussing their translations, providing an opportunity for us to further analyze the complex process of translating. And even if they did not account for those aspects that Diaz-Diocaretz addresses as being important for the translator to consider, the archives reveal the what and the why of their decisions, or their nescience. To fully understand their actions, however, we must first look more closely at the figure who compelled them to the translation table or to include and share her poetry in a wider context.

ANNE HÉBERT, HER POETRY, AND THEIR TRANSLATION

Anne Hébert is both an important and fascinating figure in Québécois and Canadian letters. Her career spans a time of great upheaval in Quebec. Her first collection of poems, *Les Songes en équilibre*, appeared in 1942, during the height of Canada's (and Quebec's) involvement in the Second World War. Jeanne L'Archevêque-Duguay, in a review, stated that when "[un] livre est beau et grand quand, en le méditant, nous sentons qu'il enrichit l'esprit, élève l'âme, enchante l'oreille. *Les Songes en équilibre* remplissent cette mission" (10; a book is beautiful and significant, when, as we peruse it, we sense that it enriches our spirit, lifts our soul, enchants our ears. *Les Songes en équilibre* fulfills this mission). Eleven years later, in 1953, Hébert published *Le Tombeau des rois*, which firmly established her as a new and important poetic voice emerging from Quebec, and prompted Gilles Marcotte in *Le Devoir* to call her "un grand poète." This collection was published during the *grande noirceur* (great darkness), the period when Maurice Duplessis was premier of the province and when rural, Catholic values dominated the social and political narrative in Quebec, while the population nonetheless became more urban and secular. Duplessis died in 1959, the Quiet Revolution began in 1960, and that same year, after having published her first novel, Hébert released *Poèmes*, a book containing the poems from *Le Tombeau des rois* as well as a new collection, *Mystère de la parole*, for which she won a Governor General's Literary Award for Poetry. At this point, frustrated by her inability to find a publisher in Quebec, Hébert had relocated in Paris, becoming a part of a generation of Quebec authors who chose to flee the oppressiveness of Quebec society at the time. Hébert would publish poems only sporadically after that, concentrating instead on prose writing, until 1992, when *Le Jour n'a d'égal que la nuit* appeared, which was a collection of older, uncollected poems, as well as new ones. Grazia Merler outlined the evolution that had taken place in this new collection: "À la différence, cependant, des trois autres recueils qui tracent un parcours intime et spirituel de la mort vers la vie, celui-ci explore différentes attitudes à l'égard de la vie et de la réalité quotidienne, différents états d'âme et impressions" (110). One year later, *Œuvre poétique: 1950–1990* was published,[7] containing all of her collections of poems, except *Les Songes en équilibre*. Her final collection of poems, *Poèmes pour la main gauche*, was published in 1997. André Brochu noted the full circle Hébert had completed: "L'auteur renoue avec la perfection du discours, la diction très personnelle, l'originalité profonde du *Tombeau des rois*, sans toutefois répéter l'exploit du poème-synthèse qui terminait le recueil de 1953" (259; The author returns with the same perfection of discourse, a very personal diction, and the profound originality of Tomb of Kings without ever repeating the feat of *poème-synthèse* that concluded the 1953 collection).

Her importance in Québec literature cannot be overstated. Often read as allegories to Québecois nationalism, her poems represented a new and dynamic voice that appeared at a time when there was heavy censorship of literature in Quebec by the Catholic Church. The *Dictionnaire des œuvres littéraires du Québec* offers this nationalistic interpretation of *Le Tombeau des rois*, by Pierre-Hervé Lemieux:

> *Mais la grande poésie se montre capable non seulement de recueillir mais aussi de faire crouler l'expérience commune enfouie en la mémoire…Un tel renversement, celui qu'opère le* Tombeau des rois, *est proprement historique même s'il a pu passer presque inaperçu malgré les critiques louangeuses qui revélaient en fait la fusion réussie d'une écriture toute personnelle et d'une préoccupation collective. Il est enfin significatif que cet exploit, comme le signale Pierre Emmanuel, le préfacier, s'opère 'à Québec', en cette capitale, défavorisée par tant de séquelles coloniales ou cléricales et qui regagne ainsi,—comme avec Saint-Denys Garneau, Alain Grandbois et Roger Lemelin,—quelque chose du leadership littéraire ancien qu'elle avait perdu.* (1001; But great poetry succeeds in not only gathering but also breaking down the

> collective experience buried in memory...A reversal of this kind, at work in *Le Tombeau des Rois*, is steeped in history, even though it may have gone unnoticed despite rave reviews that revealed the successful merging of an intensely personal style with an interest in collective concerns. It is significant, then, as pointed out in the Preface by Pierre Emmanuel, that this was accomplished in Québec, in this capital city, looked down upon by the colonial or clerical powers who were in charge respectively, and thus reclaims—alongside Saint-Denys Garneau, Alain Grandbois, and Roger Lemelin—some of the historical literary leadership that had been lost.)

Here we see the tendency to inflate the poems as symbols of Quebec culture and society: the oppression of "la grande noirceur." Lemieux is not the only critic who sees Hébert's poetry through this lens, as Axel Maugey,[8] René Lacôte,[9] Denis Bouchard,[10] Pierre Pagé,[11] and Pierre Popovic,[12] among others, all share this perspective to varying degree.

A more apolitical perspective was equally popular and evolved simultaneously with the nationalist stream. Within this group there are a number of sub-divisions; these sub-divisions, however, all share the tendency to abandon a political interpretation for a more general interpretation, choosing instead to link Hébert's poetic vision to larger poetic traditions. One of the more common approaches to Hébert's poetry is structuralist analysis—for instance, that of Jean-Louis Major[13] and Delbert W. Russell.[14] Other methodologies include those linking her to the modernist tradition (Philippe Haeck,[15] Marilyn Gaddis Rose,[16] Robert Harvey[17]) or the symbolist tradition (France Nazaire Garant,[18] Guy Robert,[19] Évelyne Voldeng,[20] Janis Pallister,[21] Lucille Roy[22]). These critics have all chosen a primarily apolitical approach to Hébert's poems.

These two broadly defined critical foci dominated until the 1980s, when Patricia Smart, one of the first critics to offer a new feminine/feminist reading of Hébert's poems, published an article entitled "La poésie d'Anne Hébert: une perspective féministe." Studying Hébert's first three collections, Smart attempts to give

> *une nouvelle cohérence et une portée autrement lorsque [l'œuvre poétique d'Anne Hébert] est regardée selon une perspective féminine. Les traits spécifiques de la féminité tels que définis par Clément, Cixous et d'autres—monde renversé porteur d'un nouvel ordre, subversion instaurée par le regard d'une enfant sauvage, affirmation de la puissance d'Éros contre le pouvoir répressif du Logos—sont en effet les clefs de voûte de l'univers hébertien.* (178; a new cohesiveness and a different perspective emerge when looking at Hébert's poetic œuvre from a feminine perspective. The

specific feminine traits as defined by Clément, Cixous, and others—a world reversed giving rise to a new order, a subversive perspective as seen through the eyes of a wild child, an affirmation of the strength of Eros against the repressive power of Logos—are in effect keys to the hebertian universe.)

Specifically, in dealing with *Le Tombeau des rois*, Smart points out how Hébert uses the image of the house as not just a "symbole abstrait de l'isolement et de l'enfermement" but instead as "l'habitation d'une femme onirique, sorte de Rapunzel liée à son sort par un décret de fidélité antérieur de sa volonté" (181; an abstract symbol of isolation and confinement [...] the dwelling of a fairy-tale woman, a kind of Rapunzel tied to her fate by an oath of loyalty that supersedes her will). Smart continues her analysis of Hébert's poetry in her book *Writing in the Father's House: The Emergence of the Feminine in the Quebec Literary Tradition*, comparing the poet's style with that of another Québécois poet, Hébert's cousin, Hector Saint-Denys Garneau, in order to identify the "feminine" in Hébert's style. This feminist approach was also taken up by critics such as Maurice Émond,[23] Nicole Bourbonnais,[24] Joanne Collie,[25] Lorraine Weir,[26] Kathleen Kells,[27] and Liliane Lacoste.[28] In fact, the majority of new studies devoted to Hébert's poetry are from a feminist perspective that is no less political than the early nationalist readings, but instead focuses on issues of gender and power rather than nation and power.

As the focal point of Hébert's poetry moved through various interpretive lenses, so too did the translations. As Lawrence Venuti says about the process of translation, "Every stage in the production, circulation and reception of a translation is profoundly marked by its historical moment, tracing a history that is distinct from the history of foreign text" ("Translation" 3), almost all of Hébert's early translators identified politics as being one of the chief motivating factors behind their choices to translate her poems. For example, F. R. Scott, her most important translator in English, was, among other things, an active social democrat who believed in a bilingual and bicultural Canada. Translating poetry and attempting to promote understanding of the "other" was important to him, as described by D. G. Jones: "[The translations] may serve, not only to open a window on another culture or country, as Scott makes explicit in his Introduction to his *Poems of French Canada*, but to open windows on the unknown country as ourselves as English Canadians" ("F. R. Scott" 163). In Scott's case, the politician was never very far from the translator. Hébert's poems (or at least the political interpretation of the poems) reflected Scott's own views on the political situation in Quebec leading up to the Quiet Revolution, a period of profound cultural, political, and social change in the province. As Jones noted: "There has been no love lost between F. R. Scott and the Quebec of Maurice Duplessis" (160). As expanded by Sandra Djwa in her biography of Scott, "Not only did 'Le Tombeau des rois' express the same metaphysical concerns that had so often preoccupied Scott...but Hébert saw Quebec society as he did" (380).

The anthologies that contain a significant number of Hébert's poems tend also to approach her poetry from a political perspective, seeing as they appeared during a time of great political upheaval in Quebec, but also during a time of national identity-building in English Canada. Glassco states in his introduction to *The Poetry of French Canada in Translation* that "It will be seen that the poetry of French Canada is a poetry of exile—from France and North America alike—and that the note of desertion, of nostalgia, of the dépaysé, recurs constantly, forming a kind of ground-bass to themes of avoidance, retreat and escape" (xvii–xviii). G. R. Roy, although not commenting on the poems themselves, echoes the sentiments of Miller, Scott, and Poulin:

> Canada, one of the few countries which officially recognizes more than one language, has a duty to make each race known to the other. This cannot be accomplished on the floor of a bilingual Parliament; it can be accomplished in the home of the private citizen. For this reason it was felt that a sampling of modern French-Canadian verse in translation would help fill a cultural need. (v)

The act of translating and anthologizing Hébert was a political endeavour for many.

While it was the 1980s before the critics began to consider Hébert from a feminist perspective, translators themselves were identifying with her as a "woman poet" as early as the 1970s. *The Other Voice: Twentieth Century Women's Poetry in Translation* (1976), *The Penguin Book of Women Poets* (1979), and *A Book of Women Poets from Antiquity to Now* (1980) obviously identified with the female voice in Hébert's poetry. As stated by the editors (one of whom translated Hébert's poetry) in the preface to *The Penguin Book of Women Poets*, "There are several contexts that condition the work of every writer: national history, cultural milieu, individual experience. We have tried to illuminate the additional context of sexual identity as it may affect the poetry of women across the lines of time and culture" (Cosman et al. 33). This sentiment is echoed in the introductions to two other anthologies as well.

From a more apolitical perspective, Graham Martin, in his *Anthology of Contemporary French Poetry* (1972), places Hébert in the French surrealist movement though his inclusion and framing (see Chapter 4). In the anthology, he makes the following comment concerning the non-Parisian poets he chose: "I have included two coloured and two French Canadian poets, but practically none of their poems given here could be said to involve a possible political theme" (11). Although he acknowledges that poets from French Canada have been included, nowhere are they identified as such. D. G. Jones also seems to de-emphasize the political for simply the geographical in his introduction to the anthology *Esprit de Corps: Québec Poetry of the Late Twentieth Century in Translation* (1997, edited by Louise Blouin, Bernard Pozier, and Jones): "Clearly this collection of poems is not that of the Bloc [Québécois], of some single national voice...We may recall the nationalism of the sixties when Miron, in a foreign country, feels the memory of his own land rise like a lump in his throat, but we may find his remarks that his life is a black hole more unexpected, more striking" (9). While Gwladys Downes' translations of Hébert appeared in John Glassco's anthology, she also included them in her own book of original poetry, *Out of the Violent Dark*. Janis Pallister's translations appeared in *The Age of Koestler*, a book of poetry and translations in honour of Arthur Koestler. Here we see a very definite shift in how Hébert's poetry is understood and translated, away from either a feminist or nationalist position and toward the larger world literary canon.[29]

TRANSLATION STUDIES AND THE AUTHOR

According to Judith Woodsworth, "little attention has been paid to the influence of the writer of the original text" (47) on the translator and the translation process. I suggest this lack of attention to the author and the role that he or she may play in translations is traceable to recent theories of translation that deal with translations done "from a distance." These theories also work to reclaim (or condemn) the power of the translator. By translations "from a distance," I mean that the translational situations studied are either historically or culturally distant. One sees situations where the translator is translating a text where the author and culture of origin are both long dead, or at situations where the author and culture of origin are geographically and linguistically distant. Either way, because of limits in time, geography, or linguistic aptitude, translators often work alone with the text in question.[30]

These same theories place the translator as the central figure responsible for producing the translated text in their role as a metapoet. Whether it is to celebrate this power (e.g., Venuti) or to question it (e.g., Lefevere, and Hewson and Martin), theorists place most, if not all, of the power in the hands of the translator. When more general literary theory puts forward the argument that the author is "dead" and calls for "the birth of the reader" (Barthes 150), it is not terribly surprising that the focus moves from the author to the reader/translator and the forces that act upon him/her. This is not to say that it is impossible to incorporate the possible influence of the author on the translator; in fact, the polysystem approach leaves open the possibility of *all* influences acting on the translator. As put by Alexandra Lianeri—

> Described in Evan-Zohar's terms, a "polysystem" is inherently multidimensional. It is able to accommodate taxonomies established in the realm of literature (the division between high and low literature), translation (the division between translation and non translation), and other modes of cultural production, as well as the realm of social relations (the division between dominant and dominated social groups). The need to account for the relations between these two realms, to describe translation not as a phenomenon existing in isolation, but as an integral part of a sociocultural totality, leads polysystem model to the supposition of norms and laws of translation production. (4)

All that is required is to examine those instances where the author becomes involved in the translation, incorporating them into the larger polysystem. The polysystem approach allows for paratextual materials to be incorporated in our study and in our understanding of the translation, which includes paratextual traces left to us by the author herself, in her relationships with her translators.

Points of contact between author and translator do, indeed, exist. Myriam Diaz-Diocaretz, in her book *Translating Poetic Discourse*, analyzes her relationship to and with the author she is translating. Diaz-Diocaretz analyzes her translations of Adrienne Rich's poetry, and the translation of poetry in general, and observes, "a poetic text integrates a composite known as the poet's personality" (9). Understanding this personality is of central importance in order to ensure proper translation. In translating Rich, Diaz-Diocaretz "found it necessary to understand the poet's tradition, her 'voice' and the different perceptions reflected in her own world vision" (40). The process involved "extra-textual" materials in order to get to know the author and her world. While direct contact with the author is not addressed, it does not preclude author-translator interactions as part of the extra-textual resources examined by the translator. This complex relationship between author and translator, as well as the translators' interaction with extra-textual materials, is highlighted below, in Hébert's case, and is explored in the chapters that follow, in an attempt to understand the process of making the text and in exploring the question of who made the particular versions of the text in English.

One of the more interesting aspects in the case of Hébert and her translators is that most of her translators were poets and critics in their own right. This would seem to have an effect on the relationship both between Hébert and her translators, and between the translators and their translations. There have always been questions of authorship in regards to translated works, and the spectre of a "name" author as the translator (as well as the circumstances of the publication of said translations) can further confuse an already murky understanding of authorship. Further, the identity of the poet/translator would necessarily come into conflict with the identity of the poet to be translated, creating tensions that might not be present otherwise. As critics, the general critical approach of the translator may taint the reception of his/her translation; in other words, the attitude of the critic overshadows the poetry. At the same time, it should not be terribly surprising that Hébert was translated by other poet/critics. How these poet-critic translators, or metapoets, and Hébert herself navigate these complexities is an issue explored in the chapters that follow, linking the authors, translators, editors, and publishers in the larger process of the socialization of Hébert's poetry into English.

TRANSLATION IN CANADA

In the Canadian context of translation, the author has at least been acknowledged as being present within the system. Canada is unique in that there is an expectation, albeit erroneous, that because it is a bilingual country both author and translator will be familiar with both official languages. The bicultural situation also increases opportunities for points of contact between cultures, and between author and translator. Of course, in the case of Hébert the most obvious example is *Dialogue sur la traduction*, between the author and F. R. Scott, her noted early translator. The scholar Northrop Frye calls this exchange "fascinating," and observes in his introduction to *Dialogue* that

> it is clear that without the stimulus of the other language, Mlle Hébert would never have discovered so much about her own meaning. Translation here becomes a creative achievement in communication, not merely a necessary evil or a removal of barriers. One can hardly learn more in less compass about the kind of craftsmanship that goes into the making of poetry than is given in these few pages. (15)

In her own introduction to the book, Jeanne Lapointe calls *Dialogue* a "rencontre privilégiée entre Anne Hébert et Frank Scott que les lecteurs des pages qui suivent sont aussi conviés" (27). Hébert herself described the experience as "une sorte de prise de conscience" (Smith, *L'écrivain* 45). What is so interesting about this situation is that although seemingly generating interest and excitement (including a re-issue of the book by Bibliothèque québécoise in 2000), no other work such as this has been published, nor has there been much critical interest in the book itself.[31]

This is not to say that there do not exist other situations similar to that of Hébert and Scott. In *Mapping Literature: The Art and Politics of Translation*, edited by David Homel and Sherry Simon, writers Joyce Marshall and Robert Melançon describe the intimate collaboration they maintained with either the authors they translated or their own translators. Marshall, however, illustrates through her own experience why these collaborations rarely happen: "Gabrielle [Roy] knew a lot of English, and her knowledge of what English words meant was almost perfect, but her knowledge of English grammar and English usage was nil, and our discussions would end with my screaming, *No, no, no!*" (18). The author may not be proficient enough in the target language to maintain a meaningful dialogue with the translator. Nonetheless, Melançon shows us how useful the collaboration can be for the author: "when Philip Stratford started to translate [*Peinture aveugle*], the inadequacies just leapt off the page...His translation showed me so much that I was able to do the revisions that I have long known were necessary. The translator is the ideal reader, the one who truly reads the whole work and can show it in its entirety to the author—the translator can become what Plato called a 'diamon,' whispering verses to the poet" (23). Iren Kiss goes so far as to suggest that "translators consult the original author when they have to make difficult choices, and share the responsibility for those choices" (26). Obviously, the impact of the author on the translator, and vice versa, cannot simply be ignored, given the complexity and possible benefits of such collaboration.

The academic Judith Woodsworth analyses the influence that Mavis Gallant had on the translation of her stories into French, often blocking their publication because she was dissatisfied with the end translations. In her essay "Writers and their Translators: the Case of Mavis Gallant," Woodsworth highlights the long, drawn-out process of translating into French and then the non-publication of Gallant's short-story collection *Home Truths*,[32] largely because of the tension between Québécois French and Parisian French, as Gallant, from Montreal, was living and writing in Paris, where she spent much of her life. In a similar situation as the one described above between Marshall and Roy, Gallant would appear to overestimate her expertise in French (51), thus imposing changes to the text that were inappropriate. But Gallant also held deep-seated negative attitudes toward translation, telling Woodsworth, "There is no precise equivalent for much of anything between English and French, and that is why translations almost inevitably fall short" (53). Because Gallant grew up in French as much as in English, her choice to write in English was a deeply personal one, making it even more difficult to see her work translated. The relationship between author and translator, in this case, is ultimately a destructive one.

More recently, Jane Everett edited *In Translation: The Gabrielle Roy-Joyce Marshall Correspondence* (2005). The collection contains 208 letters written over twenty-one years and traces the relationship between the writer (Roy) and the translator (Marshall), who was also a writer in her own right. Curiously, Everett offers little critical or analytical framework for approaching the letters: "In papers presented at conferences, I have made some attempts at analysing this correspondence; I have not done so here, partly because I am reluctant to suggest ways of reading the text when my own interpretations of the letters is still evolving, but also because any conclusions arrived at would risk being partial and subject to revision" (xxi). She goes on to explain the shortcomings of such a collection, but concludes that the interest in these letters far outweighs their faults: "although this correspondence cannot provide a complete portrait of Joyce Marshall's and Gabrielle Roy's personal and professional relationship, the letters do offer thought-provoking glimpses of this partnership, as well as the creative process and of the writerly life more generally...all of which invite reflection, if not, for the moment, interpretation" (xxi–xxii). This same incompleteness exists in the case of Hébert and her translators, but nonetheless still "invites reflection" and some degree of interpretation.

Ultimately, Everett avoids answering the question "who made these texts," and so this study seeks to expand on that point, taking it a step further with Hébert. Outside of the little work that has been done on *Dialogue sur la traduction*, we are still left grappling with these questions in the case of Hébert in English. Hébert also did not leave the same wealth of archival materials of drafts and correspondences as Gabrielle Roy, making the task of the researcher trying to answer this question even more difficult. But piecing together the multiple archives and other paratextual materials gathered for this book allows us to reflect on the highly mediated process that is translation and publication, completing the interrogation, reflection, and interpretation that Everett invites.

There are a number of similarities between the situation of Roy and Hébert with respect to their translators. Both had numerous translators with whom they interacted with varying degrees of success over the course of their careers. While Everett focuses on the Roy-Marshall relationship, Darlene Kelly chooses to look at Roy's relationship with translator Harry Lorin Binsse. Kelly is specifically concerned with, as the subtitle of her article suggests, "How Their Disputes Shaped the Text." Using a variety of archival resources, including the Roy-Marshall papers, she reconstructs the complex interaction between author and translator, ultimately leading to Roy's "firing" of Binsse in 1962 (87). The use of archival resources is essential to her study, and Kelly concludes that

> When reading a fluently translated work, most people rarely wonder about how well it preserves the original, the translator's voice being indistinguishable in their minds from the author's own. A similar equation of Binsse with Roy might have occurred, had not long-overlooked archival documents, like a lost piece of film footage, exposed their old quarrels, in the process of both illuminating both the texts and Roy herself... Archival data also permits us to attribute a more complex motive to Roy's dismissal of Binsse than was suggested by her vague complaint about "tiraillements." (101)

Here we see the potential of archival research to move us far beyond reflection and into the realm of interpretation and insight in the field of translation studies, bringing into the field elements of textual analysis, asking and answering more explicitly, who made these texts?

Yet, despite these and many other examples (David Homel and Dany Laferrière's long-time collaboration, as well the interactions between English and French Canadian feminists immediately come to mind), there exists very little theoretical work regarding these relationships. Sherry Simon perhaps comes closest to offering a reading of the Canadian phenomenon of collaboration between author and translator when she asks the question in the introduction to *Culture in Transit*: "how does the dialogue between communities (political, linguistic, cultural, literary) influence the dynamics of translation?" and offers the answer: "the translator's mandate is grounded in a commitment to both the author and the social movements which give energy to his or her work" (9). Simon is also one of the few scholars who consistently identify these points of contact and collaboration within the Canadian context. I would contend, however, that Simon is not going far enough in her analysis of the situations where the author is involved somehow in the translation of his/her work. Using a modified polysystem approach, I will put forward a theory that takes into consideration the author's possible influence that also relies on available archival information.

THE PARATEXTUAL AND TRANSLATION

Although Godard, in the quote at the beginning of our introduction, refers to them as "paritextual," Gerard Genette names the materials that surround and inform a given piece of literature "the paratext," defining it as such:

> A paratextual element, at least if it consists of a message that has taken on material form, necessarily has a *location* that can be situated in relation to the location of the text itself: around the text and either within the same volume or at a more respectful (or more prudent) distance. Within the same volume are such elements as the title or the preface and sometimes elements inserted in to the interstices of the text, such as chapter titles or certain notes. I will give the name *peritext* to this first spatial category—certainly the more typical one... The distanced elements are all those messages that, at least originally, are located outside the book, generally with the help of the media (interviews, conversations) or under cover of private communications (letters, diaries, and others). This second category is what, for lack of a better word, I call *epitext*... As must henceforth go without saying, peritext and epitext completely and entirely share the spatial field of the paratext. In other words, for those who are keep on formulae, *paratext=peritext+epitext*. (5)

Particularly in the case of translations (and anthologies of translations), the peritextual materials (title, preface, notes, etc.) become important framing elements, in particular because of the "foreigness" of the text the reader is about to access; if the reader spoke the original language, translation would be unnecessary. As well, it reinforces translation as critical act, but also imposes the presence of the translator on the final work. As put by Sherry Simon, "Dans le cas des traductions, la préface à une autre function spécifique. C'est de mettre en valeur le nom du traducteur, de donner au traducteur ou à la traductrice un lieu de parole" ("Volontés" 98; In the case of translations, the preface has another specific function, and that is to emphasize the role of the translator, to give the translator a place to speak).

Simon continues on the importance of the translator's preface, outlining two other critically relevant pieces of information they provide: They "renvoient aux mechanisms politiques et commerciaux qui soutinennent et contrôlent la production et la diffusion de l'écriture" (102; highlight the political and commercial mechanisms that support and control the production and distribution of the work); a preface also "établit des valeurs qui nous permettent d'historiciser les subjets de l'écriture" (103; establishes the values that allow us to historicize the subjects of the work). The question of economics is not a minor consideration; in many cases, the issue of money became more central to the ability to publish (or include) Hébert's poetry in English translation. Also, how Hébert was not only translated but also contextualized and framed is important in understanding her evolution as an author in English.

Another dynamic paratextual influence on her image is how the English publications, the translations, were received by the critical and general community, both in terms of sales and reviews. Douglas Babour outlines the challenges presented to us in the study of reviews, particularly poetry reviews.

> One major question, then, is: Do reviews really have any noticeable effect upon a poet's popularity or sales? The evidence is not all that clear... Did these articles, which appeared only in the Canadian edition, serve to increase the popularity of the poets they covered, or did they simply signal to the general populace that those writers had already achieved sufficient fame to merit *Time*'s attention? Even if we accept the latter conclusion, does it not seem likely that a story in *Time* (or later in *Maclean's*) would do more to promote a poet's popularity than any number of favorable reviews in small literary journals? ("Re: Viewing" 53)

He posits further on in the essay, "Is it possible that much of the making of canons occurred in the review columns of our literary magazines? If so, it is almost impossible to map the whole process" (59). Nevertheless, while imperfect (and sometimes unavailable), reviews and sales figures aid a larger understanding of the historical moment and values of that time, to paraphrase Simon. Also, one cannot underestimate the cultural capital to be found in a literary review. As put more recently by poet Lori Nelson Glenn, addressing the imbalance of women writers and poets being reviewed in Canada:

> The world of reviewing is a microcosm of the larger story of women and language. Women write and publish as frequently as men in Canada, and yet women's books are less frequently reviewed, and women reviewers are less frequently published. A casual glance at contemporary reviews shows differences in tone and approach by gender. The pie charts and counts you see on this website tell us that when social and political forces gain momentum, they keep it. To paraphrase the homily: all it takes to perpetuate inequity is to do nothing. Some of us believe that the onus is on women and gender/queer communities to interrupt the conversation,

> take the editorial reins, insert themselves into the discourse ("you could have asked"); some of us believe that the gatekeepers need to take a close look at their gates, how they've built them, and rebuild them ("you could have noticed"). Many of us fall somewhere between those stances. What is clear is that doing nothing is no longer an option.

Reviews are indeed a complex, but no less important, paratextual resource for the study of translation more generally and of Anne Hébert's evolution in English.

USING DIALOGUE AS A MODEL OF LITERARY TRANSLATION

E. D. Blodgett is one of the few theorists to use *Dialogue sur la traduction* for a larger inquiry into the process of translation.[33] In his "Towards a Model of Literary Translation in Canada," Blodgett looks more broadly at a number of translational situations in the country, but begins his process with *Dialogue*. Applying Kristeva's theories of geno-text and pheno-text to translation, Blodgett shows how Canadian translators put varying degrees of emphasis on the source text (pheno-text 1), the author (geno-text 1), the translator (geno-text 2) and the target text (pheno-text 2), but argues that power to place the emphasis on any one of these four areas remains with the translator. Nonetheless, taking what Blodgett has said a step further, the author, to varying degrees, will maintain a privileged position: while the translator eventually creates the poem (the independent pheno-text), he/she will only ever be able to create a secondary geno-text. The level of authority given to that geno-text will vary, as will the level of authority given to the first geno-text. But simply stating that there exists a second geno-text will always imply that there was once a first, housed in the author.

This is important because it finally takes into consideration the role the author may play in the process of translation. Blodgett's "hypothèse de travail" (203) ensures that the author remains present in some form, if only as an acknowledgement. Blodgett also offers evidence that the power remains with the translator: Ultimately it is Scott, Godard, and Brault who choose to "abandon" the translation and who decide which of the four "texts" to privilege, and ultimately looking at the geno-text in some way, "one might infer that Brault avoids the movement towards geno-text 1, which both Scott and Godard make, except to find possibilities for transposition" (203). Blodgett manages to maintain the empowerment of the translator while privileging the author at the same time.

Marcel Voisin also looks to *Dialogue* to expand our theoretical understanding of the process of translation. In his article "Le dialogue auteur-traducteur au service de la poésie et de la culture," he outlines how a translator must carry on a "dialogue fictif mais intime" with the author of the poem, with the goal of achieving "une communion spirituelle [qui] devrait transcender...et permettre le petit miracle d'une réécriture capable de susciter des émotions et un plaisir analogues à ceux que procure l'original" (205; a fictional, yet intimate, dialogue [...] a transcendent spiritual connection that allows the small miracle of a rewriting that instills analogous emotions and pleasures to the ones produced by the original). Voisin goes on to state: "Un dialogue authentique est un bénéfice pour chacun," (an authentic dialogue is mutually beneficial) and uses *Dialogue* as the ideal example of such a collaboration. These collaborations would lead to a new ethic of translation. This ethic would allow the translator to transcend "la prégnance du moi et de l'ethnocentrisme culturel qui ne cessent de rétrécir notre vision du monde" (212; the primacy of the self and the cultural ethnocentrism that continually obscure our view of the world). The power still remains with the translator, because it is only through a change in the way the translator views the authority of the author that such an ethical shift may occur.

A THEORY OF POWER AND AUTHORITY

I have chosen my terminology quite deliberately in the foregoing discussion in preparation for the explanation of my approach to studying the translations of Hébert's poetry. Out of the fifteen or so translators who have translated her poems, only three known correspondences took place between author and translator (F. R. Scott, Alan Brown and Alfred Poulin Jr.). One can easily conclude that these translators placed a fair amount of authority in the author—privileging the author, as Blodgett would say. But this does not negate the other forces that may have acted on those translators; nor does not corresponding imply that the author/source text held little authority. I would argue that translators are in a position of power, with a number of authorities or forces acting upon them. These authorities can range from cultural norms and expectations of the target language to the knowledge the translator possesses of the source culture. The level at which these authorities are privileged by the translator is controlled centrally; ultimately, the translator has the power to decide how he/she is going to proceed with the translation.

My shift in theoretical focus and terminology takes Blodgett's theory a step further in terms of applicability and complexity, but uses his introduction of the author as authority as its starting point. I borrow, obviously, from polysystem theories that attempt to look at all forces that work on the translator. However, I also combine polysystem theories with postcolonial theories that show that the translator does have a great deal of power over the final product. This combination of polysystem and postcolonial theories emphasizes the *power* that the translator has over the text. Translation studies made a "cultural turn" in the 1970s with polysystem theories, but we there was a "power turn" in the 1990s, as outlined by Edwin Gentzler and Maria Tymoczko in their introduction to *Translation and Power*. In other words, my analysis will take into consideration the specific historical moment of the translation or anthologization. However, the focus of my study will remain on the individual actors involved in the production of the text, examining their relative power and authority within the given system. This theoretical approach can be applied to a number of translational situations, interrogating the various "whos" that acted on Hébert's poetry.

The idea of power and authority is also useful when considering the role of editors, publishers, critics, and others in the creation, and, perhaps more importantly, the dissemination of a translation. As the chapters concerning Anne Hébert in English-language anthologies demonstrate, the power of the translator is often precarious, if present at all. Translators (if they are not the editor as well) are at the mercy of the editor's preferences, while editors must endeavour to satisfy publishers who, in turn, evaluate market considerations. Nonetheless, many translators take steps, sometimes radical steps, to ensure that they maintain power over their translation.

Chapter One of this study will look at F. R. Scott and his power in terms of the influence he exerted in the translation and image of Anne Hébert into English. No more than a few degrees of separation exist between Scott and the others who translated or anthologized Hébert in English. His attitude, both toward Hébert and toward translation and poetry in general, shaped not only his output, but also influenced Hébert's own view of her translations and translators. The chapter will also examine the effect *Dialogue sur la traduction* had on subsequent translators and translations. Chapter Two deals with the four collections of Hébert's poetry in English: *The Tomb of Kings*, translated by Peter Miller (1967); *Poems*, translated by Alan Brown (1975); *Anne Hébert: Selected Poems* (1987) and *Day Has No Equal but Night* (1994), translated by Alfred Poulin Jr.; and *Day has no equal but the Night* (1997), translated by Lola Lemire Tostevin. Chapter One not only looks at the circumstances surrounding the translating and publishing of the collections, but also compares the collections and poems found in them. Chapters One and Two deal with Anne Hébert's anthologization in English. Chapter Three deals with Hébert as a French Canadian/Québécoise and Canadian, while Chapter Four addresses Hébert outside the Canadian context. Though those anthologies published outside of Canada may well have had a larger influence on Hébert's image as an author internationally, the domestic anthologies are important in exposing Hébert to readers (and other editors and translators) who might not have known her otherwise. It's vital to look at the anthologization of Hébert in part because, as put by Anne Ferry, "The anthologist as author of the book supplants the author of the poem in choosing how it should be presented, with interpretive consequences" (2). I organized these chapters in chronological order, in order to facilitate approaching Hébert's poetry, and also the anthologies themselves, and according to a few perspectives: time period, theme, and approach. In the conclusion, I propose some new directions for studies of Canadian literature in translation, both here and abroad.

I would argue that the history of the translations of, and the publications thereof, a particular author can also be read as a narrative—like a story, so to speak. Lawrence Venuti states: "A history of translation, then, like any history, endows translation practices with significance through a specific narrative form or mixtures of forms" ("Translation" 812). The aim of this book, then, is to tell the story of Anne Hébert's poetry in English; the story of an author who moves from the local and provincial to the global and universal; and of those in the middle who rewrote her in English. Answering the question "Who made those texts?" also helps us to understand the social, political, economic, and historical conditions that informed the making of those texts. This book is not only a story of Anne Hébert, but also a history of Canadian letters over the past sixty years, moving from the local and provincial into the international and global.

NOTES

1. The correct term for people from or living in Quebec is "Québécois," but, before the 1970s, the term that was typically used in English was "French Canadian."
2. James McGann, *The Textual Condition*, Princeton: Princeton UP, 1991.
3. Martha Nell Smith, "The Human Touch Software of the Highest Order: Revisiting Editing as Interpretation."
4. See Itamar Even-Zohar's seminal work "Polysystem Theory" and "The Position of Translated Literature within the Literature Polysystem."
5. *Traduction littéraire et sociabilité interculturelle au Canada (1950–1960)*, University of Ottawa Press, 2004.
6. *Gabrielle Roy traduite*. Claude La Charité, editor. Québec: Éditions Nota bene, 2006, pp. 15–68.
7. All quotes from Hébert's poetry in French come from this edition, unless otherwise noted.
8. Maugey, Axel. *Poésie et société au Québec (1937–1970)*. Québec: Presses de l'Université Laval, 1972.
9. Lacôte, René. *Anne Hébert*. Paris: Seghers, 1969.

10. Bouchard, Denis. *Une lecture d'Anne Hébert: La recherché d'une mythologie*. Montreal: HMH, 1977.
11. Pagé, Pierre. *Anne Hébert*. Montréal: Fides, 1965.
12. Popovic, Pierre. *La contradiction du poème: poésie et discours social au Québec de 1948–1953*. Montreal: Balzac, 1992.
13. Major, Jean-Louis. *Anne Hébert et le miracle de la parole*. Montréal: Presses de l'Université de Montréal, 1976.
14. Russell, Delbert W. *Anne Hébert*. Boston: Twayne, 1983.
15. Haeck, Philippe. "Naissance de la poésie moderne au Québec." *Études françaises* vol. 9, no. 2, 1973, pp. 95–113.
16. Rose, Marilyn Gaddis. "Hébert's "Le Tombeau des Rois" (1953): A Modernist Manifesto." *Translation Perspectives*, no. 3, 1987, pp, 32–39.
17. Harvey, Robert. "La modernité comme travail du sujet chez Anne Hébert." *Les cahiers Anne Hébert* 2 (2000), pp. 27–43.
18. Garant, France Nazaire. *Ève et le cheval de grève: Contribution à l'étude de l'imaginaire d'Anne Hébert*. Québec: CRELIQ, 1988.
19. Robert, Guy. *La poétique du songe: Introduction à l'œuvre d'Anne Hébert*. Montréal: AGEUM, 1962.
20. Voldeng, Évelyne. *Lectures de l'imaginaire: Huit femmes poètes des deux cultures canadiennes (1940–1980)*. Orléans, Ont.: Éditions David, 2000.
21. Pallister, Janis L. "Thanatos and Logos in the Poetry of Anne Hébert." *The Art and Genius of Anne Hébert: Essays on Her Works: Night and Day Are One*. Ed. Janis L. Pallister. Madison: Fairleight Dickinson University Press, 2001, pp. 139–45.
22. Roy, Lucille. *Entre la lumière et l'ombre: L'univers poétique d'Anne Hébert*. Sherbrooke: Editions Naaman, 1984.
23. Émond, Maurice. *Le récit québécois comme fil d'Ariane*. Québec: Nota Bene, 2000.
24. Bourbonnais, Nicole. "Femme Métonymique, femme métaphorique: La poésie d'Anne Hébert et de Renée Vivien." *Atlantis* 11.2 (1986): 108–14.
25. Collie, Joanne. "Anne Hébert's *Écriture Féminine*." *British Journal of Canadian Studies*, vol. 3, no. 2, 1988, pp. 285–92.
26. Weir, Lorraine. "'Fauna of Mirrors': The Poetry of Hébert and Atwood." *Ariel*, vol. 10, no. 3, 1979, pp. 99–113.
27. Kells, Kathleen. "From the First 'Eve' to the New 'Eve': Anne Hébert's Rehabilitation of the Malevolent Female Archetype." *Studies in Canadian Literature*, vol. 14, no. 1, 1989, pp. 99–107.
28. Lacoste, Liliane. "Transgressions sexuelles et textuelles dans la poésie d'Anne Hébert." *RLA*, no. 6, 1994, pp. 116–19.
29. This study excludes the author's novels translated in English, as it would require its own book-length study, but cannot ignore the influence that Hébert's novel *Kamouraska*, its English translation, and movie adaptation had on her visibility and popularity internationally. As the winner of the Prix des Libraires in 1971 in France, the rights for the novel were almost immediately bought by Crown Publishers, a large American publishing house, and translated into English by an American, Norman Shapiro. The

film adaptation by Claude Jutra was released the same year as the English translation (1973), and was a critical success both in Canada and abroad, increasing Hébert's visibility. The content of the book (and the movie) also seems to have attracted a more feminist reading and thereby a whole new range of scholars to her work. One notices a sharp rise in interest in and a shift in approaches to Hébert after the novel and movie are released, particularly in the United States.

30. This observation is echoed by Wolfram Wilss in *The Science of Translation* (1982). He expresses the idea slightly differently: "Frequently the translator does not know, at least personally, the author, on whom he is working, and to make things worse, in many cases he does not know the destination of his translation product either... [therefore] close collaboration between [source language text] author, translator, and [target language text] reader seems to be rare" (144).
31. Patricia Godbout's critical edition of *Dialogue* appears in *Œuvres complètes d'Anne Hébert, Tome I—Poésie suivi de Dialogue sur la traduction à propos du Tombeau des rois*, edited by Nathalie Watteyne, Montreal: Presses Université de Montréal, 2013.
32. Woodsworth's article appeared in 1988 and there still isn't a published translation of *Home Truths*, first published in 1981.
33. This is not necessarily surprising, given that Blodgett himself participated in a similar dialogue with Jacques Brault, in *Transfigurations*, a book of translated poetry, so to speak, that Sherry Simon calls "a sequel to *Dialogue sur la traduction*" (*Translating Montreal* 140). Again, there has been very little critical attention paid to this "sequel."

1

The F. R. Scott Effect

Francis Reginald Scott might have been the first person to translate Anne Hébert's poetry, and while not the most prolific, he is, as this chapter will show, the most important and influential translator of Hébert's works. Without Scott and his obsession with the poem "Le Tombeau des rois," without his groundbreaking work connecting English and French poets, and without his tireless advocacy for the rights of translators as artists, we would not only have a much different image of Hébert in English, but a much different image of French Canadian poetry more generally. According to André Lefevere, "In the past, as in the present, rewriters created images of a writer, a work, a period, a genre, sometimes even a whole literature" (5). There is perhaps no better way to describe the influence of F. R. Scott, not only on the image of Hébert in English, but possibly as concerns English Canada's understanding of French Canadian literature more broadly. This chapter will trace just how influential Scott was in creating and shaping the image of Hébert in English, her poem "The Tomb of Kings," the modernist movement in Quebec, and French Canadian literature in general. He started everything.

Scott established himself as an important voice for Canadian politics and poetry during the 1940s.[1] In the 1950s, as outlined by Patricia Godbout, Scott became influential as a translator or, perhaps more accurately, a cultural interpreter. One cannot underestimate the importance of Scott's choosing Hébert as one of his first subjects to translate to her subsequent popularity in English. Scott, through his standing as a poet, editor, and public intellectual, had the cultural capital in order to immediately place Hébert in the minds of English Canada as a talented poet of great significance. The June–July 1952 issue of *Northern Review* contains the "first" translations of Anne Hébert, taken from *Le Tombeau des rois*: "La fille maigre" and "En guise de fête." The first letter between Scott and Hébert appears (at least, according to Scott's archive) at the very end of 1952, on December 31 (FRSF, vol. 26, file 6). The two would begin a literary friendship that lasted over the next twenty years and would have a tremendous impact on how the rest of Canada read Anne Hébert's poetry in English.

Over the next thirty years, Scott's translations, and the subsequent *Dialogue sur la traduction*, influenced, directly or indirectly, virtually every translation of

Hébert's poetry. While his translations "haunt" the reader looking at Hébert in English, but so too does Scott's influence behind the scenes, so to speak, shape many of the collections and anthologies that included Hébert in the coming years. Indeed, six degrees of separation are not necessary when trying to connect Scott to the translators and editors who worked on Hébert; one degree is often all that is needed. What we begin to see in a close analysis of these relationships is the extent of Scott's influence on these editors and translators in shaping their own translations and choices regarding Hébert's poetry. But Scott's influence is not limited to his fellow English-language colleagues; in reading the relationship between Hébert and Scott, the extent of Scott's impact on the French-language poet becomes clear, especially in regards to Hébert's relationship to future translators. More generally, Scott's work, both as a lawyer and a critic, to ensure proper recognition for translators in Canada made it possible for many of these anthologies and translations to even see the light of day.

F. R. SCOTT, TRANSLATOR

Scott's first translations of Hébert's poetry appeared in 1952.[2] It was not until ten years later that Scott's "complete" translations of Hébert's poetry appeared in book form. *St-Denys Garneau & Anne Hébert* was published by Klanak Press, a small press based in Vancouver, in 1962. Bilingual in format, the collection included nine poems by Hébert: four from *Le Tombeau des rois* (1953), two from *Poèmes* (1960), and one from her first collection, *Songes en équilibre* (1942). It is a testament to the relationship that Scott and Hébert shared that Scott was able to publish a translation from *Songes en équilibre*, as Hébert disliked her first collection of poetry.[3] Scott provided a "Translator's Note" at the beginning of the text, and Giles Marcotte provided an introduction. The Hébert poems included were, in order of appearance, "The Lean Girl," "As If for Holiday," "Manor Life," "The Closed Room," "There Is Certainly Someone," "The Two Hands," "The Tomb of Kings," "Blind Season," and "Snow."

The project began in haste in 1961, with a letter to Scott from his friend W. C. McConnell, editor at Klanak Press. Arguing that Western Canada should be exposed to this new generation of poets, McConnell was looking for an editor to produce a collection of French Canadian poets in translation and contacted Scott in the hopes that he would either take up the challenge or recommend someone for the task. Eventually, the collection would evolve to contain translations of only Saint-Denys Garneau and Hébert, in a bilingual format, with no expense spared on the layout and typography (Djwa 376). In a letter dated November 1, 1961, McConnell writes to Scott regarding the progress of the publication:

> I completely forgot to mention the most important point of all—the poetry is magnificent! And the translations, well, I can see the tremendous amount of dedication which went into them. To translate as well yet so faithfully is in effect creating new poems! I have no doubt about the volume's success. To hell with the bank—a first run of a thousand copies it must be. (FRSF, vol. 53, file 10)

One thousand copies was a significant number for a collection of poetry published by a small press at that time. But the friendship between the translator and the publisher, as well as McConnell's faith in the quality of the translations, would seem to have outweighed the high costs of such an endeavour.

The reception of the collection is very positive. G. V. Downes, another future translator of Hébert, reviews the book for *B.C. Library Quarterly* and calls it "a welcome and brilliantly successful attempt to bridge this gap [between English and French Canada/Western and Eastern Canada]" (FRSF, vol. 53, file 10).[4] In discussing Scott's translations of Hébert, Downes observes, "What is so satisfactory, and so unusual, is the way the English text—particularly in the case of Anne Hébert's work—does carry the real 'courant magnétique' of poetry," and concludes with, "One is grateful to the Klanak Press for bringing such fine translations of such fine originals" (FRSF, vol. 53, file 10). In *Canadian Forum*, Laure Rièse compares the Christian imagery in both Garneau and Hébert's poetry, and notes, "Mr. Scott, in his translations, brings out the intricacies both of language and thought. But remaining true to his models he loses nothing and embellishes nothing" (FRSF, vol. 53, file 10). Rièse sums up, "St-Denys Garneau [sic] and Anne Hébert have distinguished themselves by the maturity of their experiences, the harmonizing power of their mind and art, and one can be grateful to Mr. Scott for having brought them to the attention of the Anglo-Saxon world" (FRSF, vol. 53, file 10). In *Queen's Quarterly*, Gérard Tougas says, "There can be no doubt that Anne Hébert has been magnificently served by Frank Scott" (450). Robin Skelton, in *Tamarack Review*, observes that in Scott's translations, "much of the music is lost, but the basic perceptions remain," (81) and concludes: "This is wonderful poetry. It can stand up in any company and be proud of itself" (82). In *Canadian Literature*, Leandre Bergeron calls Scott's translation "absolument littérale" but praises this quality because "elle nous donne vraiment l'impression qu'un canadien-français est en train de nous parler dans sa langue seconde" (75; it really conveys the impression that a French Canadian is speaking to us in his second language). CBC Radio ran a review of the book for their series "Critically Speaking," where George Whalley finds himself "spellbound at once by the force and integrity" of "The Tomb of Kings," and observes, "I should like to read them all" (FRSF, vol. 51, file 7).[5] It should also be noted that almost all the reviews point to the letters recently (1962) published in *Tamarack Review* between Scott and Hébert as a point of interest relating to the translation of the poem "The Tomb of Kings." These letters would eventually become *Dialogue sur la traduction*, which will be addressed later in this chapter.

The impact of this collection on Canadian letters should not be overlooked. Two of French Canada's most celebrated poets, translated by one of English Canada's most influential poets, is a significant event. The 1960s in Canada and Quebec witnessed a huge shift in both politics and attitudes, and this small collection played a part by participating in these shifts. The first run of the collection sold out, and on February 5, 1978, McConnell writes Scott to discuss publishing a second edition.

> The reason for the proposed second edition of The Translations [*St-Denys Garneau & Anne Hébert*] is that it is out of print and it continues to be on University and other courses in various parts of Canada. Consequently we are breaking our rule of one limited edition of each book we publish. It would be a pity if this magnificent poetry were kept from a generation of students.
>
> The proposed number of copies is 1,000, my estimate of a 5–7 year supply. (FRSF, vol. 51, file 8)

The subsequent work that people like Glassco, Downes, Cogswell, and others did in translating and publishing French Canadian poetry was in no small part influenced by this initial collection of translations by Scott.

In 1977, Blackfish Press, also out of British Columbia, published *Poems of French Canada*, which collected all of Scott's translations into one volume for the first time. Scott's nine translations of Hébert's poetry reappear here, although a few are modified. Scott provides a lengthy introduction to the collection, which is part tutorial on the history of French Canada, part autobiography. The rise in Quebec nationalism and other recent developments in Canadian politics weigh heavily on Scott, and this is reflected in his introduction as well as the choice of title: while elsewhere new anthologies of poetry were calling themselves Québécois rather than French Canadian, Scott remains firmly with the older nomenclature. Or as put by Kathy Mezei, "This defiance underlines his introduction; it is perhaps 'an old man's frenzy,' perhaps an anachronistic gesture, perhaps the pain of a man who sees his dreams of the creative co-existence of two cultures dissolve into petty semantics" ("*Poems*" 106). As Scott states at the end of his introduction, "Translation is not only an art in itself, it is also an essential ingredient in Canada's political entity" (vi). This particular section of the introduction gave Scott some difficulty, as an early draft reveals. The draft is slightly different, focusing not on the political, but on the cultural. "That translation is itself an art and for Canada a cultural necessity is, I think, an established fact" (FRSF, vol. 70, file 17). The final version would seem to illustrate Scott's continuing concern with the political situation.

Alan Safarik, editor of Blackfish Press, spared no expense in producing and promoting what he felt was an important book for Canadian letters:

> We are planning three editions...twenty-six numbered and signed copies (boxed) in super bind, 100 signed editions on different paper in a different bind and then a fine trade edition of 1000 copies....
>
> While we are printing the book we will also print a brochure to be sent on a prayer out on our 3000 individual mailing list... We will mail the posters out to about 100 bookstores across the country. We will also run an ad in Books in Canada and I anticipate sending out 50 copies for review... (FRSF, vol. 70, file 17)

At this point in Scott's career, however, the mere mention of a "new" collection of works by him inspired book orders: "Word travels fast. I have already back ordered 30 copies of the book from strange places across the country... The whole book will go in less than a year. Much less" (FRSF, vol. 70, file 17). This was not exactly an accurate prediction, but not far off. On April 12, 1978, Safarik writes Scott that there are only about four hundred copies left of the book, and that the book was also in consideration for the Canada Council Prize for Translation (FRSF, vol. 70, file 17). Critical reaction to the anthology is limited, but very positive. Mezei writes in her review for *Canadian Literature* that "the translations are very good—Scott is a meticulous craftsman" (104) and notes how the "publication of F. R. Scott's translations is a timely recognition of Scott's importance as a translator" (103). Philip Stratford, for *Quill & Quire*, celebrates that Scott's "beautifully translated French Poems" had finally been collected, and observes that "the quality is high" (FRSF, vol. 70, file 17). Perhaps the highest accolade for the book and the translator is the Canada Council Award for Translation that Scott would indeed receive for his translations in 1978.

The two collections of Scott's translations and their timing are bookends of a sort for Scott's career as a translator, but also bookends for a time of great political upheaval in Quebec: 1962, the beginning and optimism of the 1960s, with a rise in Canadian nationalism, and 1977, with what could be seen as the end of a dream for Scott and his bicultural vision of Quebec's place in Canada, given ascendant nationalism and separatism in Quebec. But the legacy he would leave with these collections and his work as a translator would be felt for many decades to come.

F. R. SCOTT, LAWYER

In a letter dated April 27, 1955, Scott writes to Hébert:

> You seem to be pursued by translators. This is the penalty for writing good poetry. As you know, I think translations should be encouraged for it helps the understanding of cultures, but I quite realise how necessary it is to keep control over it so that you reduce to a minimum the degree of distortion which inevitably takes place in the process.
>
> I have assumed that you permit me to make further translations of your work, provided I should show it to you before publication, but I have not felt that I had a right to tell other translators what they should do. On the other hand, if you wished me to have some exclusive right in translation so that you can more easily control what is published, I would be willing to accept this role as a favour to you. Personally, I do not think one's reputation can ever be damaged, even by bad translations, since the original work is what counts and remains unchanged. (FRSF, vol 26, file 8)

As a poet, Scott was always concerned about artists' control over their poetic voice, but he was also concerned with making sure that the artist was properly compensated; not just the poet, but the translator as well. In the F. R. Scott fonds, there is an entire section devoted to "Permission," which includes a copy of all cheque stubs and receipts Scott received as compensation for the poems, letters, and writings reproduced in anthologies and collections. His archives also contains copies of (seemingly) all requests to include his work in anthologies, and his responses that clearly outline how much he expected to be paid for each poem/translation. As early as 1957, with the appearance of A. J. M. Smith's third edition of *Book of Canadian Poetry*, through Gage Publishing, Scott was enquiring on the status of certain translations that were included in the anthology. In a letter dated May 20, 1958, Scott writes to Enid Thornton at Ryerson Press (who held the copyright at that time for his poetry) to enquire about the publication, among others, of "Ancestral Manor" in Smith's anthology, "Did they get permission from you?" (FRSF, vol. 26, file 10). Thornton replies, "Since Gage did not ask for the use of 'Ancestral Manor,' I assume that this poem was in the first edition of their book. This means that no new permission would be required" (FRSF, vol. 26, file 10). It is interesting to note that in both editions of Smith's anthology, Scott's translation of Hébert's poem "Ancestral Manor" is not credited as a translation, but as an original Scott poem. Gage would not have held copyright for that particular poem, as the translation had not yet been published in an anthology or collection. The grey area posed by the question of translation, as well as the issue of control, concerned Scott a great deal.

Scott and Hébert would seem to have resolved the situation soon after. Scott purchased the rights to his translations from Hébert, for the publication of *Saint-Denys Garneau & Anne Hébert*, in 1962. In a letter to her, dated February 21, 1962, Scott offers $100 for the exclusive rights to his translations of her poems (FRSF, vol. 64, file 14). This is advantageous in a number of ways. Editors no long had to contact both Scott and Hébert in order to reprint a poem. This also allowed him to "control," as he explained to Hébert, the translations that were published, without inconveniencing the author. But it meant that Scott began charging the same amount of money as he would if the poem had been an original. It also allowed for Scott to control how much he was compensated for his translations. Publishing houses at that time did not adequately compensate the translators for permission to publish their translations (if they paid the translators anything at all), and Scott's ownership of his translations allowed another level of control, which often led to battles with publishing houses.

One such battle took place between Scott and Penguin Publishing for the permission to publish four of his translations in *Canadian Writing Today*, edited by Mordecai Richler, which included "Manor Life" by Hébert. According to the archives, Scott was charging his standard $25 per poem, while Penguin, in a letter dated June 16, 1969, was offering a compromise of $15 per poem for "non-exclusive English language world anthology rights" (FRSF, vol. 66, file 1). Scott replied to this in a letter dated June 26, 1969.

> I am afraid the "compromise" you suggest is not acceptable by me. You are asking for world rights; even for Canadian rights I receive $25 at least per poem. It is also apparent that you only want me to be represented by translations. This is not the form of verse for which I am best known in Canada, and rather than have your anthology misrepresent me I think I would prefer to be omitted entirely. (FRSF, vol. 66, file 1)

This letter was forwarded to Richler, who apparently contacted Scott personally, as there is no letter in either of their archives that discusses the compromise. There is a letter in Richler's archive from the editor at Penguin dated July 22, 1969, stating, "I am very relieved to hear you have mollified Frank Scott" (MRF, MsC 36.10.33), and in Scott's archive there is a receipt for $60, for $15 per poem for *Canadian Writing Today*. This sort of control was obviously important to Scott, and focused not only on compensation but also on artistic integrity. Although he had refused elsewhere to have his poems or translations published due to unfair compensation, again, according to his archives, this never seemed to happen in regards to a translation of a Hébert poem. The situation with Penguin is the closest Hébert (as translated by Scott) ever came to being excluded in English because of money.

F. R. SCOTT, FRIEND

As stated in the letter to Hébert quoted previously, Scott was also very loyal to her. He wrote a letter on behalf of Hébert on April 11, 1953, in order to assist her in acquiring a Royal Society of Canada scholarship, which he repeated again in 1954.

> I cannot think of a poet in Quebec more fitted to receive your help. She already writes enough first-rate poetry to prove her originality and devotion in the practice of this art… My own opinion of her writing is perhaps best indicated by the fact that she is the first French-Canadian poet whose poems I have felt moved to translate. (FRSF, Vol. 26, file 7)

This literary friendship and the mutual respect shared by the two authors shaped many of the future translations and publications of Hébert's poetry in English. In the early 1960s, Peter Miller was thinking of producing a bilingual edition of *The Tomb of Kings*. Hébert wrote to Scott on February 17, 1962, in regards to a possible translation by Miller: "Ryerson Press aimerait publier une cinquantaine de poèmes, traduit par Peter Miller. Ouf! Toute mon œuvre poétique, quoi!… Connaissez-vous les poèmes de Peter Miller? Les aimez-vous?" (FRSF, vol. 64, file 14; Ryerson Press would like to publish some fifty poems translated by Peter Miller. Ouf! That's pretty much my entire poetic oeuvre! … Do you know Peter Miller's poems? Do you like them?). Scott responds in a February 21, 1962, letter: "As for the book of Ryerson's, translated by Peter Miller, I have heard nothing about this. It seems to me you may want to make sure that if you are going to be published in translation, there should not be too many people attempting to do it. On the other hand, Peter Miller writes quite good poetry and I think is a responsible person" (FRSF, vol. 64, file 14). Miller eventually approaches Raymond Souster and Louis Dudek, with whom he ran Contact Press, about publishing the Hébert translations. Souster contacted Scott by mail to solicit his advice and opinion on the translations. Scott responded in a letter dated June 2, 1965: "I have decided, in view of my relationship with [Hébert] and the fact that we worked together on my translations, not to intervene in any way with respect to Peter Miller's proposed volume. Let him approach her directly if he wants to" (FRSF, vol. 65, file 3). Both Miller and Dudek contacted Hébert and obtained permission to publish the full collection of her poems, and the collection was published by Contact Press, in 1967.[6] It can be inferred that Hébert took Scott's advice about Miller to heart in allowing her poems to be translated by him. As well, she would seem to have heeded Scott's advice about not allowing too many translators to have access to her poems. One can contrast the situation with Miller and a situation that had arisen ten years earlier with another possible translator of Hébert's poetry.

On April 8, 1955, fellow poet and editor Cid Corman, who was at the time living in Paris, wrote Scott the following:

> In my 16th issue of ORIGIN...I had planned to use 4–6 poems by Anne Hébert in translations by Gael Turnbull and a French friend of his. The versions are quite satisfactory. But I recently wrote to Miss Hébert asking permission and hoping also that she were in Paris so that I might have her direct suggestions towards possible improvements. She writes me that you are her authorized translator (at least, of LES TOMBEAUX DES ROIS); that being the case, I write you for permission to print the versions I now have. I am of the belief that the importance is the poetry and that so long as the versions are honest and true, they should be made available as soon as possible. (FRSF, vol. 26, file 8)

Note here how Hébert has named Scott the "authorized translator" of her poetry, trusting him not only to translate but also seemingly to decide who translates her poems, as well as where those poems will appear. In a letter dated two days later, Turnbull himself wrote to Scott, again asking for permission to publish his translations of Hébert, reassuring Scott that "it is unlikely that more than half a dozen people in Canada read [*Origin*]," and thus such "would not conflict with any plans you have for publication of your versions, in this country" (FRSF, vol. 26, file 8). Turnbull also stated in the same letter that he and Jean Beaupré were currently working on translating a number of French Canadian poets, in the hopes of publishing a series, and that they wished to include Hébert. Scott responded to Turnbull in a letter dated April 13, 1955, expressing a great deal of interest in the project, and says of the Hébert translations, "I naturally would like you to go ahead and publish where ever and whenever you can. Of course you must clear with Anne Hébert, since she owns the copyright" (FRSF, vol. 26, file 8). Turnbull replies to Scott that he will re-inquire with Hébert about permission, hoping to be able to publish the translations. On April 27, 1955, Scott sends a letter to Corman, and copies both Hébert and Turnbull:

> I have been in touch with Gael Turnbull about the translations. I have no objections, of course, to anyone publishing anything they want to, only I feel you must have the actual versions approved by Anne Hébert. I think Turnbull is submitting his to her. I don't quite know what she means by "authorised translator"; I have assumed merely that I have the right to make my own translations with her approval and to hold copyright in them. Perhaps she wishes some person more familiar with English than herself to check the translations also. In this case we should be in some difficulty as regards to time. I can quite understand, however, that a poet would wish to control rather carefully what is published in another language over his name. I am sure we can work this out eventually. (FRSF, vol. 26, file 8)

Attached to this letter was the one quoted above concerning Scott's possible "exclusive right in translation." Scott's loyalty was rewarded, as Turnbull was never granted permission by Hébert to publish his translations of her poetry. It is unclear here why Turnbull was denied permission, although Scott does not seem to actively endorse Turnbull to Hébert as compared with his later assessment of Miller. Almost simultaneously, G. R. Roy was writing to Scott to enquire about an anthology he was assembling, which would become *Twelve Modern French-Canadian Poets*, published by Ryerson Press in 1958. Roy's anthology would include translations of Hébert's poetry, and he obviously was able to obtain permission. Although there is nothing in the archives, perhaps it is because Roy's father was a well-respected professor at the Université de Montréal, and thus a larger part of the Montreal circle, that Scott did not work to discourage this particular translation.

It is also interesting to note Scott's insistence in this particular situation with Turnbull that Turnbull solicited Hébert's advice on the translations. Hébert's own knowledge of English was limited at that time (see Godbout, *Traduction littéraire*), but so too was Turnbull's knowledge of French, as he states in a letter to Scott dated April 15, 1955, writing, "I don't have any more than a very rudimentary school-boy French, and have to depend on Beaupré here, for the idioms" (FRSF, vol. 26, file 8). Did Scott not trust Turnbull with the translations after an admission that his French was not very good? Did Hébert see the drafts and not approve of the translations? The archives do not reveal the reasons for Hébert's eventual refusal of Turnbull's request, but from the tone and content of the letters between Hébert and Scott, as well as those between Scott and Turnbull, one can certainly hypothesize that it would have something to do with the loyalty and friendship these two artists felt toward one another.

There seems to be one other early incident where a translation other than Scott's might be used in which Scott took an active interest. McClelland & Stewart in 1961 wrote to Scott about a planned collection of Hébert short stories and poems in translation, asking him to possibly write the introduction. At this point, Scott was about to release his own collection of translated poems by Hébert and thus could not accept the invitation. He does conclude his response, dated October 16, 1961, by stating, "I would be interested to learn who is going to do the translations, and whether Miss Hébert had given her approval. Perhaps you would write me again when you hear from her" (FRSF, vol. 64, file 13). The publishing house obviously did contact Hébert, as she writes to Scott in the February 17, 1962 letter:

> *McClelland and Stuwart [sic] voudraient publier, dans un même recueil, quelques nouvelles et quelques poèmes... Personnellement je ne trouve pas que ce soit une bonne idée de publier des nouvelles et des poèmes dans un même volume. Il me semble que le lecteur ordinaire qui pourrait s'intéresser aux nouvelles sera rebuté par la presence des poèmes. L'idéal ce serait de publier séparément les nouvelles et les poèmes!* (FRSF, vol. 64, file 14; McClelland and Stuwart [sic] want to publish a few short stories and poems in one volume...Personally, I don't think it's a good idea to publish them together. It seems to me that a casual reader who might be interested in the short stories would be put off by the presence of the poems. The ideal situation would be to publish the short stories and the poems separately!)

Scott responds in the February 21, 1962, letter: "They have asked me to edit it. I am not sure I want to do this. I rather agree with you that a mixture of prose and poetry may not be too good...You must realize that you are now looked upon as a kind of goldmine which English publishers can exploit... It is all very flattering but a little disconcerting" (FRSF, vol. 64, file 14). Hébert apparently never granted permission as the project did not materialize, and the first translations of her short stories, *The Torrent: Novellas and Short Stories*, translated by Gwendolyn Moore, appear in 1973 through Harvest House Press. Miller's (and Alan Brown's) translations of her poetry were released separately from the short stories, just as Hébert had wanted. One cannot discount the influence that Scott had on Hébert's decisions regarding her translations into English.

Hébert's friendship with Scott would not be the only relationship that she would forge with one of her translators. Both Alan Brown and Alfred Poulin Jr. would communicate extensively with Hébert about their respective translations of her poems.[7] Hébert would seem to have developed a literary friendship of sorts with both men, meeting with Brown to discuss his translations and the relationship between author and translator more generally (ABF, box 1, file 5), while Poulin and Hébert met frequently both in Montreal and Paris (AP-BOAE, box 10) with Hébert having a number of collections of Poulin's own poetry in her personal library (FAH, H2.195). As a result, the collections of these translators became privileged to a certain extent, with editors and publishers having to appeal directly to the author herself for permission to use translations other than Brown's or Poulin's. A case in point concerns Willis Barnstone and his attempts *not* to use the Brown translations in the anthology *A Book of Women Poets from Antiquity to Now* (Barnstone MSS). Janis Pallister as well sought to assemble a collection of Hébert's poetry in translation, but could not manage to obtain the poet's permission.[8] Part of the problem was perhaps Pallister's desire to include the poems from *Songes en équilibre*, a collection that Hébert herself refused to ever see republished. It may also have been the poor quality of the translations that convinced Hébert not to allow Pallister to attempt to translate her entire poetic œuvre. But one senses that Hébert was continuing to heed Scott's advice of not allowing too many translators access to her work, and given that both Brown and Poulin had provided (to that point) almost complete collections of translations that met her approval, the idea of a new collection may have seemed superfluous to the author.

F. R. SCOTT, COLLABORATOR

Of course, as mentioned, one cannot discuss Scott and his impact on the translations of Hébert's poetry without acknowledging *Dialogue sur la traduction*. The experience not only had an impact on future translations of Hébert's poetry but also on future translations of contemporary French Canadian poetry generally. As can be seen in his letters both to Hébert and other translators interested in working with her, he actively encouraged collaboration between author and translator in creating translations. When Miller, Brown, and Poulin contact Hébert looking for advice regarding their translations, her subsequent feedback can be seen as a direct consequence of Scott's influence.

The correspondence between Scott and Hébert discussing Scott's translation of "The Tomb of Kings" first appeared in 1960, in *Écrits du Canada français*, and was reprinted in *Tamarack Review*, in 1962. The publication in the two different journals is important because "cette double publication...a permis de faire connaître Frank Scott et Anne Hébert à de nouveaux publiques" (Watteyne 43). Included with these letters in both periodicals is an introduction by Jeanne Lapointe. In 1970, Éditions HMH published *Dialogue sur la traduction: À propos du "Tombeau des rois,"* which consisted of the letters, Lapointe's introduction, along with a new preface by Northrop Frye, and a third translation of the poem by Scott. The year 1985 saw a second edition of the book, in honour of HMH's twenty-fifth anniversary. In 2000, Bibliothèque québécoise reprinted *Dialogue sur la traduction* once again, and a revised, critical edition of *Dialogue sur la traduction*, edited by Patricia Godbout,[9] is included in *Œuvres complètes d'Anne Hébert, Tome I* (Watteyne). The impact of these letters on how critics read Scott's translations of Hébert's poetry was significant, as is illustrated in many of the reviews of *St-Denys Garneau & Anne Hébert*. In particular, critics began to draw attention to "The Tomb of Kings," which subsequently has become her most anthologized poem in English. Robin Skelton, in his review of Scott's translations, closely associates the letters between Scott and Hébert with what he calls Hébert's "finest poem" (81). It is no accident that that same association was made in the minds of many English Canadian critics.

Critical commentary on the letters began to appear as early 1962, the same year when the letters appeared in the *Tamarack Review* and closely coincided with the release of *St-Denys Garneau & Anne Hébert*. Laure Rièse praises Hébert's "lucid analysis," which "made Mr. Scott aware of all the linguistic and philosophical intricacies of her artistic output" (FRSF, vol. 51, file 7). George Whalley outlines how the dialogue "shows how scrupulously difficult this literalness of Scott's can be" (FRSF, vol. 51, file 7). When *Dialogue* is released in 1970, it is to positive reviews, almost exclusively in French, with both *Le Devoir* and *La Presse* running glowing reviews (FRSF, vol. 70, file 16). Jean Delisle provides a review of the book for the translation journal *Meta* in 1975. Again, the review is positive, with Delisle stating "Un dialogue comme celui d'Anne Hébert et de Frank Scott nous fait pénétrer au cœur de la création poétique et nous fait saisir en même temps à quel raffinement de langage doit viser le traducteur qui veut entreprendre la traduction d'une œuvre poétique" (229; A dialog, such as that between Anne Hébert and Frank Scott helps us to penetrate into the heart of poetic creation and, at the same time, makes us grasp the sophistication of language the translator must have in order to undertake the translation of a poetic work). A year later, in *Meta*, Pierre Marchand offers a rebuttal to Deslisle's positive review, concerning himself primarily with the shortcomings of translation the dialogue provides to the reader.

> *Après avoir vu toutes les difficultés qu'ont soulevées les différents aspects phoniques de l'œuvre à traduire, il semble bien qu'il soit impossible de parler de traduction, au sens où l'on entend généralement ce mot. La différence des caractéristiques phoniques des langues ne peut qu'engendrer des poésies radicalement différentes et indomptables.* (160; Having witnessed all the difficulties that translating various phonetic aspects brings forward, it would seem impossible to talk about

> translation, at least in the sense that we generally understand the term to mean. The different phonetic characteristics of the languages are indomitable and thus will only produce poetry that is radically different.)

These types of debates, which *Dialogue* inspired, are no doubt what leads Kathy Mezei to point to the book as being an important part of "the beginning of an aesthetic of translation in Canada" ("Poems" 103). E. D. Blodgett uses *Dialogue* to develop "a model for the practice of literary translation in Canada" (189), while Marcel Voisin looks to *Dialogue* to provide a new ethical standard for translations wherever possible (211). Not only has the collection stimulated translators, but it has stimulated translation theorists as well.

What the *Dialogue* and the close contact between Scott and Hébert also represented was a certain privileged status for Scott personally. Almost every early translator interested in translating Hébert first contacted Scott. This included G. Ross Roy, Gael Turnbull, Gwladys Downes, Peter Miller, and John Glassco. But others read *Dialogue* and acknowledged its influence on their translations, including Alfred Poulin, Kathleen Weaver, and Alan Brown. Scott's translations would become the standard to which all other translations would be held up against. D. G. Jones states: "while...Alan Brown [has] translated larger collections of [...] Anne Hébert, they cannot be said to have replaced the translations of Scott... Yet speaking more personally, I may say though Alan Brown may be a fine translator I cannot read his version of 'Vie de Château' without hearing that of Scott echoing through, especially at the end" ("F. R. Scott as Translator" 162). Critics may like or dislike Scott's translations (particularly in Canada, to be discussed further in subsequent chapters), but it is almost always his versions of Hébert's poems in English they return to as a point of departure.[10]

But the broader concept that Scott popularized was the idea of collaboration within the process of translation. He writes in his introduction to *St-Denys Garneau & Anne Hébert*, "As I have been assisted in these translations at various times and in various ways, especially by Micheline Ste. Marie, Jeanne Lapointe and by Anne Hébert herself...I am only part author of the English versions" (9). Perhaps the person most influenced by this idea was John Glassco, reflected in his work on *The Poetry of French Canada in Translation*. In a letter to Downes, dated March 6, 1969, Glassco offers feedback to Downes on some of her translations and notes, "I hope you don't find these suggestions intrusive. Frank Scott, Arthur Smith, George Johnston and many others, as well as myself, all mutually submit our translations to each other, and always benefit of the final version. Of course, this is mainly because we are constantly meeting" (JGF, container 2, file 21). But it is not just collaboration between and among translators which Glassco values; in browsing through Glassco's archives, one finds that Glassco contacted and solicited the advice of every single living poet he wanted to include in the anthology, often sending them the translations he had acquired, or asking if there were any translations the authors themselves were fond of. This list included Jacques Brault, André Brochu, Paul Chamberland, Robert Choquette, Cécile Cloutier, Eloi de Grandmont, and Alfred Desrochers, among others. Some declined to offer feedback on the translations, but a good many did, and Glassco worked hard to accommodate their requests. One such occurrence took place with Glassco acting as a go-between for Downes and Fernand Ouellette: "Could you oblige him? I like the poem ["Psalms for Shelter"], but in these cases I think we might stretch a point for one, and hope that you can come up with something that will please him" (JGF, container 2, file 21). This is just one example of how Glassco tried to create a collaborative environment under which to create his anthology of French Canadian poetry; there are many others, but this gives an idea of the influence Scott had on subsequent editors and translators more generally.

The archives of many of Canada's most important translators reveal that Scott was not alone in collaborating with the author in order to create translations. While translating their poetry, Peter Miller was soliciting feedback from Alain Grandbois, Octavio Paz, and Gaston Miron (CPR, box 1).[11] Alan Brown's archives reveal that he was not only in contact with Hébert, but also with Gabrielle Roy, Hubert Aquin, Jacques Godbout, Naïm Kattan, and André Langevin. These types of collaborations within the realm of translation were further explored by E. D. Blodgett and Jacques Brault in their production of *Transfiguration* (1998), and in the work of the translations and collaborations of those involved in the feminist literary theory periodical *Tessera*, which included Barbara Godard, Nicole Brossard, Daphne Marlatt, Susanne de Lotbinière-Harwood, and others. These are just some examples that illustrate the legacy of *Dialogue sur la traduction* on Canadian letters.

F. R. SCOTT, INSTIGATOR

And now we have come full circle to Scott's influence on the dissemination of Hébert's work in English translation. Let us take the opportunity to briefly examine the connections between Scott and those who would later translate or anthologize Hébert's poetry in English. Starting with the translators, G. R. Roy contacted Scott directly in regards to his input toward his anthology. In a letter dated July 3, 1955, Roy writes the following to Scott:

> I am taking the liberty of writing to you because I know that you have expressed interest in our project—a bilingual anthology of modern Canadian poetry in its original and in translation.
>
> In order to make as representative a selection as possible of the work of those poets which we include I feel that I should read all the poetry magazines published over the last 10 years. There is little of this material available here in our Montreal libraries, but I am informed that you have a great deal of it. I have applied for and was given a Modern Language Association grant to pay for having these magazines microformed; I must find them before this can be done. Would you allow me to look over your collection and have the necessary items microformed? (FRSF, vol. 26, file 8)

Although there is no reply from Scott in his archives, Roy did include a phone number where he could be contacted, and one imagines they did make contact. In fact, Scott planted the seed in John Glassco's head to produce an anthology of French Canadian poetry. In a letter dated November 12, 1957, Glassco writes, "I would like very much to talk with you about your wonderful idea of a bilingual anthology of Quebec poets: although to date I know only Garneau, [Jean-Guy] Pilon & [Giles] Fournier. I want to know more" (FRSF, vol. 26, file 9). It was through Scott that Glassco would become acquainted with many French Canadian poets and poetry, and in 1958, Glassco would be introduced to both Hébert and her poetry at a cocktail party at Scott's (Godbout, *Traduction* 202). G. V. Downes wrote to Scott in 1962 to inquire about translating French Canadian poetry, so as to not overlap with other translators. In her letter, she describes her views on translations: "I had very purist ideas about translation (ie [sic] impossible)," but, according to Downes, Hébert accommodates this tension by "[writing] poems similar to the French ones to give non-French readers an idea of the atmosphere" (FRSF, vol. 64, file 14, emphasis in the original). She continues to discuss her own views on *Dialogue* regarding "The Tomb of Kings," and even sends Scott copies of some of her translations, apologizing for "trying to improve on you and Anne Hébert" (FRSF, vol. 64, file 14). Daniel Sloate, in an interview in Montreal on February 19, 2003, acknowledged that it was Scott who insisted that he read Hébert's *Tombeau des rois*. It was a student of Sloate's at the Université de Montréal who seems to have introduced Scott to Sloate's work. In a letter dated September 9, 1971, Michel Germain writes, "étant vous-même écrivain, poète et 'traducteur' vous connaissez sans doute M. Daniel Slote; ce dernier a publié récemment sa traduction des Illuminations de Rimbaud"[12] (Scott fonds; given that you are a writer, poet and 'translator' yourself, you no doubt know M. Daniel Slote; he recently published his translation of Rimbeaud's Illuminations). On June 21, 1971, Scott writes to "Mr. Slote"—"I am delighted with your translation of 'Illuminations,' and have been reading it with the greatest pleasure" (FRSF, vol. 66, file 5). Fred Cogswell knew Scott through his poetry and would seem to have first contacted him on December 19, 1953, on behalf of the literary journal *The Fiddlehead*, "I, for one, am a great admirer of your work and would like to see it represented in The Fiddlehead" (FRSF, vol. 26, file 7). Ralph Gustaphson would also have known Scott through his poetry and through Glassco. Peter Miller may not have known Scott directly, but he obviously read his translations, and contacted Scott through closer friends of his, Dudek and Souster. Alan Brown's work as a translator would also have put him in contact with Scott's translations, and while it is unclear if the two men knew each other personally, we can see Scott's influence in Brown's contact with Hébert in order to solicit her feedback on his translations.

As for those who edited anthologies in Canada, contact with Scott was also close. Louis Dudek, as he was about to start teaching at McGill, writes to "Professor Scott" on August 29, 1951, in regards to the current crop of poets in Canada (FRSF, vol. 26, file 6). The two would maintain a friendship until Scott's death; indeed, Dudek delivered the eulogy at Scott's funeral (LDF, box 18, file 7). Mordecai Richler also had a friendship with Scott, who wrote in support of Richler in grant applications (MRF, MsC 36.12.6). Robert Weaver was an editor at *Tamarack Review*, where the letters that would eventually become the *Dialogue* were originally published, but his friendship with Scott dates as far back as his time at CBC Radio in Montreal in the 1950s (FRSF, vol. 26, box 6). William Toye was editor at Oxford University Press, where Scott had published a number of books. Leslie Monkman took classes at the Université de Sherbrooke from D. G. Jones (who co-founded the translation journal *Ellipse* with translator/editor Philip Stratford), a poet and translator in his own right, as well as founder of *Ellipse*, and close friend to Scott. John Robert Colombo also knew of Scott's translations and work as a poet, and they knew each other as fellow poets. Raymond Souster would have known Scott through Dudek, but also again as a fellow poet and editor. P. K. Page was also a part of the early Montreal movement, along with Souster and Dudek. Barry Callaghan would have known of Scott, most likely through his father, the novelist Morley Callaghan.

The relationships among the editors, poets, and translators in Canada would seem fairly natural; most of the authors and translators listed here are from the same generation, roughly speaking, and most were based at one point or another in or around Montreal, where Scott spent almost all of his professional life. Those translating Hébert later and outside Canada may not have had direct contact with Scott; his influence can still be seen in their translations, though. Katherine Weaver, Alfred Poulin Jr., and Janis L. Pallister all acknowledge knowing about the existence of *Dialogue* and to having used it a varying degree. While neither Willis Barnstone nor Graham Dunstan Martin knew of the existence of Scott and Hébert's *Dialogue*, there are nonetheless possible points of connection. Martin lived in Edinburgh, where Gael Tunbull would spend the second half of his life, and Barnstone was friends with Poulin, having published poetry at BOA Editions, Poulin's publishing house. While it is not a direct connection, these two translators were nonetheless no more than two degrees from Scott.

One cannot also discount Scott's indirect (and accidental) influence on the feminist translation movement in Canada. As put most recently by Alessandra Capperdoni:

> The notion of translation as "cultural bridge" has been at the centre of Scott's translational practice and informs his theoretical stance in his dialogue with Anne Hébert... As Godard (1984, 2002) and Mezei (1986) point out in relation to this creative exchange, the dialogue between poet and translator is symptomatic of the blindness to the sexual dimension of hierarchical power structures. On that occasion, Hébert critiqued Scott for not realizing that her poem *Le Tombeau des rois* (1953) is about a ritual rape and the subject of her poem is a young girl. (Capperdoni 247n3)

This oversight also forced the conversation about translation in Canada to move past the ideas of nationalism and identity building toward more inclusive and dynamic theories of translation. It inspired translators, as well, to look at the specific social circumstances from which the poetry originated: "Anti-colonialist resistance, so pertinent in the Quebec field of cultural production, is concealed in the English translation which presents this specific dispossession as stemming from a universal human condition requiring no political intervention to counter it" (Godard, "Literature in the Making" 89). As Godard and others point out, Scott's translation and subsequent discussion highlighted the ways that he misread the poems as much as the ways he got them "right."

CONCLUSION

Scott's influence on Hébert's image as an author in English Canada and beyond is unmistakable. His fingerprints can be found on just about every incarnation of Hébert's poetry in English. The face of translation in Canada would be much different if not for Scott's work and *Dialogue sur la traduction*. Nor perhaps would Hébert be best known for her poem "The Tomb of Kings" if it were not for the *Dialogue* book. Long recognized for his influence on English letters and poetry, as well as translation, we can now see the influence Scott had on one particular French Canadian poet. Patricia Godbout points out that Hébert's (self) image as a poet in her own language was also influenced by *Dialogue*:

> *[C]'est dans le retour de son œuvre—que la traduction lui aura permis d'accomplir—, et sur elle-même—dans ses rapports avec son propre milieu...sa lettre sur la traduction lui donne l'occasion de revenir pour ainsi dire sur ses pas et donc de revisiter les lieux de l'expérience sensible ayant donné naissance au poème. Ce retour au réel, qui n'est pas un chemin vers son point de départ mais une redécouverte d'un soi transformé dans et par le regard de l'autre, est favorisé par les remarques et questions très pointues du traducteur averti et homme de terrain qu'est Scott.* ("La dialogisme" 68; It is in this return to her œuvre, which is provoked by the process of translation, and thus a self-examination, with her relationship to her environment... her letter on translation gives her an opportunity to retrace her steps and revisit the place of the original emotional experience which gave birth to the poem. This return to the real, which is not a straight path to the beginning but instead a rediscovery of a self transformed in and by the gaze of the other, is facilitated by the pointed remarks and questions of the attentive translator and learned man, Scott.)

The shape of Anne Hébert in both languages is marked with Scott's influence.

While Scott's immediate circle of influence was Montreal—as a part of the so-called McGill Movement or McGill Group that championed modernist poetry, and then while a professor at McGill as an intellectual, author, and translator—his ultimate impact reached far beyond the borders of the island city. Sherry Simon, in her book *Translating Montreal: Episodes of Life in a Divided City* (2006), looks at Scott's attempts to create a bilingual literary scene in Montreal. She concludes: "Frank Scott arrived too early. He tried to create a scene, but the mix would not take hold. It is hard not to see Scott's crosstown journeys as something of a failure" (52). Barbara Godard puts it differently:

> Scott's practice introduced a new model for translating poetry (the field of marginal production) which in the English-Canadian tradition has subsequently been "literalist." Although a privileged interlocutor or rewriter for Hébert, Scott did not have the kind of widely recognized prestige of an Edmund Wilson to make her poetry pertinent in the field of restricted

> production, but only in the field of marginal production of left-wing and avant-garde periodicals. ("Literature in the Making" 86)

Perhaps Scott failed to create a larger, more unified literary movement or influence; nonetheless, he not only became "the defining influence for the next generation of English-language translators" (Simon, *Translating Montreal* 53), but also played an important, if not seminal, role in Hébert's popularity in English. Anne Hébert, the poet, would not be the same in English if not for F. R. Scott.

But we also see the broader role Scott played in setting up fair compensation for translators, and also helped to rewrite copyright laws as to be more favorable for translators. A tireless cultural crusader, his work also helped to establish a dedicated, federally supported funding system that would allow for works to be translated and published. We see his struggles with copyright and compensation, as well as his tireless promotion of French Canadian letters during an important and formative time in Canadian literature. The canon was up for debate, and he was trying to make sure that French Canadians were included. He may have indeed been "too early," but for Anne Hébert and Canadian letters, his impact was to be felt for a long time afterward.

Notes

1. See *The Making of Modern Poetry in Canada*, Louis Dudek, 1967; *The McGill Movement*, Peter Stevens, 1969; *On F. R. Scott*, Sandra Djwa and R. St. J. Macdonald, 1983; *The Politics of Imagination*, Djwa, 1987; *The Montreal Forties*, Brian Trehearne, 1999.
2. For a complete analysis of these first two translations and Scott and Hébert's early relationship, see Godbout, *Traduction littéraire et sociabilité interculturelle au Canada (1950–1960)* (75–84) and Djwa (371–83).
3. Gael Turnbull had previously attempted to get permission to publish translations of poems by Hébert, and in a letter dated April 3, 1955, Hébert wrote to Turnbull: "Ce recueil [*Songes en équilibre*] date de trop longtemps, et, je ne tiens pas du tout à le ramener au jour. Je préfère l'oublier" (Godbout, *Traduction* 98).
4. The clippings themselves can be accessed using the call number MG30-D211 at Libraries and Archives Canada (collectionscanada.gc.ca/pam_archives/index.php?fuseaction=genitem.displayHierarchy&lang=eng&rec_nbr=121879).
5. Scott's archives also contain a review from *La Presse*, dated sometime in early October 1970. Unfortunately, given that the archives are now only available through microfiche, the article is almost illegible.
6. Chapter Two will include a close analysis of Miller's translations.
7. Both translators, and their subsequent contact with the author, will be dealt with in detail in Chapter Two.

8. See Chapter Four for further analysis of this situation and Pallister's translations of Hébert's poetry.
9. Patricia Godbout also has an extended analysis of *Dialogue* in her essays "La dialogisme chez Anne Hébert," *Cahiers Anne Hébert* 10 (2011) and "L'espace du Dialogue sur la traduction entre Anne Hébert et Frank Scott," *Cahiers Anne Hébert* 9 (2010).
10. See the next two chapters on the extent of this comparison when dealing with later translations of Hébert.
11. Contact Press published two of the three collections of translated poetry; the translations of Miron's poetry remain unpublished (Contact Press Records).
12. Daniel Sloate was the name used as a writer and translator, while Daniel Slote was the name used as a professor.

2

Anne Hébert—The Collections

This chapter examines the circumstances around the English-language translation, publication, and reception of Hébert's collections of poetry. Most importantly, we will see the many hands that shaped these collections from inception to publication and beyond. Wherever possible, I have tried to document some of the dialogue that took place between the various parties involved in the process, to underscore the social nature of these translations and publications. The question of who made these texts is often a difficult one to answer, as we will see. Focusing separately on the collections allows for us to closely read the process, as well as the conditions under which they were produced and received. A larger, if incomplete, picture of translation and publishing in Canada (and, to a lesser extent, the United States) will emerge, as well as how Hébert's image was beginning to take shape in English.

Anne Hébert's introduction to the French Canadian literary scene was first and foremost through her *collections* of poetry; while she had published a few uncollected poems in small literary journals, it wasn't until her collections were published that the literary establishment took notice of her, for better or for worse, with publishers in Quebec refusing to publish her second collection, *Le Tombeau des rois* because of the controversial (at the time) images and subject matter. But Hébert was very conscious that she was creating a cohesive *book* of poems, even with her later collections that brought together many previously published but uncollected poems. Her archival records show that she was very deliberate in curating the poems and order of those poems for each complete collection.[1] Even in her discussions with translators (as we will see), Hébert made sure that her poems were not assembled in a way that violated the spirit of the original French-language publication. Critics also noted the coherence in her various collections, the poems often reflecting back on themselves as the poetic narrative progresses (Watteyne, 45). The importance of this coherence, this poetic vision for each of the complete collections, makes it important that they appear as complete collections in English; if not, her image would remain incomplete.

Hébert's first collection of poetry, *Les Songes en équilibre*, was published in 1942,[2] followed eleven years later by *Le Tombeau des rois*. French poet and family friend Pierre Emmanuel provided the introduction. Hébert had a great deal of difficulty finding a publisher in Quebec for her second collection, and moved to France as a result (Harvey, "Les années"). Les Éditions du Seuil in Paris published *Poèmes* in 1960, which consisted of two parts: Part one was a reprint of the poems found in *Le Tombeau des rois*, while part two, "Mystère de la parole," contained a brief treatise by Hébert on writing poetry, called "Poésie, solitude rompue," and fifteen new poems. After 1960, Hébert focused her attention on her prose writing, while still sporadically publishing poems in magazines and journals. It was not until 1992 that *Le jour n'a d'égal que la nuit*, which consisted of uncollected poems published between 1961 and 1980 and new poems written between 1987 and 1989, along with another meditation on writing poetry, "Écrire un poème," appeared. One year later, in 1993, *Œuvre poétique: 1950–1990* was published, which comprised poems from *Le Tombeau des rois*, *Poèmes*, and *Le jour n'a d'égal que la nuit*. Finally, in 1997, *Poèmes pour la main gauche*, Hébert's final collection of poetry, was published.

In English, Contact Press published Peter Miller's translation of *Le Tombeau des rois* in 1967 as *The Tomb of Kings*. Alan Brown's translation, *Poems by Anne Hébert*, was printed by Musson Books in 1975. Alfred Poulin Jr. published *Anne Hébert: Selected Poems*, in 1987, and *Day Has No Equal but Night*, in 1994, both through BOA Editions. Anansi Press released Lola Lemire Tostevin's translations of that same collection, but as *Day has no equal but the night*, in 1997. Surprisingly, *Poèmes pour la main gauche* has not yet appeared in English translation. Hébert herself refused to see her first collection of poems ever reprinted or republished in French, let alone in English translation. Thus we are left with five collections of Hébert's poetry in English translation for analysis and comparison. Let us now see who made these texts.

PETER MILLER, THE TOMB OF KINGS[3]

Peter Miller is not one of the best-known names in Canadian literature. Nonetheless, he played an invaluable role as an editor/business manager for Contact Press, a small press devoted to poetry, during the 1960s. With Louis Dudek and Raymond Souster, Miller helped shape the face of modern poetry in Canada by helping keep the press financially viable. He published two collections of his own poems through Contact, as well as three collections of translation, *The Tomb of Kings* by Anne Hébert, *Selected Poems* by Alain Grandbois, and *The Sun-Stone* by Octavio Paz. The Contact Press collection of manuscripts and editorial correspondence, located at the University of Toronto, also contain a completed, unpublished manuscript of translations of Gaston Miron's early poetry.[4]

Miller was born in London, England, moved to Toronto in 1939, and served in the Canadian Army until 1946. He worked for a bank in Toronto until 1960, whereupon he quit and travelled around the world. He started writing in 1956, and in 1959 was invited to join the editorial team at Contact Press, joining founders Dudek and Souster (CPR, box 2, folder 3). In a letter to Dudek dated April 2, 1963, Miller explains how he became interested in French poetry from Quebec: "It sprang from an expression of interest from Weaver and Colombo of *Tamarack* [*Review*] in translations from the Québécois...it was a useful suggestion." Further on, Miller explains to Dudek, "my philosophy [for translation] is—do not translate as an exercise, but give full attention to translation if the original text seems to demand translation—if the work is a necessity" (CPR, box 2, folder 3). Responding to the letter (and a subsequent phone call), Dudek writes to Miller on April 3, 1962: "This kind of undertaking [translation] has its incidental uses in bringing us together, while at the same time fanatics are beginning to throw bombs and derail trains. We have a very good feeling of common cause with these French Canadian poets, and I plan to arrange further friendly meetings" (CPR, box 2, folder 4). While Miller's philosophy of translation stemmed from a place that could be described as pure poetry, the spectre of the political realities at that time was never far from any of their minds. As he puts at the end of a letter to Dudek dated December 23, 1964, "I do believe that there is a need for [translations] in the field of biculturalism" (CPR, box 2, folder 4).

In an undated letter, probably from sometime in 1964, Peter Miller writes the following to his two fellow editors:

> For years I have felt that this central poetry collection of Anne Hébert's is an indivisible classic which should be available in full English... Frank Scott's fine translations in the Klanak selection of Hébert-Garneau include only six poems from Le Tombeau des Rois [sic]. My versions differ somewhat from his.
>
> How would you two feel about this as a Contact bilingual edition, if permissions can be obtained? (CPR, box 2, folder 4)

Attached was a copy of Miller's manuscript of his translations of Hébert's poetry. Souster seemed to have replied almost immediately, and offered Miller some feedback in what Souster calls Miller's "inversions." For example, in "Les grandes fontaines," the French line reads "N'y plongent aucune image" (Hébert, *Œuvre* 15), which Miller translates as "Plunge into them no image," and Souster instead suggests "Plunge no image into them" (Contact Press collection). Further along in the poem, the French reads "Où veillent les droits piliers / De ma patience ancienne," which Miller translates as "Where watch the straight pillars / Of my longtime patience," and Souster suggests changing to "Where the straight pillars of my longtime patience watch," without the line break. It should be noted that neither of these changes was incorporated in the final version of the translations. As Miller explains to Dudek in a letter dated December 23, 1964, "I can only say that the word-order is in every case quite deliberate, to achieve a particular effect that I am after: a feeling, if you will, that accords with that of the original without violating rules" (CPR, box 2, folder 4). Overall, however, Souster lends his support to Miller's work, calling the translations "a beautiful job."

Dudek takes much more time to respond to Miller, but finally, on May 23, 1965, he sends Miller twenty-eight pages of handwritten comments on the translations, and another typewritten page dated two days later with additional comments (CPR, box 2, folder 5). Louis Dudek's archives, at Library and Archives Canada, in Ottawa, contain Miller's handwritten corrected manuscript that was sent back to Dudek for approval, on June 4, 1965. Dudek makes an interesting comment to Miller in one of his opening remarks on Miller's translation of the poem "The Tomb of Kings," in regards to how Dudek viewed his role in the process of translating and publishing the collection: "Any differences between *our* versions and Scott's..." (CPR, box 2, folder 5, emphasis added). Dudek took his role as editor at Contact Press very seriously, and while Miller was the translator, the collection was to be published by the press that Dudek had helped found. Dudek shared Souster's enthusiasm for the translations, writing, "You've got a great book here, very important, and a permanent part of Canadian literature" (CPR, box 2, folder 5).

In his introduction to his translation of *The Tomb of Kings*, Miller writes, "To my fellow-editor and good friend Louis Dudek I offer my best thanks for having studied the translations in minute detail, and for his resulting suggestions towards corrections of errors and improvements of language. A great many of his recommendations have been adopted in the final versions" (12). This points to the close and intimate influence Dudek, a colleague, it should be noted, of Frank Scott's at McGill, had on Miller and the translations of Hébert's poetry. Dudek, in his feedback dated May 23, 1965, points Miller to Scott and Hébert's dialogue in *Tamarack Review* in an aside at the beginning of his comments on the poem "The Tomb of Kings":

> Don't forget that [Scott] has consulted Anne Hébert on many points. Have you checked both his translations of his correspondence with A-H published in Tamarack Review? Any differences between our versions

and Scott's—in the sense of the words—<u>must be confirmed by superior research or consultation with the author</u>. Otherwise you will be caught wrong where the means to correct reading was available to you. (CPR, box 2, folder 4)

Dudek places the emphasis on being able to consult with the author as a resource in order to create an accurate translation. Miller agrees, and at the top of his annotated and corrected manuscript he writes, addressing Dudek, "Some of these changes result from your own excellent suggestions; others from AH's own explanations in <u>Tamarack</u>" (LDF, Box 14, file 17). In the spirit of *Dialogue*, the following is a reconstruction of the more salient points of the conversation between Dudek and Miller about "The Tomb of Kings." The information is taken from the Contact Press collection, letter dated May 23, 1965 (CPR, box 2, folder 4), and the Louis Dudek fonds, letter dated June 4, 1965 (LDF, Box 14, file 17). The layout followed here will mirror the format used in *Dialogue*, starting with the original line in French, then as translated by Miller, followed by Dudek's comments, then Miller's, and finishing with Miller's final translation of the line.

Line 3: Le taciturne oiseau pris à mes doigts
Trans: With the taciturn bird captive at my fingers
LD: "Pris à mes doigts" must mean there that the bird is "gripping my fingers" (I've just confirmed this from F. R. Scott's translation.)
PM: Yes, as you point out, Anne H explains "pris à" in <u>Tamarack</u>. Apart from a wish to avoid crass imitation, I think maybe <u>taking</u> has the edge over <u>gripping</u>, as it is a closer translation of <u>prends</u> and has the double sense of <u>catching</u> and <u>holding</u>.
Final trans: "With the taciturn bird taking my fingers"

Line 4: Lampe gonflée de vin et de sang
Trans: Lamp swollen with wine and with blood
LD: Read "A lamp swollen..." In English this apposition would require an article, and it is the bird who is a lamp.
Final trans: A lamp swollen with wine and with blood

Line 7: Étonnée
Trans: Astonished
LD: Astonished could be "Myself surprised" to make clear that it is not the kings who are astonished or surprised. (The French of course is clear; i.e. "myself" would correspond to this inflection)
Final trans: Astonished

Line 10: Au long des dédales sourds?
Trans: Along the dulled labyrinths?
LD: "Through the silent labyrinths?" Dulled is not so good.
PM: I can't help using FRS's muted, it is the only good word.
Final trans: "Along the muted labyrinths?"

Line 13–14: Cette enfant fut-elle liée par la cheville/Pareille à une esclave fascinée?
Trans: Was that child bound by the ankle/Like a fascinated slave?
LD: Possibly "Like a slave in fascination" or "Like an astonished slave" (better)—if you have not used "astonished" in line 7.
Final trans: Was this child bound by her ankle/Like a fascinated slave?

Line 16–17: Presse le fil,/Et viennent les pas nus
Trans: Presses on the thread/And the naked footsteps come
LD: "Pulls on the thread" might be just as correct for "presse"—and more apt.
PM: If AH had intended pulls she would have said tire. Accuracy demands presses for presse—one can picture it—by pressing on the thread the footsteps are made to come. [Miller provides two sketches to make his point]
Final trans: Presses on the thread/So come the naked footsteps

Line 22: Suinte sous le pas des portes
Trans: Oozes under the doorsteps
LD: "Leaks at the sill of doors" might be better. I do not see odours "oozing"; thought it is better than "sweating." Leaks is also a dictionary equivalent for suinte.
PM: Leaking at the doors would be very uncouth manners? You're right. Larousse says "le pas de la porte" is seuil, or sill, not a step. Thanks.
Final trans: Seeps from the sills of the doors

Line 23: Aux chambres secrètes et rondes
Trans: By the secret round rooms
LD: Why "By"? These are the doors of rooms in the Tombeau des Rois. Say—"Of the round and secret rooms" (or chambers).
Final trans: Of the rooms, secret and round

Line 24: Là où sont dressés les lits clos
Trans: Where the sealed beds are poised
PM: AH explains about the beds. FRS could not improve on closed but I hope enclosed brings out her meaning more clearly.
Final trans: Where the enclosed beds are arrayed

Line 25: L'immobile désir des gisants me tire
Trans: The unmoving desire of the effigies draws me
LD: "The stilled desire" would be wonderful for "l'immobile désire." How about—"The stilled desire of the dwellers draws me" (Why call them "effigies"? She is thinking of them as quite aware, ghosts in fact)
PM: Gisant is (Larousse) "une statue d'un personnage rendré." Therefore the representation draws her not the body inside.
Final trans: The still desire of the effigies draws me

Line 26–27: Je regarde avec étonnement/À même les noirs ossements
Trans: I look with astonishment/As upon the black bones
LD: "As even on the black bones" (Je regarde at line 26 might be enforced with I gaze)
PM: Still and gaze are two fine suggestions. Thanks. AH's own explanation satisfies me that "as upon black bones" gets her image across. À même here is purely positional, not emphatic, so I have thought best to simplify. No—changed my mind to "as set on the black bones"—deliberate ambiguity.
Final trans: I gaze with astonishment/As set on the black bones

Line 30: Sur la poitrine des rois, couchées
Trans: On the breast of the kings, laid out
PM: For couchées I am much tempted to use displayed. Only a frenzy for strict accuracy prevents me.
Final trans: On the breast of the kings, laid out

Line 31: En guise de bijoux
Trans: By way of jewels
LD: "en guise"—"by way" is weak. "In the form of jewels." "In the guise of jewels."
Final trans: In the guise of jewels

Line 37: Offrande rituelle et soumise
Trans: Ritual and submissive offering
LD: The "and" could be omitted: "Ritual submissive offering"
Final trans: Ritual and submissive offering

Line 44: Semblable au vent qui prend, d'arbre en arbre
Trans: Like the wind that catches, from tree to tree
LD: "Like the wind that lifts/stirs, from tree to tree" better?
PM: Surely catches is exact for prend. Stirs doesn't have the same connotation. Incidentally, AH points out the relationship to fire which prend (catches).
Final trans: Like the wind that catches, from tree to tree

Line 45: Agite sept grands pharaons d'ébène
Trans: Stirs seven great ebony pharaohs
LD: "~~Disturbs~~ ~~Touches~~ Shakes (Yes!) seven great pharaohs of ebony"
PM: Shakes is too violent a word for agite
Final trans: Stirs seven great ebony pharaohs

Line 46: En leurs étuis solennels et parés
Trans: In their solemn ornate caskets
LD: "In their solemn ornate tombs" for rhythm.
PM: (étuis) AH points outs that these boxes or cases fit neatly, following the shape inside.
Final trans: In their solemn ornate casings

Line 51: En un cliquetis léger de bracelets
Trans: In a light tinkling of bracelets
PM: FRS has "tinkle" (one tinkle) but I see the racket as being continuous—hence tinkling.
Final trans: In a light tinkling of bracelets

Line 52: Cercles vains jeux d'ailleurs
Trans: Vain rings games of elsewhere
LD: "Vain rings elsewhere games"
Final trans: Vain rings games of elsewhere

Line 53: Autour de la chair sacrifiée
Trans: Around the sacrificed flesh
LD: "About the flesh once sacrificed." (This would be entirely true to the original: "once" simply emphasizes the fr. tense)
Final trans: Around the sacrificed flesh

Line 54: Avides de la source fraternelle de mal en moi
Trans: Thirsty for the brotherly source of evil in me
PM: AH says "avide" is more general than thirsty (or hungry)
Final trans: Craving the brotherly source of evil in me

Line 56: Sept fois, je connais l'étau des os
Trans: Seven times, I know the vice of bones
LD: "Vice" is too ambiguous in English. How about "the vice-press of bones," "the screw-press"?
PM: American usage permits spelling vise for the tool, thus enabling avoidance of ambiguity of vice.
Final trans: Seven times, I know the vise of bones

Line 59: Les membres dénoués
Trans: My limbs unknotted
PM: AH explains this sense of dénoués
Final trans: My limbs unfettered

Line 61: Quel reflet d'aube s'égare ici?
Trans: What gleam of dawn strays here?
PM: FRS again. All honor to him.
Final trans: What glimmer of dawn strays here?

Louis Dudek's remarks about the poem conclude with "A fantastic poem of entry into 'death's other kingdom.'" Miller adds his own concluding paragraph to the end of his annotated and corrected version of "The Tomb of Kings."

> This is undoubtedly AH's greatest poem. Difficult even in French, but worth the challenge. Of course, Frank Scott's translation is so superb that a new one is not needed, but one has to be made for presentation of the book in its entirety. And I have hazarded a version which does differ from his in some respects. The purpose is not competitive, but purely towards a definitive version in English for which he is mainly responsible, with additions of your thoughts and mine.

What is interesting here is Miller's mixture of resources: Dudek, Scott's translations, Hébert's comments, as well as Miller's own aesthetic preferences. He certainly does create his own version of the poem in English despite the pressure from Dudek (and indirectly from Scott) to translate otherwise.

One of the reasons that the publication of the book took place more than a year after permission was granted was the care both Dudek and Souster showed in producing a book of the highest quality. Miller first expressed his concern over their ability to obtain permission to publish translations of Hébert's poetry in a letter to Dudek dated December 23, 1964. "If you approve the ms., the question of permissions will be especially tricky, as I think Anne Hébert is quite reluctant re translations, from what I hear" (CPR, box 2, folder 4). Dudek does in fact approve the manuscript and, in a letter dated May 25, 1965, suggests "we use all our big ammunition of support at one time, so as not to risk a refusal...We want her to know that she has the best translator and the best publishing outlet that could be hoped for" (CPR, box 2, folder 4). Among his suggestions: both Dudek and Souster contacting the poet to speak to Miller's quality as a translator, sending copies of Miller's previous translations, contacting Scott directly and soliciting his support, and sending a copy of the manuscript for Hébert's approval. In the end, Dudek supplies a letter to Hébert, while Souster contacts Scott for his support. In his letter to Scott, dated May 19, 1965, Souster writes,

> Peter [Miller] has translated the whole of the The Tomb of Kings [sic] in what I read as a very smooth translation, but which you would be a better judge...
>
> I have heard it said that you are the sole authorized translator of Anne Hebert's [sic] work, and you have certainly done her justice in English. So it really boils down to how you feel about this other translation, whether you feel it should appear, whether you would be willing to approach the lady to get authorization for Peter's translations. I think that this is an important book which should be more widely available. (CPR, box 2, folder 4)

As shown in the first chapter, while Scott does not directly endorse Miller's translations to Hébert, he does not openly object to them. Dudek attempts to reassure Hébert of Miller's quality as a translator in his letter dated June 7, 1965—

> Having examined these translations with the greatest of care, in every word and phrase, I can tell you that I think they are sensitive, true to the spirit of the originals, and reliable as verbal equivalents. One feels again the highly personal, deeply spiritual, and authentic awareness of the borderline between the realms of matter and spirit which is your poetry. There is no touch of the kind of literalism or realism in translation that would destroy the poetic and symbolic intention. (CPR, box 2, folder 4)

Hébert was already aware, through Scott, of Miller's quality as a translator, but of course it was impossible for Dudek or Miller to know that Scott had long ago lent his tacit support for Miller's translations. Finally, in Miller's letter to Hébert dated June 12, 1965, he chose to focus on the importance of seeing Hébert's complete collection published in translation.

> *On pourrait dire—je le dis moi-même—que les traductions admirables de Frank Scott, faites avec votre propre collaboration et conseil, soient définitives: qu'on n'a plus besoin de versions alternatives. Cette assertion pourrait bien se constater quant aux poèmes déjà traduits. Il m'a semblé pourtant que ce livre soit une totalité, divisible si nécessaire, mais qui n'offre sa beauté complète que par sa forme totale. Ces vingt-sept poèmes, réunis, se renforcent et se présentent en petit chef-d'œuvre. En traduisant, on devrait en reproduire cette forme dans la perfection de sa totalité. Il existe peu de livres de poésie, de n'importe quelle langue, auxquels on pourrait payer un compliment semblable, d'en vouloir garder ensemble chaque poème.* (CPR, box 2, folder 4; One could say, and I do say, that the admirable translations done by Frank Scott with your collaboration and council are the definitive versions, and that we don't need any alternative versions. The same could well be said about the poems already translated. Yet it would also seem to me that this book is a complete work, divisible if necessary, but one whose full beauty is only realized through its complete form. These twenty-seven poems, presented together, reinforce and present themselves as a complete tour-de-force. Through translation, we should recreate this form and in the perfection of its totality. There are few books of poetry in any language to which one could pay such a compliment, to want to preserve the presence of each and every poem.)

The three letters, read together, use every trick in the book, so to speak, in order to convince Hébert to give her permission to publish the translations.

Hébert's reply does not appear until October 1, 1965 (due, as she explains in the letter, to her mother's death), and it would seem that Miller appealed to the perfect sensibility in Hébert. The original manuscript included a translation of "Poésie, solitude rompue" as an introduction to the collection. This was Hébert's major problem with the manuscript as it stood at that moment:

> *L[a] seule remarque que je puisse faire, pour le moment est que "Poésie, solitude rompue" n'est pas une introduction au "Tombeau des Rois" [sic], celui-ci étant préfacé par Pierre Emmanuel. "Poésie, solitude rompue" sert d'introduction au "Mystère de la Parole" [sic]. Les Editions Seuil ayant réuni, dans un seul volume "Le Tombeau des Rois" et "Mystère de la Parole," il y a parfois confusion. Mais cela demeure deux œuvres tout à fait autonomes, écrites à des époques différentes, en temps et en expérience humaine.* (CPR, box 2, folder 4; The only comment I have to offer at the moment is that "Poésie, solitude rompue" is not an introduction to "Tombeau des Rois" [sic], which was prefaced by Pierre Emmanuel. "Poésie, solitude rompue" serves as an introduction to "Mystère de la Parole." Les Éditions Seuil combined "Le Tombeau des Rois" and "Mystère de la Parole" in a single volume, which sometimes causes the confusion. But they remain two completely autonomous works, written at different epochs, both in regards to time and human experience.)

Miller concedes the point in a response to Hébert dated October 8, 1965, stating that the situation can be "facilement régler." It is another long wait for Hébert's next reply. In a letter dated January 14, 1966, she apologizes yet again for the extended delay in a response, due to family obligations and moving between Paris, Quebec City, and Montreal. But she finally gives her blessing to the translations, stating:

> *Votre traduction me semble juste et fidèle. Cette recréation poétique à partir d'une telle fidélité au texte original est vraiment étonnante. Cela me touche profondément. Merci de tout cœur. Je serais très heureuse si vous envisagiez encore (malgré le temps écoulé) de publier vos traductions de mes poèmes.* (CPR, box 2, folder 4; Your translation seems to me to be true and faithful. That you were able to recreate the poetry with such a faithfulness to the original text is truly amazing. It is profoundly touching. I offer you my heartfelt thanks. I would be very happy if you still wish to publish (despite the time lapse) your translations of my poems.)

What is striking here is her deep appreciation for Miller's translations, not just the quality, but the time and effort put into recreating her poems in English, not to mention the overall reverence that Miller expressed in regards to her poetry. Her permission is granted, and sets the ball rolling to have the translations published the following year.

For Peter Miller, producing *The Tomb of Kings* was truly a labour of love. One of the reasons that the publication of the book took place more than a year after permission was granted was the care that he took in ensuring that the book also *looked* perfect. Miller and Robert Feher, from Three Star Printing, Montreal, exchanged a number of letters regarding how the poems would appear on the page. The collection was to be bilingual, with the French on the left-hand side and the translations on the right. Early in 1967 (February 21, to be exact), Miller insisted that a page be reprinted: "I am sorry, but as I want this book to be as perfect as possible I must ask you to REPRINT PAGE 66, closing up the stanza 2 to agree exactly with the English and adjusting the spacing on the rest of the page" (CPR, box 2, folder 6). Miller achieves his goal, and, in 1967, the complete bilingual edition of *The Tomb of Kings*, complete with a translator's note and Pierre Emmanuel's original introduction translated into English is published. As Miller writes in the translator's note, "The present publication of *The Tomb of Kings* results from my being haunted by this text for a good many years...To provide the complete text in bilingual edition has been an insistent ambition of mine" (11).

Immediate criticism of the collection is limited. Miller's translations of Hébert, however, are critically examined later when reviewers begin to compare the various versions of her poetry in English. In a review published in *Culture*, in 1968, Toivo Roht praises the bilingual format of the book and says of Miller's translations, "To make readable poetry out of something which appears disarmingly simple is, as any translator knows, an extremely difficult thing to do, and Peter Miller should be commended for his work" (258). John Glassco, however, was not fond of Miller's translations, having selected none of them for his landmark anthology *Poetry of French Canada in Translation*, published in 1970.[5]

The publication of *The Tomb of Kings* was an important event in the history of translation in Canada. An average of only six titles were published in translation from French Canada per year, and the majority of those were novels. Émile Nelligan and Alain Grandbois were the only two French-language poets whose collections were available in English up to that point, with Miller and Contact Press providing the Grandbois translations; *The Tomb of Kings* was only the third published translation of a volume of French-language poetry into English in Canada. While poets such as Scott and Glassco,[6] among others, were working on their own translation projects at that time, most of the work was being published in small literary magazines. The only anthology in English available with Anne Hébert's poetry was *Twelve Modern French Canadian Poets* (1958), edited by G. Ross Roy, but this represented only a sample of Hébert's works. Miller and Contact Press provided, for the first time, a complete collection of one of her works of poetry. While an accident of timing, it is nonetheless significant that the collection was published in 1967, the year of Canada's centennial celebrations, and in the midst of the continued rise of nationalist sentiment in Quebec.[7] It was also the year that Hébert was awarded the Molson Prize by the Canada Council for the Arts. Miller's translations provided a point of discovery for an audience for Hébert's poetry that would perhaps not have known her works otherwise.

ALAN BROWN, POEMS

In 1975, the Musson Book Company published *Poems*, translated by Alan Brown. Brown is perhaps best known for his much-maligned translation of Gabrielle Roy's *Bonheur d'occasion* (*The Tin Flute*, 1980), but he also won the inaugural Canada Council Translation Prize in 1973, for *The Antiphonary*, by Hubert Aquin.[8] According to *Poems*' dust jacket, Brown was director of Radio Canada International at the time of publication, and began his translations after spending nine years in Europe with CBC's Armed Forces Service. He primarily translated novels, which included *Blackout* by Aquin, *Hail Garlarneau!* by Jacques Godbout, *Chain in the Park* by André Langevin, and *Garden in the Wind* and *Cliptail* by Gabrielle Roy. *Poems* was Brown's only translation of poetry.

By 1975, Hébert was widely known as a novelist, especially given the publication of *Kamouraska*, in 1970, and the subsequent movie adaptation, directed by Claude Jutra. And while there were many more anthologies available that contained Hébert's poetry in translation, there did not yet exist a volume of her complete poems in translation.[9] Brown's translations contain the two collections of the original French *Poèmes*, and "The Tomb of Kings" and "The Mystery of the Verb." Unlike Miller's collection, his is unilingual, with only the English translations appearing in the book. Brown does not provide an introduction or translator's note of any kind. The archives are unclear as to how the project was initiated, but it would seem that Musson bought, at the very least, the Canadian English-language rights to Hébert's poetry and commissioned Brown to do the translations.[10] Musson contacted Hébert in regards to Brown's translations, and in a letter dated April 22, 1975, she writes to Colleen Dimson, trade editor:

> *Cette traduction me semble très bonne et j'en félicite M. Brown. Toutefois il est regrettable que nous n'ayons pu nous rencontrer tous les deux et discuter ensemble. Je me*

> *contente de faire quelques petites remarques sur le texte anglais et de poser des questions à M. Brown.*
>
> *Je ne voudrais pas à mon tour en lisant le texte de M. Brown faire office de traducteur et me mêler de ce qui n'est pas mon affaire. Peut-être n'ai-je pas toujours très bien saisi les intentions profondes du traducteur? Le malentendu peut exister dans les sens, auteur-traducteur et traducteur-auteur?*
>
> *Cela me ferait très plaisir d'avoir l'avis de M. Brown à ce sujet?* (ABF, box 1, file 5; This translation seems very good to me, and I congratulate Mr. Brown. I regret that the two of us could not meet and discuss this together. I am happy to provide a few small comments on the English text and questions to Mr. Brown.
>
> I do not wish to impose myself as an expert on translation and to get involved where I do not belong. Perhaps I did not always fully grasp the deeper intentions of the translator? This misunderstanding can exist in either sense: author-translator and translator-author?
>
> I would enjoy knowing what Mr. Brown thinks of these matters?)

With the letter, Hébert includes three typewritten pages of comments concerning the first half of the collection ("The Tomb of Kings"). Particularly interesting is her shifting attitude toward translations. Now with a number of her works having appeared in English,[11] Hébert would seem to be no longer humbled by the thought of being translated and is taking a more active interest, not only in the translation of her poems, but the process itself.

Alan Brown responds directly to Hébert in a letter dated May 17, 1975.

> I was delighted to see from your letter...that I had managed to do something acceptable in translation of your poems. I wasn't at all sure before I started that I could, and was even less certain when I had finished. I could have submitted a list of my uncertainties, which might have been longer than your list of questions, and in some cases (not all!) quite a different one. But I'm pleased now to have your list, though a day's conversation would have been both more pleasant and (perhaps) more effective. Maybe that can still happen, as there's a chance I'll be in Europe in June, but I'm not sure yet. (ABF, box 1, file 5)

What follows is five pages of questions and explanations to Hébert in regards to the first section of his translations. It would seem that Brown did manage either to meet with Hébert or at least to speak with her, as the letter is annotated with additional changes and modifications. As well, the archives contain three pages of notes on the second half of the translations, “The Mystery of the Verb,” a heavily edited manuscript of the poems, and an undated page of handwritten notes in French on the nature of the role of the translator. It is unclear if the notes are a result of a conversation with Hébert or preliminary thoughts in preparation for such a conversation, but they prove to be enlightening in either case. The following is transcribed directly from Brown’s handwritten notes:

Trad.—re-creation du paresseux—pas d’invention, de la re-invention—on peut arreter n’importe où.
Poesie—extreme limite de la trad. lit.
Original: suspension volontaire de l’incrédulité, avoué d’avance: “je vais tricher, tu vas le savoir, tu vas me ccroire quand même.”
Suprème confiance du beau mensonge reussi.
Comment re-tricher tout ça dans une autre langue? (la beauté de la langue, son des mots, rhythme, metaphore, jeu d’idées, jeux de mots)
—Mots concrets |
> les chevaux qui tire la poesie
—Emotion vrai |
Rapport écrivain: traducteur—adversaires (temporaire, on espère) (ABF, box 1, file 5;
Trad.—lazy re-creation—no invention, only reinvention—we can stop no matter where.
Poetry—extreme limit and lit. trans.
Original: voluntary suspension of incredulity, admitted in advance: “I will fool, you will know, and you will believe me anyway.”
Supreme confidence in a successful beautiful lie.
How to re-fool all this in another language (the beauty of the language, the sound of the words, rhythm, metaphor, play of ideas, word play)
—Concrete language |
> the horses that pull poetry
—Real emotion |
Relationship writer: translator—adversaries (temporarily, we hope))

It would certainly seem that the two became collaborators, to a certain extent, as opposed to adversaries. It is also incredible that the collaboration was able to take place at all, as these conversations took place the same year as the publication of the translation. Pressure from the publishers rushed Brown in his work, as he writes to Hébert in a May 17, 1965, letter: “I’m probably doing this too quickly, but the publishing people are in Montreal for the book fair and want to take this back with them to send to you, as Montreal's mail is uncertain. I'll go over it again for improvements later" (ABF, box 1, file 5).

And make improvements, Brown did. His archives are particularly interesting because of the two different drafts of the poems, as well as Hébert and Brown's own commentary. The final versions are found in the eventual publication, leaving three different versions of the poems with commentary. In his review of *Poems*, David Walker writes, "When Frank Scott translated the poem 'Tombeau des rois,' Anne Hébert responded in detail. It would be interesting to know her reactions to this fine translation of the work of one of Canada's most outstanding poets" (39). We can. What follows is an exchange between Hébert and Brown, along with the original and final version of his translation, taken from Brown's archives, and, wherever relevant, the annotations he later added to the letter.

Line 1: J'ai mon cœur au poing
Trans: Perched on my wrist my heart
AH: Je n'aime pas beaucoup le mot "perched" qui me parait trop prosaïc et compromet ainsi le début du poème. Le mot "hart" [sic] vient trop tard, en fin de ligne, ce qui fausse l'idée originale d'un départ immédiat avec "le cœur au poing."
AB: If I translate literally "I have my heart on my wrist" it's an incredibly clumsy construction, but there is no way in English of avoiding the annoying repetition of "my" if I follow your construction. Poing, of course, is fist, not wrist, and sounds indeed prosaic in English. Perched, on the other hand is fairly elegant (according to my own impressions) and the metaphor gains even in surprise by having "heart" in its middle rather than at the beginning. I'd like to keep this as it stands.
Annotation: ?
Final trans: Perched on my wrist, my heart

Line 3: Le taciturne oiseau pris à mes doigts
Trans: The taciturn bird held in my fingers
AH: Le mot "held" parait faible pour signifier que l'oiseau est pris, agrippé avec ses serres aux doigts qui le portent.
AB: You're right: this should read "The taciturn bird clutching my fingers."
Annotation: OK
Final trans: The taciturn bird clutching my fingers

Line 9: Quel fil d'Ariane me mène
Trans: What Ariadne's thread guides me
AH: Il me semble que "guide" fait un peu trop touristique? N'y-a-t-il pas un autre mot en anglais pout signifier cela?
AB: Virgil was Dante's guide, that is the word used, and it becomes a tourist word only in a touristic context. I think your context is so classical that no reader would think of the guide bleue.
Annotation: [paragraph stuck through] "draws me"
Final trans: What Ariadne's thread draws me

Line 24: Là où sont dressés les lits clos
Trans: Where the enclosed resting-places rise
AH: En français "lits clos" désigne un type très particulier de lit breton, une sorte d'alcôve se fermant comme une armoire. "Enclosed resting-places" rend très bien cette idée.
AB: Is not designed to change text—we agree.
Final trans: Where the enclosed resting-places rise

Line 25: L'immobile désir des gisants me tire
Trans: The still desire of the sleepers draws me on
AH: Les gisants sont des statues de pierre représentant des personnages nobles et que l'on plaçait sur leurs tombeaux. Le mot "sleepers" est faible et ne rend pas cette idée de statues funéraires et ne donne aucune impression de rigidité et de pierre. Ceci est pourtant très important pour la compréhension de tout le poème "Le Tombeau des rois" qui est une lutte contre le désir de mort. "The still desire" ne convient guère plus, me semble-t-il. En français il n'est pas question de personnages vivants et endormis qui désirent encore, mais de statues de pierre qui représentent la mort. Ce sont les morts qui appellent les vivants. C'est la tentation de la mort (éprouvée par les vivants) qui s'échappe des statues allongées dans la rigidité de la mort.
AB: Still means immobile, desire is desire, but perhaps something can be done...I knew exactly what you meant here, and perhaps I haven't succeeded. How about: "The still desire of the stone sleepers draws me on." But: the line gets much longer and clumsier than yours, which I've tried to avoid, in general. Again, the word "sleepers" demands more of the reader than "gisants" but I think anyone likely to read the poem would know, even from my original line, that the desire is no human desire, that it is an

attraction exercised on the human by the dead, especially as the next line but one talks of black bones...
Final trans: The still desire of the stone sleepers draws me on

Line 37: Offrande rituelle et soumise
Trans: A humble ritual offering
AH: "humble ritual." Il ne s'agit pas d'humilité, mais de soumission passive et fascinée.
AB: I agree with you. Humble is the wrong word. Suggested new line 37: "~~Resigned~~; a passive ritual offering."
Final trans: A humble ritual offering

Line 40: L'ombre de l'amour me maquille à petits traits précis
Trans: The shadow of love makes-up my face with tiny careful strokes
AH: "Makes up" est trop moderne, trop ordinaire. N'y-a-il pas un autre mot pour évoquer ce maquillage très spécial? "Tiny" est trop gentil, alors qu'il s'agit d'une façon aïgue et sans pitié de procéder.
AB: Instead of "makes up" (there is no word for it, precisely) I could say "paints"—how would it look? "The shadow of love paints my face with careful needle-strokes."
But it seems here you're asking for more precision of the translation than you demand of yourself: petits traits précis does not suggest more than care to me, hardly "sans pitié" ...and tiny does not have to be a child's word...
Annotation: [Second section struck though]
Final trans: The shadow of love paints my face with careful needle-strokes

Line 56:[12] Ils me couche et me boivent
Trans: They make me to lie down, they drink of me
AH: "They drink of me" est moins fort et moins direct que "They drink me"?
AB: "Drink of me": the rhythm, when read aloud is clumsy without "of." Unless the sense if that "I" am drunk out of existence, drunk completely dry and disappear in the process, drink me would be wrong, as it implies drinking dry.
Annotation: [Entire section struck through]
Final trans: They lay me down, they drink me

Line 57: Sept fois, je connais l'étau des os
Trans: Seven times I feel the tightening vice of bones
AH: "Vice" me parait un peu trop technique. Il s'agit de donner une impression d'étouffement.
AB: Again, it seems you ask more of the translation than of the original: an Étau is a vice, and in neither language is it a device for smothering, a process for which bones are less adapted than feather pillows. As it's bones going to work in both cases, and as for you they make an étau, I don't see why they shouldn't make a vice for me.
Annotation: Stet
Final trans: Seven times I feel the tightening vice of bones

Line 60: Les membres dénoués
Trans: My knees disjointed
AH: "Les membres dénoués" cela veut dire que les membres se sont débarrassés et libérés de l'éreinte des morts et non que les genoux sont désarticulés et disloqués.
AB: Good. Thank you! Suggested new line: "My limbs set free"
Annotation: OK—Example of what only author knows.
Final trans: My limbs set free

Brown concludes his letter to Hébert with:

> I think your remarks and mine about the translation indicate some differences of temperament, and as the point of the exercise is to translate Anne Hébert and not to do an adaptation (I don't trust either the word or the process in most cases) I was delighted to have your explanations and comments. I think in some of them your fears were caused by a one or two dimensional knowledge of English, which has many dimensions beyond those one learns in a casual way, even with a good command of it. But most of your comments were real enlightenment for me. I hope we may see each other in Paris before the book reaches a frozen stage. (Brown fonds)

It is interesting to note as well that Brown would seem to have been preparing his versions of "The Tomb of Kings" and the exchange with Hébert for publication in some format; the last two pages of his letter to Hébert, along with the pages of the manuscript that contain the poem, are numbered separately, in handwriting, while Hébert's comments (which appear over two pages in the original letter to Brown) are consolidated onto one page.

Brown mentions in his notes that the relationship between the author and the translator is that of "adversaries," and one certainly gets the impression that Brown treats Hébert as an adversary, to a certain extent, given the tone and content of his comments, especially in comparison with Scott's. In particular, one can look at Brown's translation of the first line, and his attempt to "improve" the metaphor by having the word "heart" appear at the end of the line. Or when he seemingly takes the author to task for her suggesting that perhaps "vice" was the wrong word to use in line 56/57. More interesting, however, is what Hébert does not say: Note how Brown nowhere identifies the protagonist of the poem as female, and Hébert does not mention the omission in her comments.

There is a good deal of critical reception of Brown's translations (most of which he preserved in his archives, and which he sent to Hébert, as one can see in her personal archives). Brown's archives show that almost every major English-language newspaper in Canada ran a review of *Poems*, reflecting both the expanding interest in translation and in the other "solitude" (francophone Canada), and the backing of a major publishing house, as opposed to the smaller Contact Press.[13] The reviews are universally positive in their assessment of both Hébert's poetry and Brown's translations. It is interesting to note that often the two, the translations and the poetry, are conflated as being one and the same: Within the review, the translations and Hébert's original poems are used interchangeably (ABF, box 1, file 5). Hébert was better known at this point in her career, with *Kamouraska* appearing in French in 1970 and in English in 1973. Many of the reviewers praise the new availability of her poetry in English. The newspaper reviews are written by what seems to be staff writers, and perhaps not at all knowledgeable about translation. This is not the case in the reviews published in the more literary and scholarly journals.

Six different literary journals published reviews of *Poems*: Barbara Godard for *Waves*, Daniel Sloate for *Meta*, Larry Shouldice for *Matrix*, D. G. Jones for *Queen's Quarterly*, G. V. Downes for *Canadian Literature*, and David Walker for *Canadian Forum*. Of the six reviewers, David Walker is the only one who was not an academic and translator (he was a novelist). Reading these six reviews in tandem reveals a very interesting development within the history of translation studies in Canada: The reviews become as much reflections on translation, specifically the translation of poetry, as they are a review of Brown's work. Sloate and Godard begin by discussing the structural and phonetic challenges in translating poems, and both go into an analysis of Brown's attempt to recreate Hébert's structure and sound in English. Both praise the results of Brown's efforts. Shouldice and Walker focus on the history of translation in Canada, contextualizing Brown's role within that history. Both these reviewers, too, congratulate Brown on his translations, highlighting Brown's ability to recreate "the spirit if not letter of the original" (Shouldice 23) and "the refine yet violent intensity of the original poems" (Walker 38). Finally, Jones and Downes criticize Brown's "sparse" translations of Hébert's poems: "This may...leave the lady too stark in her bones" (D. G. Jones, "*Poems*" 151), leading Downes to conclude that readers "will certainly not understand why [Hébert's] reputation stands so high" (G. V. Downes, "Hébert in English" 89). This collection of more critical reviews and the less literary newspaper reviews reflect a growing interest in both Quebec poets and translation more generally, but also Hébert more specifically. With the existence of *Dialogue*, the discussions of her poetry in translation become not only more common, but also more complex. Brown's translations add another layer, another approach to Hébert's work, stimulating debate and fostering interest in the author herself.

ALFRED POULIN JR., *SELECTED POEMS* AND *DAY HAS NO EQUAL BUT NIGHT*

In 1987, BOA Editions published *Anne Hébert: Selected Poems* in the United States, translated by Alfred Poulin Jr.[14] The collection included thirty-eight translations of Hébert's poems; sixteen from *Tombeau des rois*, ten from *Poèmes*, and twelve uncollected poems. While *Selected Poems* was not a complete collection of her poetry, as the title indicates, it did represent the first significant publication of Hébert's translated poems in the United States. The majority of the poems included in the collection had previously been published in English, translated by Poulin, in 1980 in the American *Quarterly Review of Literature*. In 1994, Poulin, again through BOA Editions, released *Day Has No Equal but Night*, a translation of *Le jour n'a d'égal que la nuit*. Both of the BOA editions are bilingual. Poulin was a poet, translator, and professor of English at the State University of New York at Brockport, as well as the founding editor of BOA Editions.

The son of French Canadian immigrants in Maine, Poulin grew up speaking French at home before learning English at school. As he writes in his afterword to *Selected Poems*, "we spent the better part of our adolescence and early childhood working feverishly hard at negating and trying to erase all traces of our Québécois heritage" (152). It was only in the early 1960s that Poulin discovered the world of Québécois poetry, and through Michel Gaulin, a professor at the University of Ottawa, he was introduced to Anne Hébert's poetry. Poulin continues in his afterword to describe his interest in Hébert's poetry as both personal and political.

> [T]he world of these poems is the physical and emotional landscape where a vital part of my personality as a person and an artist is rooted, that part I'm attempting to graft back onto my total self...
>
> My interest in Anne Hébert's poetry turns out to be political, too, in so far as the poems themselves are political in the most profound sense of that word. No less than the work of her contemporaries around the world, Hébert also speaks of a national "anguish and isolation" that is as much a political reality as it is a psychological and/or emotional presence in one's personal, ethnic history. (153)

Poulin's personal and political interest in Hébert's poetry mirrors Scott's dual interest in the poet, who spoke to the two men in very similar ways.

In his prefatory note to *Selected Poems*, Poulin writes, "I am also profoundly grateful to Anne Hébert for her patience, her many suggestions [and] her graciousness" (14). Their literary friendship and correspondence began on June 27th, 1979, when Poulin sent to Hébert, via her publisher, a copy of his translations set to appear in the *Quaterly Review of Literature* and asking her to provide a prefatory note to the work.[15] As he puts in the letter, "Like so many other poet-translators, I have taken certain liberties with some of your texts; I desperately hope that such liberties will not offend you" (AP-BOAE, Box 10). Hébert responds on October 1, 1979, apologizing for the delay because of a recent stay in Canada. Bringing up an issue that would plague the publication of these poems in English in the States until 1987, she reminds Poulin that the English rights of the translations belong to Musson Books. She also addresses the "liberties" that Poulin alluded to in his letter: "Cela me touche beaucoup que vous ayez traduit mes poèmes avec autant de ferveur, quoi-que 'ces certaines libertés' que vous avez prises avec mes textes m'inquiètent un peu" (AP-BOAE, box 10; I'm very touched that you have translated my poems with such fervor, although the 'certain liberties' that you took with my texts do cause me some concern).

Two sets of letters and feedback, dated October 12 and October 17, 1979, followed. Hébert, as she had with Scott and Brown, provides typed line-by-line comments to Poulin. The first looks at the poems from *Le Tombeau des rois*, and the second at the later poems from *Poèmes*. In the first letter, she states, "Vos equivalences potiques (sic) sont le plus souvent très belles et justes." (AP-BOAE, box 49; Your poetic equivalences are often very lovely and true.). In his response, Poulin writes, "One of the first books I bought after reading Poemes (sic) was Dialogue sur la traduction by you and Frank Scott. Never did I imagine even the remote possibility of my engaging in a similar dialogue with you." (AP-BOAE, box 10). Included in Poulin's archives are his own handwritten responses to her comments, as well as his annotations on her comments, but unfortunately, not the original manuscript of the translations as they were originally sent to Hébert. As with Brown, I have recreated the dialogue between the translator and the author around the discussion of the poem "The Tomb of Kings" as best as possible given the missing draft version Hébert was working from (AP-BOAE, box 49).

Line 10: Au long des dédales sourds?
AH: "le long des dédales sourds" indique déjà que le son est étouffé et prépare le vers suivant "L'écho des pas s'y mange à mesure" ce que ne fait pas "secrets labyrinths".
AP: Yes, "muffled" better word
Final Trans: Through the muffled labyrinths?

Line 24: Là où sont dressés les lits clos
AH: "Walled-in beds" signifie-t-il bien "lits clos," c'est à dire des lits enfermés dans une sorte d'armore, comme on en trouve quelquefois en Bretagne?
AP: walled-in beds
"enclosed resting-places"—Brown
Final Trans: Where the walled-in beds are raised.

Line 59: Livide et repue de songe horrible
AH: "foul" ne traduit pas très bien "horrible," il ajoute une idée de saleté et de malpropreté trop prosaïc et concrète.
AP: "foul" strong than horrible, not necessarily "saleté"
Final Trans: Livid and satiated with foul dreams

Line 63: D'où vient donc que cet oiseau frémit
AH: "Shiver" me semble trop fort pour traduire "frémit" qui est plus secret, à péne perceptible, un tout petit frisson à fleur de peau.
AP: "Shiver" is frisson à fleur de peau. Goose bumps.
Final Trans: Why does this bird shiver

Line 65: Ses prunelles crevées?
AH: "Gouged" rend plutôt une idée d'yeux arrachés, alors qu'il s'agit d'yeux "crevés"
AP: gouged or burst or split or shattered
Final Trans: Its punctured eyes

It should be noted that in *Selected Poems*, Poulin changed the last line back to "Its gouged eyes." While Poulin certainly considers Hébert's advice, in this poem, in particular, he sticks to his own interpretation.

And yet, Hébert allows the translations to be published, and the two maintained a long and warm relationship, with Hébert even insisting that Poulin be the translator for her novella *Héloïse*[16], written to him in a letter dated June 12, 1980 (AP-BOAE, box 10). This offer was made following a meeting between the two in Montreal over the Christmas holidays in 1979 (AP-BOAE, box 49). The two continued to meet in both Montreal and Paris over the years as well. But while Hébert was generally supportive of Poulin's translations, she was still insistant on a number of things. The first was that her poems be presented as they were published in *Poèmes*, properly organized, ordered, and titled, including the brief essay, *Mystère de la parole*. (AP-BOAE, box 49). As well, she continued to insist, repeatedly and firmly, that her first collection of poems, *Les songes en équilibre*, were not to be republished or translated, despite Poulin's repeated insistence.

Despite those limitations placed on Poulin by Hébert, he kept working tirelessly to try and find a way to publish his translations of her poetry at a literary press. One of the main obstacles, given Hébert's rising success, was the price that *Éditions de Seuil* and General Publishing in Canada were asking for the English rights to her poems. Poulin's archive is filled with his requests for funding as well as submissions to various publishing houses, all of whom turned him down due to lack of funding and interest in publishing poetry translation (AP-BOAE, Box 54). He did secure a $1500 grant from the Canadian Embassy in 1984 (AP-BOAE, Box 49), and had Hébert's support in his continuing negotiations with the publishers (AP-BOAE, Box 54 and 55). Poulin also wrote to Hébert about his continuing health issues, which slowed his progress on publishing the book of translated poems. One way around the price of publishing the translations of her poems was to include a number of uncollected poems whose rights still stayed with Hébert.

In 1987, *Anne Hébert: Selected Poems* was finally published by his own press, BOA Editions, in no small part due to Hébert's own advocacy for the collection in general and Poulin's own dedication to the work. She even relaxed her stance on her poems being presented in their complete and unaltered form; other than Scott's translations, this is the only collection of selected poems of hers to be published in either language. The book ended up winning a number of translation awards, including a Translation Award from the Columbia Translation Center (AP-BOAE, Box 49). The Association of Literary Translators of America (ALTA) and the Delegation of Québec organized a number of readings in New York City, one at the historic Poets House, in the Fall of 1988 (AP-BOAE, Box 49). The book was received warmly, with the poet herself heavily involved in the promotion of the collection.

It's unclear from the archives why there is no correspondence between Hébert and Poulin about his translations of *Day Has No Equal* in the archives. What is available is a discussion of the translations with Michel Gaulin, as well as a number of drafts of the manuscript with a significant amount of annotations.

A draft dated February 5, 1993, was sent to Gaulin accompanied by three pages of questions. Gaulin responded with a fax, dated February 18, 1993, that included three pages of comments. "La page blanche" is one of the poems which Gaulin and Poulin discuss (AP-BOAE, Box 114). Below is the original French poem, followed by the original draft, followed by what was a handwritten version added in the margin of the manuscript, and ending with the final version of the poem, as published.

La page blanche Devant moi N'espère que toi Sur la feuille nue	The white page In front of me Wants nothing more Than you on the naked page	The blank page Before me Asks for (hopes for) nothing more Than you on the bare sheet	The blank page In front of me Wants nothing more Than you on the naked sheet
Lisse neigeuse à perte de vue Belle page étale Ne vient que la finesse de tes os Subtile apparition	Smooth woman swimming out of sight Lovely display page Nothing surfaces but the delicacy of your bones Subtle apparition	Smooth (lithe) limitlessly snowy Lonely page on display Emits merely the finesse of your form Subtle apparition	Lithe woman swimming out of site Lovely smooth page on display Nothing surfaces but the fineness of your bones Subtle apparition
Grand squelette debout En filigrane gravé Au bout de mes doigts Sur la transparence du jour.	Tall standing skeleton The watermark At my fingertips On the day's transparency.	Tall upright skeleton Its watermark etched At my fingertips Over the day's transparency	Tall standing skeleton Watermark At my fingertips On the day's transparency

In his questions to Gaulin, Poulin asks about two parts of the poem: "Belle page étale: Lovely sound in French, but is it simply the absence of punctuation or is there such a thing as a 'page étale'—something like a display page? If so, not in my dictionary," and "Grand squelette debout/En filigane gravé: Now, is the tall skeleton standing *in* the watermark; or is it a matter of 'a tall standing skeleton/In the watermark...' or simply, "Tall standing skeleton/Watermark..." Gaulin responds to the two questions as follows: "Étale: My dictionary (Le Petit Robert) gives: sans mouvement, immobile; sans aucun agitation. Synonyms are (among others): calme, fixe, stationnaire. I think the analogy, in this poem, is to a still body of water," and "Grand squelette etc: There is no question in my mind that the skeleton is standing upright, posed (??) in *filigrane* fashion on (in?) the page, at the tip of her fingers" (AP-BOAE, Box 114). It is interesting to note how because of Poulin's original translation of the lines "Lisse neigeuse à perte de vue/Belle page étale," Gaulin continues with the water image, even though this is a blatant mistranslation of the lines. It would further seem that Poulin caught his own mistake in the draft copy, but returned to the mistranslation in the final version, at Gaulin's insistence. Besides the mistake, the translation challenges Poulin to try and recreate the sparseness of Hébert's verse, with varying degrees of success.

There was quite a bit of critical reaction to the two works. *Selected Poems* was widely reviewed on both sides of the border. In her review for *Québec Studies*, Marilyn Gaddis Rose calls Poulin's translations "a genuine *tour de force*" ("*Selected Poems*" 132), while Anna Balakian, for *Translation Review*, praises Poulin's success in "preserving [the] semblance of weightlessness Hébert's French creates" (54). Evelyne Voldeng in *Canadian Literature* outlines a number of small errors in translation, but overall claims that: "Thanks to his creative talent Poulin has, however, added a valuable contribution to the translations of Anne Hébert's poetry" ("Literal Translation" 177). In her review for *University of Toronto Quarterly*, Barbara Godard concludes that Poulin "holds his own" ("Poems" 92), while in *Fiddlehead*, M. Travis Lane says that "we should be grateful for the plainness of Poulin's translation" (100).[17] *Day Has No Equal but Night* was equally well received in the United States, with positive reviews in *World Literature Today* and *Booklist*, while Judy Clarence, in *Library Journal*, considers Poulin's efforts a failure (AP-BOAE, Box 4).

Poulin's two collections are quite important for Hébert's visibility in the United States, and thus her overall visibility as a poet. BOA Editions, although a small press, served much the same purpose as Contact Press in Canada, and shared the same type of reputation: providing quality poetry in original English and in translation; the press had recently published the 1985 Pulitzer Prize winning poetry collection *Yin* by Carolyn Kizer. Poulin's translations became the standard translations in the United States, and are included in many of the American anthologies. While the majority of Poulin's translations appeared in *Quarterly Review of Literature*, Poulin also published small selections in nine different periodicals, including *Ms.* and *American Poetry Review*. His translations of Hébert's poetry even appeared in the 50th Anniversary Anthology edition of *Quarterly Review of Literature* in 1993. According to the Poulin-BOA Editions records, BOA promoted both collections of translations quite heavily, advertising in both small and larger poetry periodicals. French Canadian poetry did not have much of an image, or even any sort of awareness in the United States at that time, but Poulin's translation helped ensure that she could be accessible and readable for a US market.

LOLA LEMIRE TOSTEVIN, *DAY HAS NO EQUAL BUT THE NIGHT*

In 1997, House of Anansi Press published *Day has no equal but the night*, translated by Lola Lemire Tostevin, who is the author of six books of poetry and four novels.[18] She has translated Michael Ondaatje's collection *Elimination Dance* into French. Born in Timmins, Ontario, to a French Canadian family, Tostevin learned both French and English as a child, and her bilingual upbringing is illustrated in her semi-autobiographical novel *Frog Moon*. She studied comparative literature at the University of Alberta, and has taught creative writing at York University and the University of Western Ontario. *Day has no equal but the night* contains no translator's note or introduction, and presents the poems in English only.

In an e-mail exchange discussing her translations of Hébert, Tostevin admitted to trying to "respect the [original French] text as closely as I could while keeping a poetic quality to the English translations." Tostevin had long had an interest in Hébert's work, and had previously interviewed the author for *Brick* magazine,[19] but it was Anansi's idea for Tostevin to translate Hébert's latest collection of poems, as Anansi was publishing all of Hébert's later novels in English. Tostevin agreed. "I knew that she was getting on and that is was important to be publishing as much of her work as possible." Tostevin understood Hébert to be an important author, explaining that "her novels capture the psychological, emotional and intellectual malaise that existed in Quebec when she first began to write. While her early poetry explores the melancholia and anguish of a repressive environment, it also transgresses Romanticism through great beauty and joy" (personal communication, February 5–6, 2004).

What is particularly interesting about Tostevin translating Hébert's poetry is her reputation as an important feminist thinker and writer in Canada. Her first two collections of poetry, *The Colour of Her Speech* and *Gyno Text*, explore the uses of female language and experience, while experimentally manipulating language and the poetic form. Contrast Tostevin's style to Hébert's more traditional style and assertion that she is interested in the universal human condition. The juxtaposition between the two women poets within this context, especially in contrast to Poulin's more traditional political approach to Hébert's poetry, suggests interesting results.

Let us return to the poem "La page blanche" from the previous section. Below, accompanying the original French, is Poulin's published version, before Tostevin's version.

La page blanche	The blank page	The white page
Devant moi N'espère que toi Sur la feuille nue	In front of me Wants nothing more Than you on the naked sheet	Before me Waits only for you On the bare paper
Lisse neigeuse à perte de vue Belle page étale Ne vient que la finesse de tes os Subtile apparition	Lithe woman swimming out of site Lovely smooth page on display Nothing surfaces but the fineness of your bones Subtle apparition	Snowy weave As far as the eye can see Beautiful page at ebb-tide Emerges from your delicate bones Subtle apparition
Grand squelette debout En filigrane gravé Au bout de mes doigts Sur la transparence du jour.	Tall standing skeleton Watermark At my fingertips On the day's transparency.	Tall skeleton standing up At the tip of my fingers Engraved in the filigree Upon the day's translucence

One of the aspects that Tostevin recreates is the sparseness of Hébert's lines. She also more accurately translates "neigeuse" as "snowy," avoiding one of Poulin's more obvious errors. How Tostevin interprets and translates the second verse, however, is interesting, especially as it compares to Poulin's (error aside). In order to conserve the shorter length of Hébert's lines, Tostevin changes the first line to two lines in her version. While accurate (in fact, a direct translation), "as far as the eye can see" is not as poetic "à perte de vue." The question of how best to translate "étale" is brought to light in comparing the two English versions. While Gaulin was not wrong when defining the word for Poulin, he omitted the origin of the word, and how the word is typically used, as an adjective, in French. According to *Le Robert et Collins* (1999), "étale" is usually used to describe the sea/ocean when it is calm. Tostevin chooses to use the image of still water when describing the page, although "ebb-tide" is, again, not the most poetic expression for the image. Both Poulin and Tostevin once again have a different interpretation of the next line: "Ne vient que la finesse de tes os." In fact, the two translators have opposing translations of the line; while Poulin translates the line to mean that the bones emerge from the smooth page, Tostevin translates it as the page emerging from the bones. Given the later context of the image of the bones as engraved in the page/watermark, Poulin would seem to have produced the more accurate rendering of the line.

Overall, Tostevin makes every effort to conserve Hébert's short lines and sparse language, although sometimes inaccurately, and sometimes to lesser poetic effect. Neither of the two translators of *Day* has seemed to make as much of an effort to recreate the sound patterns of Hébert's French, either. Jane Koustas, in her review for *University of Toronto Quarterly*, observes that Tostevin "struggles to avoid a purely literal translation without over interpreting, and possibly misinterpreting, Hébert's complex poetry" ("Translations" 339). The two newspaper reviews of the collection do not play close attention to the quality of the translation, with both Barbara Buccilli for *Echo Weekly* and Libby Scheier for *The Toronto Star* praising the beauty of Hébert's poetry, with little regard for Tostevin's role (Centre Anne-Hébert). Overall, however, Tostevin's *Day has no equal but the night* is important because it was published by a small but well-respected publishing house based in Toronto as a companion to the publication of Hébert's better-known novels by that same house.

CONCLUSION

The collections of Hébert's poems available in English are important for a number of reasons. When readers discover Hébert's poetry in an anthology, or through her fiction, they may have cause to read the author further, her poetry further. In particular with Poulin's two collections, an American audience can access Hébert's poetry fairly easily, and in quality translation. As we will see in the next two chapters, having collections of her poetry already in English translation often made it easier to include her in various anthologies. Multiple translations thus invite multiple comparisons, which can lead to better translations, and certainly much discussion, critical and otherwise. Most of all, they ensure that Hébert's reputation as a poet persists, despite perhaps being overshadowed by her reputation as a novelist, especially among English readers.

What these processes also show is the social and collaborative nature of the translation and publication of these poems, and thus the shaping of Hébert's image as a poet in English. Save for Tostevin, all of the other translators received a great deal of feedback from friends, colleagues, and editors on their translations. In Brown's case, we see the importance of the publication of the novel *Kamouraska* in English in 1973, as a publisher thus approached Brown to do a translation of a volume of Hébert's poems, rather than the other way around. But the picture, too, remains incomplete. *Poémes pour la main gauche* remains untranslated, and some would call these her finest, most mature poems. This could be from a lack of interest from translators, but also a lack of funds to support the translator and publisher in the creation of such a translation. The publishing market for translations of poems seems to have circled back to a time when translators like Scott and Miller struggled to publish their translations due to financial constraints and consumer indifference. One hopes that this is not the end of Hébert's journey into English, and that other hands will come through to help translate and shape her later poetry in the English language.

NOTES

1. For a more complete analysis of the archives and the curation of her collections, see the "Introduction" in Watteyne.
2. Hébert refused to ever allow this collection of poems, or the poems contained therein, to be republished, let alone appear in translation, although a limited-run, illustrated edition did appear in 2010, after the author's death, and again in the recent *Œuvres complètes d'Anne Hébert, Tome I* (Watteyne). For a more detailed discussion of the author's attitude toward her first collection, see Watteyne 37–40.
3. A portion of this section appeared in my essay "'Any difference between *our versions* and Scott's': Collaboration, Anxiety of Influence, and a Translation of Anne Hebert's 'Le Tombeau des rois,'" published in *Open Letter*, vol. 15, no. 1, 2012, pp. 13–22.
4. Also located at the archives are letters between Miller and Paz in regards to his translations, as well as with Miron and Grandbois.
5. This anthology will be dealt with in detail in Chapter Three.
6. See Chapters One and Three for a more complete picture of the work being done in poetry translation.
7. Given that *The Tomb of Kings* was published in 1967, at the height of Canadian nationalism as well as political unrest in Quebec, it is all the more surprising that there was little fanfare for the collection.
8. The Alan Brown fonds at the University of Calgary contains drafts and letters between Brown and Aquin, as well as other drafts and letters to and from some of the translations mentioned here.
9. *Les songes en équilibre* is excluded from the complete works as Hébert refused to have the collection republished in French.
10. Brown was not the first choice for the translations. Colleen Dimson solicited John Glassco on two separate occasions to be the translator of *Poèmes*. Both times, he refused. In a letter dated August 27, 1974, Glassco says, "Alas, I must confirm my

decision not to undertake the translation of Anne Hébert's Poemes [sic]. More than ever I see they are quite untranslatable, because translation reveals in the most merciless way their intrinsic intellectual and semantic emptiness, and the verbal music, like the exquisite shimmer and nuance which are all they have, cannot be acceptably reproduced in English" (JGF, container 8, file 17). On December 14, 1974, Glassco reiterates his position, "The work is unsympathetic to me, and the task of putting her verbiage into acceptable English is quite beyond me" (JGF, container 8, file 17). This represents a major shift in Glassco's attitude toward Hébert and her poetry, but also a major shift in his attitude toward translation, both of which will be discussed in Chapter Three. Thanks to Brian Busby for bringing these letters to my attention.

11. *Kamouraska*, translated by Norman Shapiro in 1974; *The Torrent*, translated by Gwendolyn Moore in 1973; and *The Silent Rooms*, translated by Kathy Mezei in 1974. As you can see, the early 1970s was a time of great interest in Hébert in English.
12. There are two different versions of the original French poem. Line 41 in the original version reads "Et cet oiseau que j'ai respire" while the version found in *Poèmes* reads "Et cet oiseau que j'ai/respire." This causes some of the translations to have an "extra line," as the French version they are working from had changed.
13. The newspapers that ran reviews of Brown's translation of *Poems* include *The Kingston Wig-Standard*, the University of Toronto daily newspaper, *The Victoria Daily Colonist*, *The Toronto Star*, *The Ottawa Citizen*, *Winnipeg Free Press*, *The Gazette* (Montreal), and *The Windsor Star*. These press clippings are all available at the Centre Anne-Hébert at the Université de Sherbrooke.
14. Stoddard published the book in Canada.
15. My thanks to Trip Kirkpatrick for retrieving these letters for me at the Beneike Library.
16. The translation appeared in 1982, translated by Sheila Fischman, published by Stoddard books.
17. So rare was it to see Hébert's poems translated and published in the United States, when a selection of Poulin's translations appeared in 1980, in *Quarterly Review of Literature*, both *University of Toronto Quarterly* and *Books in Canada* published reviews, even though the translations appeared in a periodical, rather than traditional book format.
18. Biographical and bibliographical information has been taken from www.pathcom.com/~tostevin/index.htm.
19. The interview can be found in Tostevin's *Subject to Criticism*.

3

Anthologizing Anne Hébert in, as, and for English Canada

As stated previously, Hébert is one of Quebec's most studied and most translated authors. According to André Lamontagne's work with Réjean Beaudoin and Annette Hayward on the reception of French Canadian works in English Canada, she is one of the top three studied authors (along with Marie-Claire Blais and Gabrielle Roy). Not surprisingly, Koustas identifies these same three as the top three translated authors into English. Barbara Godard, commenting on this phenomenon, observes "plus de traduction, plus de recensions critiques, plus de capital symbolique, plus de traduction" ("Littérature en devenir" 496; more translation, more critical reviews, more symbolic capital, more translation). The translations of Hébert's poetry are also the focus of a number of scholarly articles—due in large part to the existence of the book *Dialogue sur la traduction*. Her "capital symbolique" for an English Canadian audience (and beyond) is increased further as none other than Northrop Frye, the eminent critic and theorist, provides the introduction to the letters in *Dialogue*. While there is little doubt about Hébert's status as Québécoise *auteure extraordinaire*, the manner in which she moved from being a celebrated regional author to being included in a world anthology, for example, remains largely unanswered. The purpose of this chapter is to analyze the anthologization of Hébert's poetry in English, charting the evolution of the author's "capital symbolique" from within the borders of Canada, and the role that translators, editors, and reviewers have played in that process.

There has been a growth in interest in the critical study of anthologies recently. A 2010 special issue of the periodical *Voix et Images* was devoted to the literary species that is the anthology. Jane Everett and Sophie Marcotte, in their introduction to the special issue, observe that what is selected to be included in an anthology is fraught because

> *cet extrait représente le seul contact qu'auront les lecteurs avec un ou une auteur, une œuvre, une litterature. Dans d'autres cas, ces extraits représentent le premier contact, celui qui oriente les lectures subséquentes et conditionne l'horizon d'attente des lecteurs. Dès-lors, comment render compte de façon cohérente et utile de tous les facteurs*

> *impliqués dans la production et la sélection des textes, et de ceux qui influent sur leur insertion sans les institutions littéraires locales et internationales et leur reception par celles-ci? Quelles approches, quels filtres notionnels nous permettent d'appréhender les dimensions esthétiques, éthiques et idéologiques des pratiques et des déterminants textuels et extra-textuels qui gèrent les fonctions assignées aux textes anthologisés au sein des systèmes nationaux et internationaux qui les produisent et les reçoivent? Comment penser l'anthologisation de manière productive?* ("Anthologies" 11; this selection represents the sole contact that readers will have with an author, an œuvre, a literature. In other cases, these selections represent the first contact, one that shapes subsequent readings and conditions the shape of the horizon of the readers' expectations. And so, how to articulate in a coherent and useful way all of the factors implicated in the production and selection of tests, and those that influence their inclusion without the local and international literary institutions and the reception they provide? Which approaches, which notional filters allow us to understand the esthetic, ethical, and ideological dimensions of the practices as well as the textual and extra-textual influences acting on the functions assigned to the anthologized texts by the national and international systems that produce and consume them? How can we think of anthologization in a productive way?).

Karine Cellard, in the same issue, emphasizes the importance of the framing devices, or paratextual elements, that shape an anthology (and thus the authors and selections found therein): "sa configuration révèle en creux une mise en récit de l'ensemble—géographique, générique, identitaire ou autre—dont l'ouvrage se veut la synecdoque...il s'agit bien là d'un récit, mais d'un récit en morceaux (choisis)" (44–45; its configuration reveals, at its crux, a cohesive narrative—geographic, generic, identity-based, or other—that presents itself as a synecdoche...It is indeed a narrative, albeit a narrative in (chosen) pieces). Everett, in her own essay in the issue, highlights the dual role of both the anthologist and the translator in recontextualizing a given author for and in the target language:

> *Qu'il s'agisse de traduction ou d'anthologisation, ou de toutes deux, une étude attentive des cas particuliers devrait conduire à une meilleure compréhension des phénomènes globaux...je m'attarde donc à une analyse de quelques cas dans l'espoir d'éclairer une dimension spécifique de la réécriture, soit la recontextualisation des textes, opération qui induit toujours une recontextualisation des auteurs et de leur œuvre entier... nous espérons dégager quelques-uns des enjeux reliés au phenomena de la recontextualisation et, par là, au processus de l'anthologisation.* ("Anthologies" 58;

> Be it of translation or anthologization, or both, a study that is attentive to particular cases should work towards a better understanding of global phenomena...I am attempting, then, a study of a few cases in the hope of bringing to light a specific dimension of rewriting, that is, the recontextualization of texts, an operation that always involves a recontextualization of authors and their complete body of work...we hope to expose some of the issues linked to the phenomena of recontextualization and, as a result, the process of anthologization.)

The purpose of this and the next chapter, then, is to do just what Everett proposes: analyzing the case of one specific author and her journey (reshaping, recontextualization) into English. Anthologies add a number of new layers of socialization of an author and her work; who performed these extra interventions and what impact did they have on Anne Hébert's image of an author in English?

THE "ENGLISH" FRENCH CANADIAN CANON

I borrow the coinage in the heading from an article by Cynthia Sugars that charts the anthologizing of French Canadian authors in English. The article focuses on short-fiction anthologies and outlines the complex relationship that anthologizers have had with the French Canadian canon, and the limited (and confusing) exposure that the English reader would have gained through exposure to said anthologies. Most problematic are anthologies that "silently include translated French Canadian items within a stated 'English only' Canadian context" (121). This creates, according to Sugars, an awkward and imbalanced relationship between the two "official" Canadian literatures. Sugars, however, is not the only critic to outline the shortcomings of the picture of French Canadian literature in English Canada: Jane Koustas, Barbara Godard, Kathy Mezei, Réjean Beaudoin and André Lamontagne, Annette Hayward, Paul Martin, and others have all outlined, in one form or another, the imperfect relationship between the French and English Canadian canons through the mediated form of translation and anthologization. Essentially, they all agree that there exists an "English" French Canadian canon. Koustas goes as far as to statistically compare the number of canonical Quebec texts that are available in English translation, which turns out to be around 60 percent ("Loaded Canon" 46–47). These examinations of the English-language French Canadian canon limit their studies to within the borders of Canada, and ignore the impact that the canonization practices have on the image of individual authors more broadly.

One of the primary canon-formation exercises is the creation of anthologies. According to Robert Lecker, "Anthologies of Canadian literature have always been preoccupied with the construction of nation. In this respect, they resemble other national literature anthologies, which are often devoted to solidifying or challenging an established canon" (*English-Canadian* vii). Donna Bennett calls anthologies "the most obvious acts of canon-definition" (221n1), while Leonard Diepeveen points to the significance of how the anthology has become a "narrative," and therefore is now "overtly polemical and, in some sense, anthropological" (144). Most, if not all, studies concerned with Canadian anthologies look to answer some form of Lecker's basic question: "which authors had been most popular among anthologists...and, if possible, to provide some account of the values implicit in the data" (*Making it Real* 114). The writers cited also limit their studies to the national project of the anthology and the collective role of the authors within that national canon/anthology.

Anthologies are complex creations, mediated by a number of forces: editors, publishers, authors, and in this case, translators. As Peggy Kelly observes,

> publishers, whose decisions are determined by market factors, have a major role in the construction of the accessible canon. In addition, editors of anthologies and literary histories have enormous influence not only on the shape and content of their own projects, but also on the shape and content of the traditional and curricular canons. (73)

The question addressed here and in Chapter Four is the as-of-yet unexamined role anthologies have played in the canonization of a particular author, and, in this case, her image as a poet in English. In trying to accommodate as many of the various factors as possible, the following two chapters include not only an analysis of the conditions behind the publication of the anthology—the decision to include Hébert and which translations to include—but also an analysis of the reception and, whenever possible, the sales of said anthologies. One appearance in an anthology does not make an author canonical, but the repeated appearance of Hébert in multiple English-language collections cemented her place in the Canadian literary tradition (Chapter Three) and beyond (Chapter Four).

ANNE HÉBERT AS FRENCH CANADIAN

Hébert is an interesting case study in terms of the evolution of the author's identity through anthologization. She is widely translated and widely praised. She is also undoubtedly canonical in her language and society of origin: French Quebec. The recent publication (Watteyne 2013) of a critical edition of her complete works of poetry in French and its subsequent warm reception also illustrates how central Hébert is to the Québécois literary canon, but Hébert's entry in *The Annotated Bibliography of Canada's Major Authors* (1979), while dated, also shows how widely her poetry has been anthologized in French. This is also reflected in the first (English) anthologies in which she appeared. Hence, for English Canadians her primary identity was therefore as a French Canadian poet.

TWELVE MODERN FRENCH-CANADIAN POETS, G. ROSS ROY, 1958

In 1958, Ryerson Press published the anthology *Twelve Modern French-Canadian Poets*, with G. Ross Roy as the editor and translator. A PhD in English from the Université de Montréal, Roy had also studied in Paris. In his acknowledgement, Roy thanks George Cartier, future founder of the Bibliothèque nationale du Québec, for his help "in selecting the poems to be used in this anthology" (iv). Through this consultation with an "insider" to French Canadian letters, Roy is striving for an authentic sample of the best French Canada had to offer at that time. His goals in editing this anthology are clearly outlined in a brief, two-page introduction: filling a "cultural need" by providing "a sampling of modern French-Canadian verse" in translation; contradicting the perception that "twentieth-century French-Canadian poetry does not exist"; and showing that "French-Canadian poetry has come of age in the past generation" through moving toward "universality" yet "[managing] to remain Canadian" (v, vi). The original French version of each of the poems selected appears on the left-hand side of the page, while Roy's English translation follows on the right, a popular format for French Canadian poetry anthologies.

The project started for Roy as early as 1955, if not before. As mentioned in Chapter One, Roy wrote to F. R. Scott for advice and input in selecting French Canadian poets to include in an anthology. The initial project also aimed to include both English and French poems in the anthology (the closing paragraph of the letter to Scott mentions "the possibility of getting your permission to include a selection of your own poetry"). It is unclear why the project changed—there is no response from Scott in his archives, but Roy did include a phone number in his letter. Two years later, in 1957, this project appears again in the letters of Raymond Souster. In a letter to fellow translator Gael Turnbull, dated May 12, 1957, Souster writes, "Have a mss of French-Canadian translations by G. R. Roy here and under consideration by a private press. If we can get this out it'll be a big thing" (GTF, box 6).[1] In a subsequent letter to Turnbull, dated July 7, 1957, Souster writes,

> No luck as yet as to publishing that fine volume of French-Canadian translations. The chap here in Toronto who was to be considering a private press edition I think is a dead loss and I'm going to get the mss back. May let Ryerson have a look at it. It's such a fine book that ways and means of getting it out should be found. Following up your pioneer efforts along this line, it could be an important book for Canadian poetry. (GTF, box 6)

On December 1, 1957, the good news finally arrives. "Ryerson have accepted G. R. Roy's bilingual TWELVE MODERN FRENCH-CANADIAN POETS for publication" (Turnbull fonds). Without the help and support of Raymond Souster, Roy's translations perhaps would never have been published at all.

Roy chose three of Hébert's poems from her second book of poems, *Le Tombeau des rois*: "Les grandes fontaines," "La fille maigre," and "Un mur à peine." The choice of the poems themselves reflects Roy's view of French Canadian poetry as being an extension of the French symbolist movement, as well as his central thesis that

> much of today's poetry centers around the inner self of the poet—his intimate relationship with other people, with himself, and with God. This is the stuff of the greatest of poetry, and the most universal. By telling of one person, himself, the poet tried to speak for all, just as the reader tries to bridge the gap from the poet's experience to his own. (vi)

For Roy, in 1958, recent French Canadian poetry is universal, inward looking, and primarily male. Of the twelve poets selected for the anthology, only three are women (Hébert, Rina Lasnier, Isabelle Legris). It is interesting, then, to see that he has included "La fille maigre" in his selection of poems by Hébert. One of the most gendered poems from her second collection, it clearly identifies the narrator as female (the other two poems by Hébert provide no clues as to gender). All three poems, however, reflect a certain inward-looking tendency, as the "Je" battles with and within itself. The selections, and the order in which they are placed, reflect the order and evolution that takes place in the full collection, *Le Tombeau des rois*. "Deep Fountains" takes place in an external, open setting and involves "us," but moves in the last verse toward "the inner reaches of myself" and the separation of the us into the narrator and other (61); "The Thin Girl" continues this separation between the narrator and the other, as well as sharpening the focus of the narrator internally ("I have beautiful bones," 63); and finally, in "Not Quite a Wall," of the narrator's increasing isolation and powerlessness. One wonders, however, if a reader would recognize this progression without being familiar with the entire collection.

The only direct review of the anthology (according to Kathy Mezei's exhaustive bibliography) appears in *Canadian Forum*, in 1958. In it, Laure Rièse laments that Roy "did not evaluate the poets he presents, that he has not shown how they fit into the present pattern and evolution of French-Canadian literature," and concludes that "the truth is that much of the poetry cited is still dense and dry" (286). One wonders if it is the poetry itself that is dense and dry, or the translations. In that regard, Rièse is kinder to Roy, stating that

> Certainly, Mr Roy has faithfully reproduced the physical content and the actual words. We wonder if he does not fall short sometimes of the mood and occasionally of the rhythm... The author has adhered closely to the original and has faithfully suggested what had been intended for the reader without undue elaboration. (286)

Rièse observes, in much the same way that Roy does in his introduction to the volume, that this was a "most commendable work" for "making the poetry of French Canada accessible to English readers" (286). John Glassco is less kind when mentioning Roy's anthology in his article "The Opaque Medium," which deals specifically with the situation at that time (1969) in regards to the translation of French Canadian poetry. Glassco never directly names the anthology, instead identifying Roy in his short "history of serious translation of French-Canadian poetry," as well as the date of the anthology's publication (1958), and closes the discussion with the statement that "Roy's miscellany is noteworthy as an example of poetry translation at its weakest" ("The Opaque Medium" 28). F. R. Scott refers to the anthology in a letter to G. V. Downes, and Downes responds in a letter dated August 13, 1962, calling the collection "singularly uninspired" (FRSF, col. 64, file 14). Louis Dudek and Michael Gnarowski list the anthology in their 1967 book, *The Making of Modern Poetry in Canada*, in a section entitled "Relations with French Writing in Canada." Dudek and Gnarowski (who had previously worked with Roy on a bibliography of Canadian poetry before 1950) go on to comment on the financial difficulty facing the publication of translations—"The educational and publishing machinery of the country is not yet adjusted to serve the day-to-day needs of a dual culture" (249). Roy, in his acknowledgements, thanks "the Modern Language Association of America for their grant which was used in obtaining material" (iv). This is perhaps not an illustrious introduction to Hébert for English Canada, but the fact that one of Canada's most important presses at that time (Ryerson) was willing to put out a book of translations of French Canadian poetry represented a significant and perceptible shift in priorities for that period. And this shift would begin to gain momentum going into the 1960s. This increased Hébert's accessibility in English as a French Canadian poet.

THE POETRY OF FRENCH CANADA IN TRANSLATION, JOHN GLASSCO, 1970

Although the 1960s did not see any anthologies of French Canadian poetry in translation that included Anne Hébert, the period did witness the preparation of one monumental anthology that would be released in 1970: John Glassco's *The Poetry of French Canada in Translation*, published by Oxford University Press. That another major Canadian publishing house was willing to support such a monumental project was a result of two major forces which were not totally unrelated. Politically, as a result of the Quiet Revolution and the rise in nationalism in Quebec, there was an appetite to study Quebec. Financially, there were more opportunities for a publisher to subsidize a project as expensive as publishing poetry in translation. The project received generous grants from both the Canada Council and Quebec's Department of Cultural Affairs. Preparation for the anthology began as early as 1957, at the suggestion of Scott, and for the next thirteen years Glassco would contact virtually every person who had ever put pen to paper to translate a French Canadian poem, and as many French Canadian poets and editors as he could think of. The result is an anthology that includes 193 poems by 48 French Canadian poets, translated by 22 different translators, including Glassco himself. Hébert has thirteen poems included in the anthology, translated by Scott, Downes, Ralph Gustafson, and Glassco.

Glassco had earlier published translations of five of Hébert's poems ("Petit désespoir," "Vie de château," "Les mains," "Le Tombeau des rois," "Les petites villes"), which appeared in *Canadian Forum* in October 1959. He had been introduced to the poet at Scott's home in May 1958 (Busby 151), and Hébert sent a copy of *Le Tombeau des rois* to him as a result. Glassco was so taken by her poetry that he began to translate her poems directly in the margins of the book (JGF, container 10, file 7). In October 1958, and then again in July 1959, he sent his translations to Hébert for her approval. She replied on September 4, 1959, writing that:

> *Je suis touchée de la grande attention poétique que vous avez apportée à la traduction de mes poèmes, et je vous en remercie de tout cœur. Dans l'ensemble, cela me plaît beaucoup. J'aurais aimé pouvoir vous signaler quelques détails qui me paraissent s'éloigner quelque peu du texte original. Mais comme le temps presse, je ne puis que vous assurer que je serais très heureuse que le "Canadian Forum" publie vos traductions de mes poèmes.* (JGF, container 11, file 1; I am touched by the immense poetic attention that you brought to the translation of my poems, and I offer my heartfelt thanks. Generally, they greatly please me. I would have liked to point out a few details that seem to me to distance them from the original text. But since we're running out of time, I can do nothing except assure you that I would be very happy to see your translations of my poems published in "Canadian Forum.")

Already involved in the translations of Hébert's cousin, Saint-Denys Garneau, Glassco would ensure that the translations of Hébert's poems were of the highest quality.

Throughout, Glassco was prepared either to improve his own translations or to put them aside for ones that he deemed to be of superior quality; of his five translations, only one appears in his anthology, "The Little Towns." For two of the poems ("Manor Life" and "The Tomb of Kings"), Glassco chose instead to use Scott's translations, as well as selecting Downes's translation of "A Touch of Despair," which he identifies in a letter to Downes dated August 12, 1967, as being "much better than Peter Miller's or my own version" (JGF, container 2, file 21). Convenience was not a determining factor, as Miller's translations of Hébert's poetry were readily and easily available. Glassco was not tremendously fond of Miller's translations, a sentiment reflected in another letter to Downes dated May 1, 1966, "I find Miller's work most uneven in quality" (JGF, container 2, file 21), and in his article "The Opaque Medium," where Glassco points to (but does not directly identify) Peter Miller's translation of Hébert's "Vieille image" as a "[display] of ignorance and laziness" (30). Glassco's inclusion of Gustafson's translation, "Cities in Sails," was a result of Gustafson, who has a number of other translations in the anthology, simply submitting the poem. In the October 16, 1966, letter that accompanied his submission, Gustafson wrote, "Could you find a place in your anthology for the enclosed poem of Anne Hébert?...this poem (which I found in the Canadian issue of the Atlantic Monthly) intrigued me: difficult, full of colours, and as good a capture of the act of sex as anyone's" (JGF, container 3, file 1). Glassco was excited to accept the poem, saying on October 19, "You have really re-created the poem itself: also, it is a fine example of her more recent and so to say more released work. She is at last out of those rooms and tombs and has stopped studying her hands" (JGF, container 3, file 1).

This approach to the selection of Hébert's work reflects Glassco's overall approach to the anthology. The quality of the translations themselves were of paramount importance, ultimately leading to his choices for inclusion—"this is an anthology of poetic translations rather than of translations of poetry" (*Poetry* xxiv). Glassco wanted the translations to stand alone, and chose not to include the original French poems. As he states in the conclusion of his introduction, "The translations in this collection are presented as things that must stand on their own dependent on their own poetic merits, owing to their originals nothing but the inspiration that has here found a partial rebirth" (xxiv).

That the anthology was so long in the making was not only due to Glassco's devotion to the quality of the translations (as well as the depth and breadth of the poets included), but also because of financial issues. Brian Busby, in his biography of Glassco, describes the decade-long financial struggle:

> The collection had been accepted by Oxford in 1965, originally under the condition that the press would obtain a $2500 grant from the Centennial Commission with which to pay the poets and translators involved. Although the application was turned down, the publisher remained committed. In 1967, the project received a $2000 grant by Quebec's Department of Cultural Affairs to cover permission fees for all the French texts. However, it wasn't until two years later, when the Canada Council awarded $4000, dedicated to paying the translators, that the project was finally scheduled for publication. (222)

This long delay saw a massive change in French Canadian (now, in 1970, "Québécois") society, which affected the reception of the work.

Two of the strongest criticisms of *The Poetry of French Canada in Translation* (which was, overall, well received and widely praised) had to do with Glassco's lack of more contemporaneous poetry and his attitude toward Quebec nationalism. The two criticisms are not mutually exclusive. As Glassco states in his introduction, "it is a truism that politics and nationalism have somehow never managed to make really good poetry" (xix). He explains that the poetry in his anthology reflects "that the poetry of French Canada is a poetry of exile" (xvii), criticizing as well the presence of "the dead hand of surrealism—an influence no less pernicious than any other worn-out poetic method" (xix). He further emphasizes

> that within these limits French-Canadian poets have accomplished marvels of form, insight, music and grace. The work of Nelligan, Morin, Choquette, Grandbois, Saint-Denys-Garneau, Rina Lasnier and Anne Hébert is of the first, or almost the first, order of poetry; but the measure of its worth is in its transcendence of the historical situation, of that French fact which, however fundamental to the life of the people itself, was nonetheless something that these poets assimilated and surmounted: the single-minded passion by which they did so is the measure, indeed, of their poetic stature. (xvii–xix)

This idea of the poet transcending his or her linguistic or "national" origin is important in the progress of an author beyond provincial borders; in this case, Hébert. Glassco's claims about Hébert were not ignored; in fact, placing her within a historical context brought out the quality of her poems. A review in the *Toronto Telegram* concludes, "That there are three or four poets—Nelligan, Saint-Denys Garneau, Hébert, and perhaps Grandbois, who have taken this thick, perverse, inverted nationalism and religiosity and fashioned it into poetry that transcends the moment, is all the more remarkable" (JGF, container 16, file 10). J. M. L'Heureux, in his review of the anthology for *Canadian Forum*, restates the same list of poets as Glassco in his introduction, and goes on to comment on their poems, "Significantly, they are poems which have shed almost completely the outward signs of their place of origin, like abstract cubes replacing the pines and rocks of earlier paintings. Forsaking the 'poetic' eloquence of their predecessors, they move towards more abstract, more universal themes" (182). Again, we are already seeing Hébert's image as that of a poet who transcends linguistic or provincial/national boundaries beginning to take shape. We can also see the connection between an editor's decision in writing the introduction and the reception of a particular author within the anthology; in this case, Hébert is singled out by both Glassco and the critics.[2]

One cannot underestimate the impact of this anthology on the English-language French Canadian canon. It was the first of its kind, and widely read in classrooms and homes across the country. Hébert's visibility as a poet for an English-speaking Canadian would not have been higher. Her place within both the accessible and curricular canon was beginning to become firmly established. And while critics argued about the place (or exclusion) of other poets in regards to Glassco's anthology, none found fault with Hébert's inclusion, and she would continue to find a place within the English-language French Canadian canon.

THE POETRY OF MODERN QUEBEC, FRED COGSWELL, 1970, 1971, 1976

One of Glassco's harshest critics also put out an anthology of translated poems in 1970. Fred Cogswell published, through Fiddlehead Books, *One Hundred Poems of Modern Quebec* in 1970. In 1971, he published *A Second Hundred Poems of Modern Quebec*. In 1976, *The Poetry of Modern Quebec* was issued by Harvest House as part of their French Writers of Canada series, which consolidated the first two anthologies. Cogswell levels a number of criticisms against Glassco's anthology, including his dismissal of the more nationalist poets:

> If one reads and takes seriously the work of the current Quebec nationalist writers, one will be reluctantly compelled to see...the questions before Quebec... It is a bitter choice, and it will be made uncompromisingly with blood unless men in greater number throughout Canada come to understand what the issues are. ("*New: American & Canadian*" 103)

And, as a result, Glassco's lack of contemporariness: "His anthology in this regard does not accurately reflect French Canadian poetry during the past ten years" (103). But perhaps the most scathing critique of Glassco's anthology is Cogswell's assessment of the translations themselves:

> But since I have the kind of technical competence that can put into rhymes in English anything that a poet can in French, and because I have a sensitive eye and ear for incongruity in rhythm or diction, I am irritated whenever I see sonnets whose lines do not rhyme, quatrains that keep none or half of the rhyme-schemes of the original, stanzas that add a line to the number of lines the author already had, or words and rhythms palpably out of place with regard to the whole effect. I consider such work only half-translations, and I found more to annoy me in John Glassco's book than I felt I ought to have done. (104)

Cogswell's collections can be placed in direct contrast to Glassco's anthology and in direct response to Cogswell's own criticisms of it. In his introduction to *The Poetry of Modern Quebec* (the only collection of the three to contain an introduction), Cogswell clearly states that he is interested in "the works of several major poets of the past four decades in considerable depth" (5). He is interested, specifically, in charting the "rapid change" that Quebec poetry had experienced over his chosen time period. The final anthology contains twenty poets, while the other two earlier anthologies contained thirty-seven and forty-two poets, respectively.

Although there is some overlap, a great many of the poets and poems published by Cogswell in his three books do not appear in Glassco's anthology.

Hébert is one of the few poets who stands firm through all three anthologies. It is interesting to note how Hébert, although well into her career in the 1970s, is still considered one the recent modern poets from Quebec. In *One Hundred Poems of Modern Quebec*, two translations appear, "Eve" (from *Poèmes*) and "Offended Parties" (then still uncollected). Cogswell's *Second Hundred Poems of Modern Quebec* included "And It Was Day," "Snow," "Captive Gods," "Night," and "Wisdom Broke My Arm," all from *Poèmes*. In the final anthology, "Our Hands in the Garden" is added, while "Offended Parties" is removed, for a total of seven poems. This is about average for a poet appearing in Cogswell's *Poetry of Modern Quebec*. Not much is known about the selection process used by Cogswell, or about the translation process itself. Cogswell discusses Hébert in his introduction to the final anthology, at first in relation to her cousin Saint-Denys Garneau, but then goes on to say that "Both Anne Hébert and Roland Giguère, however, having mastered the form and sensibility of this existentialist poetry were to move outward toward greater involvement with the external world in their work" (6). This is reflected in Cogswell's selection of Hébert's poems: missing are those "internal" poems from *Le Tombeau des rois* (including the well-known title poem), and included instead are the poems from that early collection that reflect a more outward-looking perspective ("Our Hands in the Garden" and "Night").

Cogswell's review of Glassco's anthology, his later introduction to *Unfinished Dreams*, and comments from his long-time collaborator, Jo-Anne Elder (who co-edited and co-translated *Unfinished Dreams* with Cogswell), provide additional clues to his choice of poems and translation style. In his critique of Glassco's anthology, Cogswell (see above) points to weaknesses in poetic form. Elder comments that Cogswell initially was a formalist, where "form was more important than content" (personal communication, July 20 2004). This dedication to form was expressed by Cogswell in a number of different forums, notably in *Ellipse*, "As both alliteration and assonance are enhancers of cadenced verse, in choosing the vocabulary in the English translation, I have used both alliterative and assonanced words in clusters, wherever possible in making my choices from the French originals" ("Strange Capture" 15), and in an interview with Laurence Hutchman, "Well, for one thing, a good translator, if he finds the thing that at the heart of the poem is a living thought or a living situation or something that might be these things, will somehow or other emphasize these things in the particular work concerned" (Hutchman 69). In a draft introduction to *Unfinished Dreams*, Cogswell comments that "some poems are more translatable than others, [therefore] the choice of poems has been dictated more by the merit of the poems in translation than by the merit of the original" (FCP, box 2, file 14). This commitment to quality through formal translation, coupled with his thesis regarding Hébert as an "external" poet, would explain reviewer John J. O'Connor's "[surprise] not to find...Hébert's 'Le Tombeau des rois,' 'Les Chambres de bois,' and 'Vie de château'" ("Translations" 1977, 413), three of Hébert's most inward-looking poems.

Cogswell's devotion to formalist methods of translation serves Hébert's poems well. Philip Stratford observes that Cogwell's "verse...is plainer, more direct, often less mannered," meaning it in a negative sense overall, but, as he observes as well, "whenever simplicity is required, or native strength, and...a kind of prosaic humility [Cogswell's] verse is better" ("Circle, Straight Line" 90). As reiterated by J. M. L'Heureux, Cogswell's "preference is consistently for the straightforward statement rather than the circumlocution, for compression rather than dilution" (183). Hébert's poems require such simplicity, such a straightforward approach, and as her verse is relatively plain and direct, and, as such, Cogswell's translations are particularly suited to Hébert's style. John J. O'Connor underlines Cogswell's translation of "Eve" as being "especially noteworthy" (("Translations" 1977, 413). However, others criticize Cogswell for his devotion to meter and rhyme. Patrick Holland calls the translations "wooden" (191), while Pierre Cloutier observes that "rhyme is a constraint which Cogswell need not have imposed on himself at all" (75). Overall, Cogswell is at his best when he remains true to his formalist tendencies. Jean-Guy Carrier points to Cogswell's translation of these lines of "Neige," "Veille mon cœur, la neige nous met en selle sur des coursiers d'écume" as "Remain awake, my heart, snow transports us on the backs of steeds of foam," as being one of his less successful translations (23).

Hébert remains at the centre of many of the reviews. From being cited as one of the "major" poets included in the anthology (Holland), to specifically underlining translations of her poems (Carrier and Stratford), to using Hébert as a poetic landmark (L'Heureux), almost all the reviews recognize the importance of Hébert, or at least attribute to her an importance above others included in the anthology. Another tendency that begins to appear in the reviews are comparisons of translations, understandable due to the relative volume of anthologies and translations that were now available. Glassco or Cogswell (*One Hundred Poems* and *Poetry of French Canada in Translation* were both released in 1970)? Cogswell or Scott (*Poetry of Modern Quebec* and *Poems of French Canada* were released in 1976)? While G. R. Roy was celebrated for simply providing an anthology, Cogswell, Glassco, Scott and others were now part of a larger tradition of anthologies and translations. Said Stratford, "I recommend the game of comparing translations as a fast and fascinating way to get into the heart of the poetry, the French as well as the English" ("Circle, Straight Line" 90). The standard had been raised, with major publishing houses and small presses alike putting out anthologies edited by some of the most important English Canadian poets of the time, all of whom agreed that Hébert deserved a place within their pages.

Scott's *Poems of French Canada*, released in 1976 by Blackfish Press (dealt with in more detail in Chapter One), is an example of a major poet/translator putting out an anthology through a smaller press. Scott collected thirty-eight of his translations of French Canadian poetry and put them together in this limited anthology. His translations of Hébert had already appeared in his 1962 collection *St-Denys Garneau & Anne Hébert*, as well as a number of other anthologies, and have already been dealt with in the previous chapter. While nowhere near as focused as Cogswell's anthology, or as comprehensive as Glassco's, *Poems of French Canada* does collect Scott's efforts in translation over the past three decades.

VOICES FROM QUEBEC, PHILIP STRATFORD AND MICHAEL THOMAS, 1977

In 1977, in part in reaction to the 1976 election of the separatist Parti Québécois to a majority government in Quebec, Philip Stratford, a professor at the Université de Montréal and respected literary translator, and Michael Thomas put together *Voices from Québec*, published by Van Nostrand Reinhold. Anne Hébert's poem "Offended Parties," translated by Fred Cogswell, is the only work by Hébert included, as part of eighty-six selections of poems, short stories, excerpts from novels, and essays from Québec and francophone writers. Her poem is listed under the heading "Politics and Protest." Other authors, including Marie-Claire Blais, Jacques Ferron, Antoinine Maillet, and Michel Tremblay, merit multiple entries, and Hébert's poems could have easily fit into other categories Stratford set, such as "Love and Fantasy," "Childhood and Family," or "Past and Present."

Stratford was known at that time for having translated *Dans un gant de fer* (1965), by Claire Martin, published in 1975 as *In an Iron Glove: An Autobiography*, as well as two important non-fiction collections of essays, *Convergence: Essays from Quebec* (1966) by Jean Le-Moyne, and *André Laurendeau: Witness for Quebec* (1973), which he edited. Stratford saw translation as an opportunity to "effectively bridge the cultural and political gap between English Canada and Québec" (Lane-Mercier 75). In his own words, Stratford puts it this way:

> Our politicians, our economists, our historians, our royal commissioners get translated. But how much more important in the long run, when it is really a question of knowing another people, how they think, feel, react,

> imagine and remember, to have our poets, dramatists, and novelists translated, our essayists and journalists. ("French-Canadian Literature" 183)

In the preface to the collection, Stratford and Thomas emphasize the uniqueness of the writing of French Canadians, and the Québécois in particular, stating that the "differences are definitely there—centuries of history, language and culture have confirmed them." (iv). But they close the preface emphasizing the more universal aspects of the literature: "we hope to have shown, by borrowing the many voices you will hear in these pages, that French Canadian experience today is not so foreign after all, but is recognizably like our own while still remaining excitingly different" (iv). It's interesting to note how they highlight simultaneously the commonality and the exotic ("excitingly different"). Quebec was, at this point in history, a mystery to much of Canada, as the Parti Québécois election is indeed described as "startling" in the opening lines of the preface (iii).

Stratford could certainly be described as an "insider" to Quebec culture as a professor at the (francophone) Université de Montréal, as well as a translator of important non-fiction texts dealing with the situation as it was evolving in Quebec. He was also an important figure in the development of literary translation in Canada, having co-founded not only the translation journal *Ellipse* in 1969, with D. G. Jones, but also the Literary Translators' Association of Canada, in 1975 (Lane-Mercier 78). Around the publication of *Voices from Québec*, Stratford also put together, with Maureen Newman, the *Bibliography of Canadian Books in Translation: French to English and English to French* (1975 and 1977). He was also friends with many of the translators and authors already discussed: F. R. Scott, D. G. Jones, and John Glassco, among others. Clearly he was familiar with Québécois literature, as well as what was available in translation, while putting together this anthology.

While Stratford does not have any available archives, one can reasonably conclude that he was familiar with the various available translations of Hébert's poetry, given that the anthologies listed previously appear in his bibliography. Stratford was well aware of her poetry and her prose; in his 1986 comparative study *All the Polarities*, Stratford compares *Kamouraska* and Margaret Laurence's *The Diviners*, and in the conclusion he mentions that "the title of several poems by Anne Hébert highlight the claustrophobia: 'The Tomb of Kings,' 'The Closed Room,' 'The Wooden Room,' 'Narrowing'; the diminishing dimensions give a spiritual twist" (99). The poems selected for the anthology, "Les offensés" (translated as "The Offended Parties"), was at that time an uncollected poem that would later appear in Hébert's *Le jour n'a d'égal que la nuit*, in 1990. Cogswell's translation was the only one available at that time. The poem itself deals with those who are oppressed and silenced finding voice: "In this extreme misery the silent came forward / A whole nation of mutes stood on the barricades" (Stratford and Thomas 171). The haunting images of the starving and powerless are stark and moving, perfectly fitting with the theme of "Politics and Protest."

Only one review of the anthology, from the *University of Toronto Quarterly*, could be found. It is very positive review by John J. O'Connor in his "Translations" omnibus review section. O'Connor describes the anthology as being "remarkably representative in every sense" ("Translations" 1978, 384) and that this "impressive organization and range of references are generally matched by the quality of the translations throughout" (385). He closes the review "by strongly recommending to all Anglophone readers of Quebec literature the respectful transformations of Stratford and Thomas" (386). It's interesting to note that O'Connor directs the recommendation only to those who are already interested or reading Quebec literature in translation. From the introduction, one would imagine that Stratford and Thomas had a larger audience in mind. Again, Hébert's poetry (which, at this point, was not being newly published, not even in French) is being introduced within the larger context of Quebec literature.

OUT OF THE VIOLENT DARK, GWLADYS DOWNES, 1978

In 1978, the poet Gwladys Downes released *Out of the Violent Dark*, published by Sono Nis Press. This would be her second anthology containing a combination of her translations of French Canadian poetry alongside her original poems. In 1973, Klanak Press released *When We Lie Together: Poems from Quebec, and Poems by G. V. Downes*, a slight, single volume which contained ten translations and four original poems. This particular collection did not contain any translations of Hébert's poetry, although Downes acknowledges the poet's influence in her preface, observing that her own poem "Mirror, Mirror," "rather reminds me of Anne Hébert" (*When We Lie Together* 11). She concludes her preface with "It is hoped that this latest volume in Klanak's poetry series will do something to bridge the gap between the two cultures in Canada" (11).

Downes reiterates this dedication to "bridging the gap" in her 1969 article "Is the Muse Bilingual," observing that "In Canada today, for example, the need of translations is obvious; the bilingual writer finds himself working in a society which is becoming more and more aware of the role the translator can play in interpreting various parts of the national dialogue" (195). In her conclusion, she echoes Glassco's point that "the need for accurate renderings in English of French poems is urgent" (199). *Out of the Violent Dark* contains twenty-seven translations and seventy-one of her own poems, with three translations of Hébert's poems, "A Touch of Despair," "The Planting of Hands," and "A Little Dead Girl," all three of which had appeared in Glassco's anthology. Although no introduction accompanies *Out of the Violent Dark*, one can deduce that Downes's aim with this collection was similar to the aim of her previous collection: bridging French and English Canada. All of the translations in the latter collection are once again exclusively of French Canadian poems and poets.[3]

It is through *The Fiddlehead* and Cogswell that Glassco would come into contact with Downes, inviting her to submit translations to his anthology. Downes is still concerned with repeating translations that already exist, writing to Glassco on April 27, 1966: "I am a little disappointed, in reading Louis Dudek's new anthology, to discover that Une Petite Morte... [has] already been translated, and so very accurately, by Peter Miller" (JGF, container 2, file 21). Glassco encourages Downes to submit her translations anyway, stating, in a letter dated April 25, 1967, that he "simply [couldn't] see [himself] preferring any version of his to yours." Glassco offers quite a bit of feedback to Downes and encourages her in that same letter to continue translating and submitting to the anthology, especially poems (such as Hébert's) that he saw were "particularly fitted to your fine 're-making' technique" (JGF, container 2, file 21).

This "re-making" technique is explained more fully by Downes as "free-wheeling if necessary, but not necessarily free-wheeling" ("Muse" 196), where the "translation sets as its ideal the literal poetic, but is ready to sacrifice literal exactness under some circumstances" (169–70). She offers an example of this technique using one of Hébert's poems, "Petit désespoir." The last two lines read "Mon cœur est rompu/L'instant ne le porte plus," which she translates as "The stream no longer bears / My tired heart" (198). Interestingly, the version of the last two lines that is finally published reads "my tired heart no longer / moves with the stream" (*Out* 43; Glassco, *Poetry* 142). The version that appears in the article was sent to Glassco as an option, but he preferred what would eventually appear in print, commending the translation of the entire poem in a letter dated August 12, 1967, as he found that Downes "re-link[ed] the poem which makes it flow and, I think, even add[ing] another dimension" (JGF, container 2, file 21). In either version, however, the last two lines illustrate Downes remaking technique.

This technique was not always easy for Downes. As she expressed to Glassco in a letter dated December 27, 1965, "I think after working on [Hébert's poems] that her poetry, being so chiseled and meticulous, probably loses more in translation which isn't careful, than that of other poets. It is fundamentally easier if one can catch a rhythm in the second language not to follow syntax than to stick to it!" (JGF, container 2, file 21). Her approach to the poems, their syntax, and their rhythm are in opposition to Cogswell, but more in line with Glassco, who, as

Patricia Godbout describes it, was interested in "le palimpseste" (*Traduction* 175), that is, the erasure, to a certain extent, of the original in favour of the translation, and hence his decision to omit the original French poems.

The title of this particular collection, *Out of the Violent Dark*, reflects Downes' own attraction to French Canadian poets. In an 1982 article, "Women Poets in Quebec Society," Downes quotes Michèle Lalonde describing the situation in pre–Quiet Revolution Quebec: "We were living under the sign of the great big NO, in a silent, asphyxiating pharisaic world of forbidden thoughts, forbidden words and deeds and passions and so on ad infinitum, until there was nothing left to be experienced except the vacuum itself" (108). Jeanette Lynes has noted the similarities between Downes's choice of French Canadian poets and her own aesthetic, illustrating the "strong parallels" such as the "descent into an underworld, sometimes associated with death and sometimes with the subconscious." (43). It is not surprising, then, that Downes quotes "Le Tombeau des rois" extensively in her article dealing with Quebec women poets.

> [Anne Hébert's] poetry is spare, subtle, elegant, pared down to the essentials—pure in the best sense of that abused and overworked terms. With the most restrained hand and ear, she draws a magic circle which pulls the reader into the poems in the same way one listens to a Mozart melody. There is no linguistic dross here, no padding. Broadly speaking, the material is the adventures of the protean psyche caught at certain moments of intensity in which no division exists between subject and object, desire and expression, speaker and language. The moment is incarnated in an image, frequently a single one whose ramifications are elaborated in language which becomes simply a clear pane of glass revealing the configurations of the poet's mind...This is not "Quebec poetry," but simply poetry, and although one of Anne Hébert's later poems "Eve" had been hailed by the feminist movement, she is not fundamentally a feminist. Her commitment is to literature. ("Women" 106–07).

As we can see from the quote, Downes shares the sentiment that Hébert transcended the regional, linguistic, and gender labels often reserved for her poetry. By the time this article was written, Hébert had received a fair amount of national and international praise as a novelist based in Paris. Downes reminds the reader that Hébert was first, and foremost, a poet, a poet of the highest quality.

The three poems by Hébert translated by Downes and published in Glassco's anthology are reprinted exactly in *Out of a Violent Dark*. Critical response to the collection focuses primarily on the work as a part of the Downes's evolution as a poet. Lynes praises Downes and her corpus, stating that "her skills as poet and translator demonstrate an admirable range of abilities, and her bringing francophone poetry to anglophone readers represents a noteworthy contribution to Canadian letters" (44). In her review, Rona Murray chooses to focus primarily and almost exclusively on Downes's own poetry, but does mention her "many exquisite translations," and singles out her translation "The Planting of Hands" for "the purity of its images, its gentle madness" (157). Kathy Mezei brings Downes's translations into sharp focus by comparing the lone female translator's versions with those by her male colleagues.[4] Focusing on language and style, Mezei outlines the differences between Hébert's translators on the level of poetic style:

> The persona [in *Le Tombeau des rois*] often resembles the frail yet lugubrious girlish figure portrayed in "La fille maigre": "Je suis une fille maigre/ Et j'ai de beaux os." Neither F. R. Scott's translation "I am a lean girl/And I have beautiful bones" or Alan Brown's "I am a thin girl/With fine bones" quite captures the desperate fleshlessness of the persona, though Scott, a fine translator of Hébert's poetry creates a sharper, more poetic rendition." ("Gender" 138)

Mezei goes on the compare Gwladys Downes' translation of the poem "Une petite morte" with Brown's, pointing out that Downes "creates a poem that is at the same time more concrete and eloquent than did Alan Brown" (139). She continues, "Downes has entered the poem, its experience, its images, while Brown stands outside, awkwardly. Downes' "curls on the sill" is more rhythmic and evocative than Brown's "struck down on our threshold"; "she is a child white in her foaming skirts" is too literal a rendering [by Brown]...Downes has a finely tuned ear to Hébert's nuances" (140). Looking at the lines in question, Brown translates them as "collapsed on our sill" and "She's a white child in her mossy skirts." One should also note that Downes changes one line in the original version to two lines in her translation: "Nous n'osons plus sortir depuis qu'elle est là" becomes "Now that she is there / We do not dare go out." The other translators maintain the one line, and even invert the word order. This is a clear reflection of Downes' remaking technique, where the focus is clearly on the target poem, rather than the original poem. It is also clear that Hébert remains central to the critics, as well as to the translator herself.

ESPRIT DE CORPS, BLOUIN, POZIER, AND JONES, 1997

There is a significant time gap between Downes's anthology and the next anthology of Quebec poets in translation. The fervour experienced during Canada's centennial year and the subsequent moneys invested into the project of national identity building, combined with the after-effects of the first Quebec referendum, as well as the relative lack of interest in English Canada for Quebec letters,[5] rendered the act of anthologizing French Canadian authors relatively unpopular. But in 1997, Écrits des Forges (Trois Rivières) and Muses' Company (Winnipeg) jointly published *Esprit de Corps: Québec Poetry of the Late Twentieth Century in Translation*. The book was edited by Louise Blouin, Bernard Pozier, and D. G. Jones and contained almost the same poems as the French anthology *Poètes québécois*, also published by Écrits des Forges, in 1996. While Blouin and Pozier were the editors of the original French anthology, Jones was brought on to supervise the translations, due in no small part to his long-time association with the translation journal *Ellipse*, published until recently at the Université de Sherbrooke.

In the introduction to the original French anthology, Blouin and Pozier provide a "petit parcours de la poésie québécoise: Archéologie de nos vers." [*Short journey through Quebec poetry: An archeology of our verses*] "The volume starts with Louis Fréchette (1839–1908) and includes ten poets born before 1915, the date when the English version of the anthology begins, with Rina Lasnier (1915). Hébert is mentioned in the introduction to *Poètes québécois* as an example of a poet from the "époque de la solitude," (period of solitude) which includes the 1930s, 1940s, and 1950s. Interestingly enough, the poems selected for the anthology are all from Hébert's later collection, *Le jour n'a d'égal que la nuit*, from 1992. The authors conclude, however, that "le poème québécois fin de siècle et fin de millénaire se fait quotidien, personnel, émotif, cherchant à redéfinir l'homme, la femme et leurs rôles" (10; the Quebec poem at the end of the century and the end of the millennium is quotidian, personal, emotive, seeking to redefine man, woman, and their roles.) Pozier has also stated that the selection of poems was "surtout en vue de proposer autre chose que les poèmes présents dans la majorité des anthologies" (personal communication, February 11, 2004; always trying to present something other than the poems typically included in the majority of anthologies).

Besides excluding the ten poets born before 1910, *Esprit de Corps* also excludes Saint-Denys Garneau and Gatien Lapointe, the latter omission noted by Amy Barrett as "intriguing" given that Lapointe was the founder of Écrits des Forges (35). Ten translators worked on the poems in the anthology, including Jones. In the introduction, Jones writes that "the view of the poetry presented here is not that of the present editor but of Quebeckers themselves—more exactly, the writers and editors associated with Écrits des Forges" (*Esprit* 9). This assures the English reader that this is a collection that carries a certain degree of authenticity. Moreover, Jones further reassures the reader, stating, "this collection is not that of the Bloc" (9), a reference to the separatist political party the Bloc Québécois, then the official opposition in the federal parliament. Jones does not refer to Hébert's poetry directly, but he does make reference to Glassco's anthology: "While one might argue that this anthology continues what John Glassco in his anthology, *The Poetry of French Canada in Translation* (1970), called a poetry of exile, it strikes me that there is yet a more positive kind of *esprit de corps* that emerges here. It is solidarity with ordinary living, and mortal, creatures" (11). Certainly, Jones's anthology does pick up where Glassco's left off to a certain extent, and fills in the gaps elsewhere, with little-anthologized poems of better-known authors, such as Hébert.

Daniel Sloate was brought to the project through his work with Guernica Editions.[6] Antonio D'Alfonso, then editor-in-chief at Guernica, gave Jones a list of translators that included Sloate. Perhaps best known for his translation of Rimbaud's *Illuminations*, Sloate has translated a number of French Canadian poets for Guernica, and was nominated for a Governor General's Award in 1997 for his translations of *Aknos and Other Poems* by Fulvio Caccia. Sloate had translated a number of poets in the anthology other than Hébert, but had no choice in the selections, as it was a reproduction of the earlier French anthology. The editors trusted D'Alphonso's judgment, and offered very little feedback in terms of the translations themselves, which appear in the anthology as Sloate submitted them. Sloate describes himself as taking a "structuralist" approach to translation, where his priorities included "reproducing form, sound, along with structural and visual elements." As he states elsewhere, Sloate believes that "a text is translatable insofar as the translator can produce a text of his own which may not be semantically identical with the original, but one which is *semantically equivalent to it*" ("Comment on Sharma" 313).[7]

Sloate also did not concern himself with much of the "extra" material on the author, be it critical or otherwise: "it keeps the gossip, the twitching of literary curtains on one side, and the poem on another side, distinct although intimately linked to the other. But this is of no ultimate importance in terms of the poem itself" ("Literary" 165). Scott had previously insisted that Sloate read Hébert's *Le Tombeau des rois*, and as a result Sloate "had been moved by her vision of things," but "of Anne Hébert the person, I knew nothing and was quite content with this ignorance" (165–66). He was aware however of other translations of Hébert's poetry, having written a very complete, if structuralist, review of

Brown's translation of *Poèmes* for *Meta* ("Literary"). Sloate quite clearly describes what he looks for in terms of a quality translation, and its application, which he calls "transcreating"—

> "transcreating" the original [uses] as many of the original elements as possible, both internal and external, in...translation. Up to a point, this method is excellent, enabling the translator to detect *unsuspected* or obscure internal structures as well as the more obvious external ones. This is the "objective" side. But it is at this point, given the multiple choices offered to the translator, and taking into account the structures of the original poem, that a "subjective" intervention must occur: the intensity and quality of this intervention is dependant on the individual translator alone. (166)

Sloate concludes, "the translator must become or be a poet himself" (168). He saw Hébert as a poet much like himself, of a specific place, not as a voice of a people, a politics, or a gender. For Sloate, Hébert transcended her place and gender to achieve Poetry.

The five poems included in both anthologies are "Homeland," "Apparition," "Scorched Earth," "Tenebrous Lesson," and "Absurd Sun," all from *Le jour n'a d'égal que la nuit*. "Terre originelle" and "Apparition" appear in the "Poèmes Anciens 1961–1980" section, and had appeared previously in uncollected form. Alfred Poulin Jr.'s translation *Day Has No Equal but Night* had appeared previously, in 1994, through BOA Editions, and Lola Lemire Tostevin's translation *Day has no equal but the night* was published by Anansi Press the same year as *Esprit des Corps*. Sloate does state that ultimately the translations are "interpretations [that] are creations in so far as they are unique perspectives upon a reality...which can be viewed from different points of reference" ("Literary" 166), which would fit with some of his decisions as a translator. Overall, however, Sloate's five translations are consistent with his own approach; Sloate has said that friends have observed that his own distinct poetic voice comes through in his translations of Hébert and have become a part of the "Sloate œuvre."

Amy Barrett, in her review of the anthology, points to Hébert's inclusion and her status as an "icon," but doesn't directly comment on the translations of her poems. Barrett has reservations about some of the translations (D. G. Jones's in particular), but concludes "*Esprits* [sic] *de Corps* provides a much needed introduction for English readers to the literary solitude that is Québécois poetry" (35). Dean J. Irvine, in his review for *Canadian Literature*, calls the anthology "a metonym for the multiple sites and histories of material culture" (170).

Focusing mostly on the cultural implications of the anthology, and the material meaning of the title, Irvine has little to say about the selection of poetry and the quality of the translations, other than "*Esprit de Corps* shows that translation is possible for French Québec poetry, and that they have attempted to translate both spirit and letter of the poetry" (170). Another aspect that Irvine points to is the collaborative effort of the anthology, between English and French publishers, editors, and author/translators. "This emphasis upon collaboration, not upon individualism or separatism, forges a real sense of community in and around the anthology," he says (170). But this does not negate the perceived fact that Québécois poetry is "other," and Irvine spends his conclusion reminding the reader about the inherent tension between source and target texts, local and colonial forces; Québec, even through translation, is constantly recreated as the mysterious other.

For an English Canadian reader who was paying attention, Hébert's importance and impact on the French Canadian/Québécois poetic canon is clear. Her inclusion and discussion in French Canadian anthologies in translation, even in the lone anthology that does not include any of her poems in translation, cements her status as an icon. To repeat what Barbara Godard has said, "plus de traductions, plus de recensions critiques, plus de capital symbolique, plus de traductions" ("Littérature en devenir" 496). One could take that one step further within this context and argue that the same theory would apply to the anthologization of an author. However, even a superficial survey of French anthologies of Québécois literature and poetry will show that Hébert's status is not simply the work of the English Canadian anthologists and critics.[8] She was, in both French and English, a part of the French Canadian/Québécois canons, the accessible, curricular, and traditional canons. More problematic, in a political sense, is her inclusion within the larger Canadian canon.

ANNE HÉBERT AS CANADIAN

Occurring simultaneously to the project to introduce French Canadian poetry to English Canada was the project to formulate a Canadian canon, mainly through anthologies. The majority of these anthologies, according to Lecker's bibliography of English-language Canadian anthologies (1997), focused exclusively on English Canadian works, excluding French Canadian authors in either their original or translated form. A handful of anthologists resisted that trend and consciously chose to place French Canadian poets in translation in their anthologies of Canadian literature. This was in part due to the availability of quality translations of French Canadian poetry and literature, but also was a part of a larger federalist vision of Canada that included both solitudes. These inclusions were not unproblematic—on one hand, the inclusion of French Canadian poets in anthologies to be used in English courses would prove to be against the linguistic divisions in academia; on the other, post–October Crisis politics (a time marked by domestic terrorism and the suspension of civil liberties) made it politically delicate to place the Québécois authors in a larger, Canadian context. Those who did choose to include French Canadian authors were often themselves in contact with the translators and the other anthologists, and thus influenced by the work of their colleagues. They canonically reinforced each other. Hébert was important to those working on French Canadian poets, and so too was she important to those studying Canada via the literary canon.

POETRY OF OUR TIME, LOUIS DUDEK, 1964

In 1964, Louis Dudek edited *Poetry of Our Time*, the first contemporary anthology of poetry that included both English Canadian and French Canadian poets (the latter in translation).[9] MacMillan published the anthology, which contained not only Canadian poets but also a selection of English-language modernist poets. As stated earlier, Dudek was one of the founders of Contact Press as well as many other poetry journals, a professor of English at McGill, and a published poet and translator himself. He adopted Erza Pound's "Make It New" slogan, which would influence both his writing and his editing endeavours (Davey 13). Dudek was also fiercely patriotic and looked to support young, avant-garde Canadian writers (16). Having grown up in Montreal's East End, he was familiar with French, and it was through his job at the Quebec Tourist Bureau that he

> came into direct contact with francophone writers, first with Maurice Hébert, who was Dudek's boss, a minor poet himself and father of Anne Hébert; and then with Yves Thérrault, who worked at the next desk. These early associations confirmed Dudek's interest in the writers of Quebec, an interest which would see him trying his hand at translating their work. (Gnarowski 13–14)

Dudek was instrumental in encouraging the publication of translations through Contact Press, and was heavily involved in Peter Miller's translations of Hébert's poetry and the unpublished Gaston Miron manuscript (CPR, Box 2, folders 3–5).

The anthology project began in the early 1960s, with Dudek shopping the idea and an incomplete manuscript to a variety of publishers. From the very beginning, he intended to include English Canadian and Québécois poetry in the anthology. In a letter to G. B. Halpin of Prentice-Hall, Dudek writes: "The Canadian selections are incomplete, at this stage only about half-finished. They would have a separate short Introduction. We must bring in a few French-language poets in Canada (4 or 5), especially in view of the present political situation in Québec" (LDF, box 13, file 7). One cannot imagine that there was much of an audience for an anthology of modern poetry that included a Canadian sampling. In a letter to MacMillan dated June 8, 1964, Dudek confides that one of the other publishing houses he approached responded with "Yes, of course, we do need this; but it is too early for it yet" (LDF, box 13, file 7). He also revealed that both Prentice-Hall and McClelland & Stewart thought that the anthology was too much of a risk. But MacMillan took that risk and agreed to publish the anthology.

Dudek divides the anthology into two sections, "Twentieth-Century Poetry" and "Modern Canadian Poetry," complete with separate introductions for each section. In the introduction to the Canadian section, Dudek treats the development of the two literatures, English Canadian and French Canadian, as separate and virtually unrelated, having been influenced by completely different traditions (British/American and French, respectively). He notes that

> English-Canadian writing is clearly following the path into reality in trying to resolve this problem [the conflict between reality and idealism], French-Canadian poetry has followed the inward path of spirituality, subjectivity, and idealism, without being any less aware of the problems of reality that produces the poetry. (196)

Hébert is given a special place in his introduction, she marking the "[beginning] of modern French-Canadian poetry" (197). Given that the Quiet Revolution was taking place at the time, it is surprising that Dudek does not mention the socio-political context in which the French Canadian poems were being created. He does conclude his introduction with: "Perhaps this freedom of mind and reliance on the opportunity of experience, without preconceptions, is the keynote of present poetry" (198). This would fit the criticism often levelled against English Canadian criticism of French Canadian literature: it is, for the most part, apolitical, ignoring the context and political implications of the works.[10]

In an enlightening piece appearing in the *Montreal Gazette* three years after the publication of his anthology, Dudek offers more reflection on how he viewed contemporary Québécois poetry generally and Hébert's poetry more specifically. Like Scott, Dudek prized Hébert's poetry because "it brings a new aesthetic to English Canadian poetry, because Anne Hébert's contemplative and inward poetry is unlike anything available in English" ("Ann Hebert" I9). He goes on to observe:

> Among the best French Canadian poets there is a great distance between the poet and the audience. From their style, neither Grandbois, nor Saint-Denys Garneau, nor Anne Hébert would expect a wide popular response...[their poems] are very much over the head of the general reader.... The result is that French Canadian poetry is deeply withdrawn into itself. It is highly introspective and inwardly-centered. Incredibly beautiful sometimes, and intensively imaging—true to itself—but lacking real roots in present society. (I9)

This interpretation and framing of Hébert (and French Canadian poetry) wilfully depoliticizes and dehistoricizes it from the social reality it came from. In his study of Québécois poetry from 1948 to 1953, Pierre Popovic draws the exact opposite conclusion to Dudek's, finding instead that Hébert's poetry in particular "travaille de manière spécifique à l'intérieur du discours social" (390). It is also insulting to a French audience that the power and beauty of Hébert's poetry would be lost on them. These are the risks and dangers of anthologization and translation: gross generalization, misrepresentation, depoliticization. But, the trade-off is the potential for a much wider audience, an audience and readership who might not otherwise read Hébert's work.

Included in the anthology are "Snow," "A Little Corpse" (both translated by Peter Miller), and "The Lean Girl" (translated by Scott), along with the original French version of each poem. The first poem is from *Poèmes*, while the other two are from *Le Tombeau des rois*. Miller's translation of "Snow" was previously unpublished, while "A Little Corpse" appeared in *The Tomb of Kings* that same year. Dudek, who intend his anthology to be used in high schools, provided an introduction, both critical and biographical, to each of the authors, as well as "Study Aids" at the end of the collection for each of the individual poems appearing in the anthology. He introduces Hébert's poetry thusly:

> Anne Hébert writes allusive poetry in the French-Symbolist tradition, a poetry in which explicit meaning is irrelevant and 'the essence of things' is communicated through the music and the connotation of words. But the human side of such poetry is nevertheless possible to grasp. Its quality of feeling is conveyed to the reader directly, even if the sense and the images remain vague and uncertain. (266)

This introduction is interesting as it associates Hébert to poetry, and not to any sort of socio-political force. But it is also a reflection of her power as a poet; much like the critics who commented on English anthologies of French Canadian poetry, Hébert is raised to a different level in terms of her accessibility and image. The study aid further focuses the reader's attention on the surreal aspects of the poems and the symbolic power of the language; emphasis is placed on the "dream" quality of "Snow" (355), the reader is encouraged to relate to "A Little Corpse" as a "fairy tale" (356), and the lover in "The Lean Girl" is equated with "the universe itself" (356).

Out of the twenty-nine Canadian poets who are included in Dudek's anthology, only six are French (Hébert, Nelligan, Saint-Denys Garneau, Grandbois, Gilles Vigneault, Jean-Guy Pilon), and of that list, Hébert is the only woman. In a letter dated January 23, 1965, Dudek writes to Miller:

> I have an unusual request, or invitation, to make, I've just finished the modern poetry textbook which I was preparing for Macmillans—a collection of British, American, and some Canadian poets, with Introductions, biographical notes, and critical questions on all the poems—a very big job. This book contains a few of the principal French Canadian poets, five names in all. With the French poems, I have an English translation in each case, so that there will be no language obstacle to reading these poems in the high schools across Canada. Now—
>
> I selected the poems without first looking to see if these are included in Frank Scott's or in your books. A few are. But I find that some still have to be translated. There are three poems that I would be happy to see you do. It would bring more of your translations into the book and keep my name from recurring too often as translator (I will be translator for four of the poems as it is).
>
> Now then, the three poems that need to be done are Anne Hébert's poem "Neige" and Grandbois' two poems "Ce qui reste" and "L'Enfance oubliée".
>
> (One other from Anne Hébert, "Une Petite Morte," I see you have in your new MS [*The Tomb of Kings*]. I would like to use that)...
>
> Time, however, is very pressing. I have intended until just yesterday to do these translations myself, but my dear friend Aileen Collins suggested the wonderful idea that I should ask you to do it. How long would it take you to do three poems? Can it be done in a week or two? (This book is already in the typesetting stage, and these last bits of copy are holding back the whole job.) Let me know anyhow. (CPR, Box 2, file 4)

Unlike Glassco and others, Dudek selected the poems to be included in the anthology first in the French, and then selected/created translations. Miller writes to Dudek that he was "plagued" by "Snow," consulted with Scott's translation, and found the poem "for technical reasons rather a bastard." He also explains some of the choices he made in translating Hébert's poem in a letter to Dudek dated January 27, 1965. Showing a concern for form as well as accuracy, Miller distinguishes in his translation between "rêve" and "songe" as "dream" and "fancy," (Dudek *Poetry*, 266–67) and tries to preserve Hébert's economy of language: "I would have much preferred to use 'becalmed white, swollen plumage' instead of whiteness, but this would have risked construction of white as an adjective agreeing with plumage, which would have sounded bad and would bugger the whole passage up" (CPR, Box 2, file 5). Dudek responds in a subsequent letter, stating: "The Anne Hébert poem sounds especially good in English" (CPR, Box 2, file 5). What remains unclear is why Dudek uses two of Miller's translations and one of Scott's.[11]

An editorial review from the *Ottawa Journal* ignores the inclusion of Canadian poets completely, instead lamenting the fact that "only 11 of the 36 poets representing 'the poetry of our time' were born in the 20th century" ("Where"). The *Montreal Star* celebrates that "modern Canadian poets are also represented" and "that several French-Canadian poems have been included, in French, with English translations on the next page" (Francis 8). No mention, however, is made regarding the selection of French Canadian authors included, even though a significant portion of the review is devoted to the choices of English Canadian poets and poems. This is perhaps a reflection of the relative lack of knowledge regarding French Canadian poets and poetry, but nonetheless, six out of twenty-nine poets is a relatively small proportion. However, as the reviewer points out, the book is significant because of its accessible format, which would provide an introduction to Canadian poetry that perhaps would not have happened otherwise.

The inclusion of Hébert in this context is important as a new and different set of readers would be exposed to her poetry, in this case, an entire generation of high-school students. The poems that Dudek selected are no more or less representative of her body of poems to that point: the inclusion of "Snow" does mark the slight departure that takes place between *Le Tombeau des rois* and *Poèmes*, in terms of form, style, and evolving subject matter. Dudek does choose to present the poems in reverse chronological order: "Snow" (1960) comes before "A Little Corpse" and "The Lean Girl" (1953). They are all poems that have been seen elsewhere, if not perhaps in that exact form/translation. With the French included, and with quality translations, the reader would have a good, albeit brief, introduction to Hébert's poetry.

While the critical reception of the anthology may have been limited to two brief newspaper mentions, MacMillan was rewarded commercially for the risk taken at the time in publishing the anthology. Dudek, upon the book's release, wrote sixty letters publicizing the new collection to curriculum supervisors and administrators across Canada. The two-page letters, all dated March 12, 1966, conclude with the following:

> Altogether, I hope that this text will be a joy for the teacher and the pupil to work with. Poetry is often reported as "the most difficult of all subjects to teach," possibly because the content and tone of the poems offered is foreign to the experience of modern youth. POETRY OF OUR TIME is designed to provide good poetry that does relate to modern life and that leads to mature thought and reflection on the issues of the modern world. I hope that you will consider it for adoption. (LDF, box 13, file 7)

MacMillan also sent a number of copies to universities across the country and received favourable feedback from almost all who replied to the publisher. All comments passed along to Dudek through MacMillan were kept anonymous, but in letters dated between May 10 and August 3, 1966, Dudek heard comments from as many as a dozen teachers and academics from institutions such as Laurentian University, the University of Saskatchewan, and the Nova Scotia Teachers College. Many of them applauded the inclusion of English and French Canadian modern poetry, as well as the anthology's accessible and affordable format. The anthology crossed the desk of a member of the Faculty of Education at the University of British Colombia, who also happened to be "on a Department of Education English Committee" (LDF, box 13, file 7). In a letter dated June 20, 1966, MacMillan passed along the following "anonymous" comments: "I think the Dudek anthology is the best of its kind in Canada...I recommended this volume in the strongest language possible to those charged with making decisions" (LDF, box 13, file 7). As it turned out, the anthology was adopted in British Colombia in 1967 as a part of the Grade 12 curriculum, leading to the sale of approximately 35,000 copies. The book had already been reprinted once, in November of 1966, having been adopted in a number of university introductory courses and high schools across the country.

Contrary to the publishers who had been unwilling to take a chance on his anthology, sales proved it was not "too early for it yet," but exactly the right time: 1967 was Canada's centennial year, and the height of Canadian nationalism, as well as the height of the 1960s generation that was also looking for ways to "Make It New." Dudek was an important and influential voice in Canadian letters, as an author, publisher, and now an anthologist. Hébert is presented in a context that allows her to be compared not only with her English Canadian colleagues, but also with the broader example of modern poetry. She is one of the few French Canadian poets to be included in this influential anthology, beginning a trend that would see her poems in virtually every English Canadian anthology that included French Canadian works in translation. Paul Martin explains the importance of an author's inclusion in an anthology, even if they are not directly assigned: "Even if they only read the texts assigned to them by their professors, [students] witness, in the physical form of the anthology, how much there is that they are not reading. Simply by flipping through the table of contents, they begin to get an idea of the larger shape of the field, that there is more out there that they can learn" (*Sanctioned Ignorance*, 183). Hébert has now been, to recall Peggy Kelly's observations, placed within the curricular canon—young readers in high schools and universities across the country now had an opportunity to read Hébert and experience her poetry within the larger context of Canadian and modern English poetry

CANADIAN WRITING TODAY, MORDECAI RICHLER, 1970

The next anthology of Canadian literature to include Hébert's poetry in translation was *Canadian Writing Today*, edited by Mordecai Richler and published by Penguin Books, in 1970, as the twelfth book in a larger series featuring current writing from regions and countries around the world. According to William French,

> The Penguin people in England are well launched on a series of paperbacks designed to reveal the state of writing in various countries and continents...Before we blush with pride, it should be noted that earlier volumes in the series have dealt with writing in Australia, South Africa, Cuba, Poland and Czechoslovakia, among other countries, but at least we're ahead of Nepal and Iceland. ("Books and Bookmen" 18)

Hébert is represented by one poem, "Manor Life" (translated by Scott), taken from *Le Tombeau des rois*. Out of forty-six authors in the anthology, there are twelve French Canadian authors who appear in translation, including Pierre Elliot Trudeau, future prime minister. The importance of the anthology was not lost on those who were reviewing it: a major international publisher putting out the anthology at an affordable price and in accessible format as a part of an already successful series of anthologies. The audience was assumed to be large and international in scope.

For those very reasons, the anthology itself generated a great deal of controversy at home, from the choice of editor to the literature included, and even the cover illustration, a reprint of the painting *Imperial Wildcat No. 3, Excelsoir Field, near Edmonton*, by Henry George Glyde, which can be seen as quite desolate. John Richmond, in his review for the *Montreal Star*, writes:

> Bleaker than the friendless widow of an improvident husband it evokes an aspect of Canada, devoid of beauty; a land polluted by the ugliness of a gimcrack technology, in an Eliot wasteland, rorshached with blobs of snow, with four human figures either on their way towards or their way from some grim task. Nothing but its glum, pointless ugliness has point. No prospect pleases. Here Kafka and Greene would have made the down-payment on their duplex. (72)

This is just the beginning of the criticism levelled at this anthology. The choice of Richler as the editor was questioned by a majority of the reviewers: at the time he was asked to edit the collection, Richler had been living in England for a considerable duration. And, as the book was to be a significant representation of Canadian writing, many had issues with the selections that Richler the expat had included, particularly in light of the title words, Canadian writing *today*. As the headlines of two of the reviews indicate, "Behind the times with Canadian writing" and "Canadian Writing Today is yesterday's news," reviewers generally shared the sentiment expressed by Barry Callaghan that "the result is a collection that is not only incomplete but it has the air of something that might have been interesting 10 years ago" ("Mordecai" 30). Richler's introduction also drew aspersions. Not one missed the comment—"Put plainly, this is an anthology of the Canadian writing I like" (Richler 23)—that Richler concludes his introduction with, either. The introduction was widely criticized, as expressed by Phyllis Grosskurth in her review for *Saturday Night*, "[Richler's] ambivalent tone implies a struggle to find anything at all to say" (33). Stated more directly by David Helwig in his review for *Books in Canada*, Richler "is a mediocre critic, largely derivative and unthinking" (8).

Richler's treatment of French Canadian writers in the introduction is interesting. He reminds the reader immediately in the second paragraph that:

> Canada, remember, is a two-headed culture. The French is cocooned by language, the English isn't. We English-speaking, but not necessarily Anglo-Saxon, Canadians make up in touchiness what we lack in militancy. We have, mind you, reason to be touchy. From the beginning,

> Canada's two founding races, the English and the French, outdid each other in scornfully disinheriting us. A few arpents of snow, Voltaire wrote contemptuously of Canada in *Candide*; and Dr Johnson described the dominion as a 'region of desolate sterility...a cold, uncomfortable, uninviting region from which nothing but furs and fish were to be had.' (15)

The rest of the introduction does not differentiate between English and French writers in Canada in any meaningful way, except to identify "new militant French-Canadian writers" in Hubert Aquin, Jean-Guy Pilon, and Jacques Godbout. Hébert is not mentioned specifically in the introduction. It is interesting to note that Richler explains that he "sought out the younger writers, those who have made their mark within the last ten, fifteen, years" (23), but uses a poem by Hébert published in 1953 in *Le Tombeau des rois*, which first appeared in 1951 in *Cité libre*. *Kamouraska* had been released and she won the prestigious Molson Prize in 1967, but Hébert had certainly made her mark on Canadian letters at least five years earlier than Richler's cut-off date. While Richler points to some "notable exceptions" to the rule (Frye, Earle Birney, Saint-Denys Garneau, George Woodcock), he does not address the issue of Hébert's inclusion in the anthology.

In a letter dated August 3, 1967, Richler wrote to Jill Norman, editor of the then-titled New Writing series for Penguin Books, England, about the upcoming Canadian edition. In it, Richler clearly outlines his intentions with the collection:

> I think we're agreed that anything going into the anthology should be up to international publication: literary excellence, not Canadian worthiness, will be the test. I will also try to make the anthology contemporary in tone, concentrating on writers who have made their reputations since 1950; both English and French Canadian.
>
> I will not be including the older generation of Canadian writers (Leacock, Maclennan [sic], Callaghan, Gabrielle Roy, etc). I will also avoid the set anthology pieces that have figured in so many centennial collections...
>
> I also hope to include at least two French Canadian stories and work by four French Canadian poets...certainly something by Marie Claire Blaise [sic] and Anne Hébert. (MRF, MsC 36.10.33)

Already, Richler has judged Hébert to be one of the handfuls of poets who fits his criteria of literary excellence and possessing a contemporary voice. It is possibly through his friendship with Scott that Richler was introduced to the poetry of Anne Hébert, although the connection is not explicitly clear. But her inclusion in the anthology was not guaranteed, nor was it uneventful. In a letter from Jill Levine in London, dated November 22, 1968, she states: "There are one or two pieces in the Anthology that I am not very happy about. They are mostly poems. I wonder whether if it may be possible to find other poems by the same people?" (MRF, MsC 36.10.33). One of the poems listed is "Manor Life." In the letter, Levine does not address why she feels the particular poem is unacceptable, although she does acquiesce to Richler's better judgment: "On the other hand, if they are poems that you like particularly, then we will keep them, since any selection like this is necessarily personal and subjective." In a subsequent letter, Richler does not address the issue of Hébert's poem, while it finally does appear in the final publication.

He had to fight one last battle before Hébert's inclusion was assured: permission from the translator. Scott refused to accept the $15 per translation that Penguin was offering, as he was accustomed to receiving $25 per translation. As previously discussed in Chapter one, Scott was resitant to his translation of Hébert being included in the collection. As described by Levine, in a letter to Richler dated July 3, 1969, "Scott...is obviously very niggled that none of his own poetry is included" (Richler fonds). Scott expresses his discontent with the situation in his own letter to Penguin: "It is also apparent that you only want me to be represented by translation" and threatened to refuse use of any of his translations (MRF, MsC 36.10.33). Richler, who was living in Montreal at the time, obviously spoke to Scott, as the next letter from Levine, dated July 22, 1969, reads, "I am very relieved to hear you have mollified Frank Scott" (MRF, MsC 36.10.33). Implicit in these letters is Richler's commitment to the inclusion of Hébert within the anthology. When the volume was finally released, Hébert's name was included on the list of authors placed on promotional materials from Penguin for the book (MRF, MsC 36.10.33).

Most reviewers were content to simply compliment Richler for his inclusion of French Canadian authors at all. Keith Fraser, in his review for *Canadian Literature*, states, "Richler's attempt to balance French and English writing is commendable" (90), and William French forgives Richler for other editorial crimes, because "he includes a sample of current French-Canadian writing in translation" ("Books and Bookmen" 18). Two reviews, by John Richmond and Peter Sypnowich, respectively, question the choice that Richler makes to include an extract from Jacques Godbout's *Knife of the Table*, as Richler had previously panned the book in a review. Phyllis Grosskurth is not as kind to Richler's selection from French Canada.

> The greatest disappointment, however, is the quality of the French-Canadian writing selected (in translation) for this anthology. With the exception of the Gothic imagination displayed by Marie-Claire Blais, much of the writing is self-indulgent, overwrought, and pretentious. There is here little indication of any literary renaissance in Quebec, of the claim made by other writers in the anthology that French Canadians are the only group in the country who possess what Neil Compton calls a "unique identity." (34)

While "Manor Life" perhaps does not express Hébert's gothic sensibility, connected more readily with *Kamouraska*, to call the poem self-indulgent simply because the speaker is mysteriously drawn—to quote the poem, "to look at oneself in the mirror day and night" (Richler 43)—is to miss the point. In fact, this poem mocks the tendency toward self-indulgence, through showing the manor in question as a type of prison, hiding dead bodies. In direct opposition, Barry Callaghan laments that only one of Hébert's poems is included in the collection: "It is simply absurd, if space is a problem...to present only one poem from such an excellent poet as Anne Hébert and one from Colombo" ("Mordecai" 30). Callaghan, it should be noted, is the only reviewer that directly addresses the inclusion of Anne Hébert in the anthology. Perhaps being included immediately after Trudeau's "The Sorry Tale of French-Canadian Nationalism" tended to distract the reader from her entry. The lone "international" review of the anthology, from the *Times Literary Supplement*, London, makes no mention of Hébert either and maintains much of the same tone and comments of the Canadian reviews: it laments the poor quality of the introduction, questions the editorial choices and their motivation, and wishes there were more French Canadian writers included.

The wide reception of Richler's anthology stands in direct opposition to the limited reception of Dudek's anthology. But the impact was just as great, simply with a different audience. Richler was a popular and recognizable name, not only in Canadian literature, but internationally as well. Penguin was a major publisher; its Writing Today series well known. While sales figures nor print runs are unavailable in the archives I consulted, accessibility was the aim of this collection, as much as it was for Dudek's collection, but with a larger intended audience. Here was an anthology that was being talked about, a different type of exposure than Dudek's anthology, which was being taught. In this situation, rather than becoming part of the curricular canon, the anthology placed Hébert within the accessible canon. In either case, Hébert was being exposed to an entirely new audience, this time through infamy.

THE OXFORD ANTHOLOGY OF CANADIAN LITERATURE, WEAVER AND TOYE, 1973

In 1973, Oxford University Press published *The Oxford Anthology of Canadian Literature*, edited by Robert Weaver and William Toye. The anthology contains eighty authors, with fourteen of those from French Canada. Three poems by Hébert are included: "The Little Towns" (translated by Glassco), "Manor Life" and "The Tomb of Kings" (translated by Scott). All three are from *Le Tombeau des rois*. Also included in the anthology is the poem "Portrait of Anne Hébert" by D. G. Jones. The anthology provides a preface by the editors, a brief bio-critical introduction to each poet, and a thematic index to the poems. The collection enjoyed another run in 1981, and again in 1983, while in 1982 the press published *Teacher's Handbook to The Oxford Anthology of Canadian Literature*, written by Shirley I. Paustian, as a companion to the editions. Weaver worked for the CBC, producing, among other shows, *Anthology*, a show that featured Canadian writers. He also founded the *Tamarack Review*, enlisting Toye as an editor, who at the time was editorial director for OUP Canada.[12] Both editors of the anthology were heavily involved in Canadian letters, and although they were not authors themselves, they played a large role in shaping Canadian literature as we know it.

In their relatively short preface, the editors address the motivation for their anthology and the selections therein, which is "to give a general view of our writing from the early days to the present" (xiii). The editors admit that "the selections represent...the tastes of the two editors" and apologize for the omissions, "particularly of some younger writers from Québec" due to space constraints (xiii). The organization of the anthology is alphabetical instead of chronological, and the thematic divisions are based in no small part on Margaret Atwood's "arresting study of Canadian literature...*Survival*" (xiii). The cross referencing is not limited to Hébert, and in fact the editors often chose entries based on their being able to trace their "original" influence (e.g., *The Journals of Susanna Moodie* by Atwood, and selections from Susanna Moodie herself). The editors conclude their preface with their hopes for the anthology and its influence: "It is our hope that *The Oxford Anthology of Canadian Literature*...will bring together even more Canadian readers and Canadian writers, offering both pleasure and discoveries and tantalizing some of you into making further investigations of your own" (xiv). The intended audience for this anthology was wide, and primarily Canadian, and its goal was to provide an introduction to Canadian authors and their writing. What kind of introduction to Hébert would the reader receive?

Aside from the basic biographical introduction listing her personal history and publications, the editors provide a basic critical introduction to her poems, focusing on their symbolic nature, as well as their relation to Quebec letters:

> Some of Anne Hébert's most memorable poems describe a retreat from reality into the solitude of a surrealistic interior world where purity and innocence are sought. It is a world of symbols—of childhood, captivity and death—that portray a subconscious landscape with disturbing clarity. The sorrow of isolation and the renunciation of the joys of life in favour of the anguish of solitude are important themes in Anne Hébert's poetry, as they are in the works of many French-Canadian poets, particularly that of Saint-Denys-Garneau. But Anne Hébert's writings trace a gradual liberation from this captivity (from all restrictive conditions of life). For example, in the closing lines of 'The Tomb of Kings' we read of the freeing of the captive poet after a confrontation with death. (205)

The editors also direct the reader to the exchange between Scott and Hébert regarding the translation of the cited poem. Within this introduction, we can see the editors universalizing her poems, offering the reader a more general and symbolic context by which to interpret them. The three poems that Weaver and Toye include reflect their view of Hébert's poetry: a journey from oppression to freedom. The two first poems, "The Little Towns" and "Manor Life," full of echoes of death and isolation, set the atmosphere for the climactic "The Tomb of Kings." Interestingly, in the thematic divisions offered for readers at the back of the book, Hébert's poems are listed under only two of the themes: Fantasy ("The Little Towns" and "The Tomb of Kings") and Prison and Prisoners ("Manor Life" and "The Tomb of Kings"). Her poems are absent from other applicable themes, such as Death, Violence, Victims, Escape, Quebec, Alienation, or Childhood and Youth. D. G. Jones's "A Portrait of Anne Hébert" is mentioned at the end of the editors' introduction to Hébert, and again in the thematic sections "Portrait" and "Poems and Poets." Even more interesting is Hébert's total absence in the companion *Teacher's Handbook*; while there are French Canadian authors cited in the *Handbook*, she is not among them. Nonetheless, what Weaver and Toye establish is Hébert's place within Canadian letters, how she fits within the larger context, as well as her influence and interrelations (Saint-Denys Garneau, D. G. Jones, F. R. Scott).

The choice to place Hébert in their anthology was easy for the editors, as William Toye explained in a letter: "As Bob Weaver and I had determined to make this anthology representative of both English- and French-Canadian writers, Anne Hébert's inclusion, as one of the leading French-Canadian poets, was mandatory" (personal communication, February 9, 2005). Toye himself chose the poems, and acknowledges his personal connection to the two translators, having published Glassco's *Poetry of French Canada in Translation*, and being a "close friend of Frank Scott's," as well as editor of *Tamarack Review*, where Scott and Hébert's *Dialogue* was originally published. Toye explains, however, that the choice to use the two translators' versions was not based on personal bias: "These three fine poems appear in [other] translations that are also fine. I say this objectively, quite apart from my friendship with the translators. I was very much aware of the dedication and sensitivity they applied to their translations." Toye goes on to explain his motivation for choosing particular poems. "I chose the poems because I thought that even though Hébert was a difficult poet, meaning in all three would not be entirely beyond the grasp of an intelligent high-school student." Quality and accessibility are thus the two criteria for selection, as well as the status of Hébert as a "leading" French Canadian poet. The idea of universality is also reinforced with Toye's observation that high-school students would be able to appreciate and understand the poems and the poet.

Evidence relating to the response to the anthology is quite limited considering the intended scope and the influence of the editors. Reviews are also contradictory. Morris Wolfe largely praises the anthology in *Saturday Night*, while Chris Scott maligns it in *Books in Canada*. Scott criticizes the limited selection of French Canadian writers in the anthology: "Add to this fact that French-Canadian literature is but sparsely represented, and then given only in translation, and the dominant impression is one of chaos" (5), and thus recommends alternative anthologies for classroom purposes. He also calls the anthology's multiple cross-references a "mutual admiration society" and that "it is hard to suppress the feeling that all these persons...are in fact one and the same writer" (5). Wolfe, on the other hand, praises the choices that the editors make, both in form and content, in particular when comparing the collection to previous anthologies. He states that "Weaver and Toye have accepted two important premises: that an anthology of Canadian literature must include writing by both English and French-Canadian writers, and that literature is the best writing on any subject in whatever form" (40). He also praises the introductions for their "breezy and informative manner [that] strikes a right balance between the scholarly and the popular" (40). Neither reviewer makes direct mention of Hébert's inclusion. One reason is that Wolfe, in his review, compares Weaver and Toye's anthology to previous anthologies that included only English Canadian writing. Scott favours those anthologies that do not combine English and French Canadian authors and their writing. Another perhaps more subtle reason is that neither of the reviewers is particularly familiar nor comfortable with French Canadian writing and authors. This is a reflection of the more complex socio-political situation that had evolved since Richler's anthology: the October Crisis of 1970 and the swift rise of nationalist sentiment in Quebec. Scott's disapproval of the works being included "only in translation" calls attention to the new linguistic tension between the two solitudes, as well as to questions of colonialism and appropriation.

But this superficial dismissal also points to the reviewers' inability to address the French Canadian texts and their accompanying introductions in any sort of depth. Those who reviewed the anthologies of French Canadian poetry in translation were often specialists in French Canadian poetry themselves, while those who are reviewing English Canadian anthologies are usually unilingual specialists in Canadian literature, which is a reflection of how Canadian literature was (and still is) typically taught in Canada: along linguistic lines. Nonetheless, the multiple reprints and *Teacher's Guide* would suggest an eager audience for the anthology, despite the limited critical exposure, further placing Hébert within the curricular canon.

LITERATURE IN CANADA, DAYMOND AND MONKMAN, 1978

In 1978, Gage Educational Publishing released the two-volume *Literature in Canada*, edited by University of Guelph English professors Douglas Daymond and Leslie Monkman. Volume One, as described in the book's preface, "extends from Jacques Cartier in the sixteenth century to Stephen Leacock and his contemporaries in the early decades of the twentieth century" while Volume Two starts from "the rise of modernism following World War I" (xii). Volume Two contains entries by eighty-four authors, fifteen of whom are French Canadian. Hébert is represented by eight poems, six from *Le Tombeau des rois* and two from *Poèmes*: "The Tomb of Kings," "The Lean Girl," and "Snow" (translated by Scott); "The Water Fishermen" (translated by Miller); "The Little Towns" (translated by Glassco); "The Wooden Room," "Life in the Castle" and "Spring over the City" (translated by Brown). The poems appear not only in chronological order by original publication date, but also in the order in which they appeared in translation; "The Tomb of Kings" thus becomes the first poem in the section. The section on Hébert begins with a basic biographical introduction that also lists a number of her publications and translations.

In their preface, which is practically identical in both volumes, the editors address the purpose of their two-volume anthology:

> *Literature in Canada* traces the evolution of Canadian literature from the narratives of exploration of the sixteenth century to the poetry, fiction and drama of the nineteen-seventies. It is intended for the English-speaking reader and emphasizes the development of Canadian literature in English.

> However, translated texts from more than two dozen authors writing in French have been included and, within the limits of translation, these selections introduce some of the major writers of French Canada. (xi)

We learn two important pieces of information from this excerpt: that the editors saw Hébert as a "major" French Canadian author and that they were conscious of the imperfect medium that translation represents. This may help to explain why the editors selected translations from such a wide variety of sources: poems by four different translators are chosen. Much like Glassco in his anthology, the editors here want to ensure the highest-quality translation is included as a representation of the original author's poem. This criterion remains a mystery, and at this point the editors certainly had no shortage of versions to choose from, as Brown's *Poems* had just been released, in 1975, bringing the total number of Canadian translators of Hébert's poetry to eight. Some of the choices appear obvious, such as the inclusion of Scott's version of "The Tomb of Kings." Douglas and Monkman agree with Dudek's assessment that Scott's translation of "The Lean Girl" was superior to any of the others available, but counter popular opinion by selecting Brown's "Life in a Castle" over the much-anthologized Scott version, "Manor Life." Brown was the only translator to that point who had tackled "Spring over the City," but most of the choices between versions came down to the choice between the two translators who had translated entire collections of Hébert's poetry: Miller or Brown for "The Water Fishermen" and "The Wooden Room," with Glassco's version of "The Wooden Room" also in the mix.

In an e-mail dated March 13, 2005, Leslie Monkman addresses some of these questions. His first exposure to Québécois culture had been through his involvement at Expo 67, and then he had "spent a research term sitting in on the comparative Canadian literature classes of Doug Jones and Ron Sutherland at the Université de Sherbrooke in 1971 while simultaneously reading as widely as [he] could in Canadian poetry and fiction in French." Monkman had an advantage over Daymond in relation to the selection of French Canadian poetry, as "Doug just worked from the translations." The inclusion of Hébert in the anthology was a "no-brainer" as she was an important member of the Quebec canon, and "her reputation in English Canada too as a writer of both poetry and fiction," as a result of Scott's translations, as well as the recent appearance of *Kamouraska*. The poems themselves were selected to "[reflect], where possible, different stages in a writer's career." For translations, however, "our judgment of the quality of available translations probably influenced some inclusions regardless of the French originals." Monkman goes on to address the unique situation that Hébert presented to the editors: "What I recall of the Hébert [sic] selections is the luxury of actually being able to choose from several different translations of a poem as well known as 'The Tomb of Kings.' Predictably, I recall our wishing that we could combine existing translations on various occasions." The resulting selections of Hébert's translations reflect "qualitative decisions influenced heavily by the principles of 'new criticism' in which we had been trained." Working from the previous books from Scott, Cogswell, Glassco, Miller, and Brown, Monkman and Daymond selected what they felt were the best possible translations of Hébert's poetry that also reflected her evolution as a poet up to that point in her career.

The poems chosen by the editors are standard for Hébert, and do provide a good introduction to her poetic vision, even if favouring her poems from the earlier 1950s over the ones that appear in *Poèmes*, in 1960. The ordering of the poems in the anthology—choosing to place the poems in chronological order according not only to original publication date but also in chronological order of the translations—is an interesting choice on the part of the editors. "The Tomb of Kings," which was the concluding poem of the eponymous collection, is first, while the other poems appear in an order that does not reflect their original ordering in the original collection. The poems themselves strike a balance between the internal and external worlds that Hébert explores symbolically through her poetry. The inclusion of "The Lean Girl" as well as "The Water Fisherman" and "The Wooden Room" introduces the reader to Hébert's more "feminine" poems, while "Snow" and "Spring over the City" reflect the freer style of poetry Hébert adopted for "Mystère de la parole," with longer lines and shorter verses, coming closer to prose than her earlier collections. Up to this point in Hébert's career as a poet, the selection, despite the ordering, provides the reader with an excellent introduction to her poetic vision.

Barbara Godard's brief review for *Quill & Quire* praises the two volumes' affordability and scope, as well as points to a few of the limitations, primarily in the area of French Canadian literature. "While it is laudable for Quebec writers to be included, the sampling of their texts is too small to allow comparative studies," she writes (31). Godard does not mention Hébert directly, nor does she discuss the quality of the translations included. Overall, she strongly recommends the two-volume set. Michael Dixon, in his review for *Essays on Canadian Writing*, also praises the collections' accessibility and affordability, as well as including "some welcome additions to the standard fare" (250) that appears in other anthologies. His only real criticism is that the anthology feels "too typical" and that it may be the beginning of a trend of "producing anthologies of anthologies" (250). Dixon also reflects on the relatively limited audience for the anthology, students, and the collections' probable inability to transcend its target market into the larger sphere. "Is it simply a matter of inept commercial distribution? Or is it because the selections are too 'difficult'...Or is there something more obscurely distasteful to the 'average' palate in any 'academic' dish?" (251). Dixon does not address the inclusion of Hébert, nor the inclusion of French Canadian authors in general in his review, which is, like Godard's, generally positive.

In comparing these two reviews, we see the linguistic divide between reviewers in addressing the issue of French Canadian authors in the anthology: Godard, a translator herself, readily comments on the French Canadian authors, if only generally, while Dixon, an English professor, ignores the French Canadian authors in his review. Nonetheless, in terms of their scope and intended audience, the Weaver and Towe and the Daymond and Monkman anthologies play a large role in promoting not only French Canadian poetry to English Canada, but Hébert, specifically, to a wider English-speaking audience. Even if the selection of French Canadian poets is limited in both anthologies, Hébert makes the cut, so to speak: selected by institutions (Gage, Oxford University Press) and by people of influence within those institutions (Toye as an editor and Daymond and Monkman as professors), she becomes further imbedded in the curricular canon.

THE POETS OF CANADA, COLOMBO, 1978

Hurtig Publishers put out their own anthology in 1978, John Robert Colombo's *The Poets of Canada*. Each of the more than two hundred poets included is represented by one poem; Hébert's contribution is "Thin Girl," in a translation by Brown, the original appearing in *Le Tombeau des rois*. There are twenty-five poets from the French Canadian tradition found in the anthology, as well as twelve poems from the "unofficial languages" of Canada: "Inuktituut (Inuit), Algonkian (Indian), Estonian, German, Hungarian, Icelandic, Japanese, Lithuanian, Polish, Spanish, Ukrainian, and Yiddish" (*The Poets of Canada* 13). The poems once again appear according to the date of publication. Colombo was well known as a poet and as an anthologist: he had twelve anthologies of various volumes of Canadiana when *Poets of Canada* was released. Called a "Master Gatherer" by Robin Skelton (qtd. in Barbour "John Robert Colombo" 1997, 226), Colombo is "a shrewd market analyst and salesman [who] has recognized from the first that his major product is not this book or that book but rather John Robert Colombo, the maker of all kinds of books" (Barbour "John Robert Colombo" 1986, 143). *The Poets of Canada* would be no exception to his aim of accessibility and commercial availability, and is an important part of Colombo's anthologizing project.

Colombo writes in his preface that his collection "offers the reader a poetic panorama rather than an in-depth view of its subjects," and that it represents "the first historical anthology in which the reader can enjoy, in a single language, the works of poets who write in the two official languages, English and French (13). His criteria for selecting the poems were not limited to "literary excellence," choosing to take "into account historical, cultural, and social considerations" (13). The poets were selected based on "[having] something to say to us today and who say it with a marked individuality of style," while the representative poem from each poet was based on four criteria:

> First, the poem would have to be strong and powerful...Second, the poem selected would have to be characteristic of the poet or representative of the author's work...Third, as much modern poetry is considered "obscure" or "difficult," the poem selected should be (I felt) accessible to the average reader on first reading...Fourth...the poems selected should not be too long. (14)

Given these criteria, one could wonder why Hébert's "Lean Girl" was selected, rather than the better-known (and arguably more accessible) "The Tomb of Kings"; perhaps it was judged too long for inclusion in the anthology. In terms of representation, "Lean Girl" certainly is a "strong and powerful" poem and represents the more female-centric nature of Hébert's poetic works. Colombo, in an e-mail, confirms that "Lean Girl" "is characteristic of the poet's attitude. As well, it could be appreciated upon a single reading and understood without documentation" (personal communication, March 17, 2005). As Colombo further related, there was never any doubt as to Hébert's inclusion in the anthology—"If an editor wishes to compile an anthology of poetry that is representative, the editor has to represent those people who are respected at the time. Anne Hébert was recognized to be an important writer (and is so today increasingly)."

In terms of Québécois poetry, Colombo writes the following in the anthology:

> Representation given to the poetry written in French is not as extensive as that given to the poetry written in English. No single volume could do justice to the two poetries, which have grown up side by side, sometimes intertwined, sometimes not. At the same time, the average English reader is not as interested in the lesser-known French poets as he is in lesser-known poets who write in his own language, for the former fall outside his experience as the latter do not. Besides, the majority of the poets of French expression regard themselves as *Québécois* rather than as *Canadiens*—as poets of Quebec rather than as poets of Canada. So when it came to choosing the Quebec poets, I applied one or more of these

> criteria: the poets should be of historical interest; his work should represent one of the number of important tendencies in Quebec poetry; or the poet should press some special claim (like prior translation) on the attention of the English reader. (15)

Colombo's contact with the poets and poetry from French Canada dates as far back as the 1960s, when he co-edited *Poésie/Poetry 64* with Jacques Godbout, co-published in 1963 by Éditions de Jour in Montreal and Ryerson Press in Toronto. Godbout, according to Patricia Godbout, "apprend l'anglais dans la rue, dans le quartier Côtes-des-Neiges où il grandit" (*Traduction* 213). Colombo's translations of Godbout's poetry had appeared in Glassco's *Poetry of French Canada in Translation*, and he knew French well, allowing the two editors to communicate effectively, as well as affording Colombo the opportunity to judge the French poems in their original language and in translation. This collaboration between Jacques Godbout and Colombo also provided excellent "exposure" for Colombo in terms of contemporary Québécois poets and poetry, although none of the six Québécois poets who are featured in *Poésie/Poetry 64* are included in *The Poets of Canada*. Colombo had also translated poetry into English in the past, from French, Bulgarian, Hungarian, Algonkian, Inuktituuk, Italian, Japanese, Polish, Portuguese, Romanian, and Spanish. *Selected Translations*, which Colombo edited, was published in 1982 as a companion piece to Poulin's *Selected Poems*, and contains sixty-five poems in translation by Colombo, among others. In a note at the beginning of the collection, Colombo thanks his collaborators, or co-translators, specifically Alexander L. Amprimoz, Irène Currie, Glassco, and Ben Shek for translations from the French (viii).

In 1970, Colombo edited *How Do I Love Thee: Sixty Poets of Canada (and Quebec) Select and Introduce Their Favourite Poems from Their Own Work*. There are ten Quebec poets included in this particular anthology, while six declined his invitation to submit their favourite poems: Jacques Brault, Gérald Godin, Hébert, Gilles Hénault, Gaston Miron, and Yves Préfontaine (xi). While Colombo does not address the reasons for their refusal to be included in the project, the list does illustrate that Colombo had a good idea as to who was important in terms of Québécois poetry at the time, as well as a familiarity with Hébert's work. The poems and commentaries by each of the Québécois poets appears in both French and English: "The translations are partly my work, partly that of Ben Shek...Each French poet checked his or her poem in English, and most of them made important revisions" (xv). Colombo also explains his choice to place "of Canada (and Quebec)" in the title of the anthology—

> This circumlocution may sound too clever by half, but I wanted younger Quebec poets to feel at home in the anthology. One of the charges a revolutionary-minded *Parti Pris* poet brought against the bilingual anthology *Poetry 64/Poésie 64*, which Jacques Godbout and I edited, was that it was "a political act" designed to keep the French in a *numerus clausus* relation to the English. So I agreed in advance to identify all the French poets at Quebeckers rather than as French Canadians. Separatism aside, the poets writing in French in this anthology obviously feel more like Quebeckers living in North America than they do Canadians living in Canada. They are part of "French North America" rather than "British North America" (*i.e.* Canada). The poetries of Canada may have developed side by side, sometimes even in the same city, but after a hundred years they have precious little in common. (xiv–xv)

While the two prefaces are similar in terms of how the Québécois poetry in contextualized, Colombo titled the second anthology studied here *Poets of Canada* and not *Poets of Canada (and Quebec)*. Nevertheless, Colombo had an active interest in the French poets of Quebec, and was well placed to select the poets to represent Quebec in his subsequent anthologies.

Colombo would have had three different versions to choose from for a translation of "La fille maigre": Scott's, Miller's and Brown's. Scott's and Miller's translations had been used elsewhere in the anthology (translations of Pierre Trottier and Marc Lescarbot from Scott and of Alain Grandbois from Miller). Colombo would at least have been familiar with Scott's translation, as he had consulted and used translations from Glassco's *Poetry of French Canada in Translation*, as well as Scott's *Poems of French Canada*. Colombo also points the reader to Miller's translation of *The Tomb of Kings* in the introduction to Hébert (143). In more recent correspondence, Colombo writes that there was "really no choice, at least no choice that I was aware" (personal communication, March 17, 2005). However, he goes on to say, in the same correspondence, that "It is probably true that she [Hébert] still awaits her principal translator, though F. R. Scott wrote wonderful versions in English." Brown's translation was selected by Colombo as follows: "I read the English text, compared it with the French original, found it to be faithful and poetic and proceeded" (personal communication, March 17, 2005). He begins the introduction in the anthology on Hébert with a quote from Louis Dudek (no source cited) describing the nature of her poetry. "Highly personal, deeply spiritual, an authentic awareness of the borderline between the realms of matter and spirit" (143), he writes, and follows with a simple biographical/bibliographical introduction to her works in English translation.

The lone review of this anthology, contained in the same review as that of Monkman and Desmond's *Literature in Canada*, in *Essays on Canadian Writing*, concludes: "Colombo's anthology has merit" (Dixon 250). There is no mention of individual Québécois authors (or any individual authors included from minority languages) or of the quality of translation, beyond this: "Colombo has put together two hundred formulaic entries, arranged chronologically...of two hundred Canadians (or near-Canadians) who have written poems in the past three-and-a-bit centuries" (249). This contradicts Colombo's claim that his anthology was the first of its kind to include poets and poems from the "near-Canadian" languages. Dixon does offer praise for the anthology, stating, "Whatever its shortcomings as a paradigm of Canada's poetic culture, Colombo's miscellany has value as a primer in the poetic spirit itself" (250). Colombo, as master gatherer, gathered Hébert into his collection of Canadiana, receiving approval from one of the institution's most prolific figures. While less visible perhaps than previous anthologies in terms of a critical audience for, a Colombo anthology was an "event," an event that provided another opportunity for Hébert to become a part of the accessible canon.

TO SAY THE LEAST, P. K PAGE, 1979

One year later, in 1979, P. K. Page edited the poetry anthology *To Say the Least: Canadian Poets from A to Z*, published by Press Procépic. Page is best known as a poet in her own right, having won the Governor General's Literary Award for Poetry in 1954 for *The Metal and the Flower*. She arrived in Montreal from British Columbia in 1941, and immediately became involved in the Montreal Movement, which included Scott, with whom she worked with at the literary magazine *Preview*. As well, she first appears outside of periodicals as a poet in *Unit of Five* (1942), where she shares the pages with, among others, Dudek and Souster. By the time this anthology was published, Page was considered a West Coast poet, having lived in Victoria for a significant amount of time.[13] *To Say the Least* was published in memoriam of Jerry Lampert, "writer and friend of writers" (Page 5), former executive director of the League of Canadian Poets. All proceeds from the book went into a Gerald Lampert memorial fund, with those poets appearing in the anthology waiving their permissions fees. There are 102 poets featured in the anthology, of which only seven are Québécois.

Hébert is represented by "Snow," translated by Scott. Every poem featured in the collection is "short"; the longest poem collected is thirteen lines. "Snow" is seven lines long in Scott's translation, as taken from *Poems of French Canada*, which is slightly different (and one line shorter) than the Scott-translated version in *St-Denys Garneau & Anne Hébert*. Regardless, "Snow" fits the criteria that Page set forward that the poem must be short, but also that it "must be larger than its mass" rendering it "memorable" (7). Page also had three different translations to choose from at the time (Scott, Cogswell, Brown), though it is not terribly surprising that she selected Scott's, given their long friendship.[14] In a handwritten comment on a typed letter to Scott, dated March 1, 1979, Page adds Hébert's poem to be included in the list of Scott's translations she wanted to use, "Communion" by Ouelette, "Greener than Nature" by Giguère, and "Snow" by Hébert (FRSF, box 67, file 3). In the acknowledgements at the end of the anthology, Page credits the wrong source for the version of "Snow" that appeared: *St-Denys Garneau & Anne Hébert* instead of *Poems of French Canada*. Page always intended on including Hébert in the anthology; in a draft letter to William Toye, dated May 13, 1976, she explains the inspiration for the manuscript: "In the course of working on the collection I discovered that the poets very nearly made an alphabet. There was Atwood and Acron and Bissett and Bowering and Cohen and Dudek and Everson and Finch and Gustafson and Hebert [sic] etc. etc." (PKPF, vol. 18, file 6). Hébert is included in the initial, incomplete manuscript, and in the original list of poets that Page outlines, she was the only French Canadian.

Page presents the authors not in alphabetical order, as her letter may suggest, nor in chronological order. Page describes her editorial choices in ordering the poems:

> In putting the book together I tried as a sculptor does to sense the form hidden in his material and, in bringing it to light, give significant shape to the whole. Within that shape I have tried too, to create an order in which each poem is linked to its immediate neighbours in such a way as to augment them. This linkage, sometimes logical, sometimes not, is never random. (7)

Hébert's poem is preceded by "Munchausen in Alberta" by Elizabeth Brewster and "Lake Harvest" by Raymond Knister, and is followed by "Canada in Winter" by Jill Hoffman and "Frost" by George Johnston. "Lake Harvest" is the only poem not dealing with winter or the cold, but does deal with natural landscape. Fitting Hébert into a larger narrative, as it relates to other authors, is important to Page, as she is looking to create a cohesive narrative. She succeeded.

The anthology was fairly widely reviewed, and very warmly received. Two reviews appeared in the *Vancouver Sun*, with Eleanor Wachtel calling the collection "a fine little book with a noble purpose" (38L), and Christopher Dafoe pointing to the anthology as an excellent remedy for the current disinterest in Canadian poetry in Canada: "I recommend it especially to those who have already decided that Canadian poetry is not worth bothering about. Some may be inclined to think again" (D7). William French, for the *Globe and Mail*, writes: "the collection as a whole is stimulating, provocative and generally successful" ("Books and Bookmen" 1979, 13). *Quill & Quire* calls the anthology "a coffer of gems, a book worth reading, worth keeping, and—so wide is its appeal—even worth giving to those who don't usually enjoy a book of poems" (Aubert 63). Finally, Christopher Levenson, in *CV/II*, praises it for being a "very varied and satisfying collection" (25). None of the reviewers addresses Anne Hébert directly, nor the inclusion of Québécois poets in translation in general, although Wachtel wonders if poets such as Joseph Quesnel would have been included if not for the requirement to account for all of the letters of the alphabet (38L).

While the publishing house that agreed to publish *To Say The Least* was smaller than some of the presses that were putting out anthologies then (Oxford, Gage, Macmillan), Page nonetheless is a major name in Canadian letters, marking another figure for whom Hébert was a poet of major importance and influence. Her choice of putting Hébert alongside English authors who were dealing with similar subject matter and poetic vision serves to include Hébert in a larger Canadian context. The introduction the reader would receive to Hébert would be a-historical and apolitical, instead inviting readers to focus on her poetic images within a larger context of Canadian poetry. The reception shows that the anthology had a more popular appeal, placing Hébert yet again into the accessible canon.

POEMS OF A SNOW-EYED COUNTRY, WOOLLATT AND SOUSTER, 1980

In 1980, Academic Press Canada published *Poems of a Snow-Eyed Country*, edited by Richard Woollatt and Raymond Souster. The anthology was designed to be used as an "introduction to the poetry of Canada's geographic regions" and "a stepping stone to a rich and varied literary world" (8) for a high-school audience. The poems are grouped geographically, and the editors provide thematic groupings in an appendix, as well as an introduction to each section and "Springboards and Bridges" at the end of each section, "designed to help you move through and beyond the poems in the book...by indicating to you different ways of looking at the poems in question" (8). The editors pull together seventy-eight different poets, with eight from the French in translation, three "French Canadian Songs in French" and three poems translated from other languages (German, Icelandic, and "Eskimo") (172). Hébert is represented by "The Little Towns," from *Le Tombeau des rois*, translated by Glassco, in the section "La Belle Province."

Woollatt was a poet and a high-school teacher in the Toronto area. Souster was a poet, editor, publisher, and influential member of the modernist poetry movement of the 1950s and early 1960s. He founded Contact Press with Louis Dudek and Irving Layton, and created a number of small, literary magazines. After Contact Press dissolved in 1967, according to Frank Davey, "Souster [spent] much time...editing school anthologies—'missionary work,' as he described it to Cid Corman—to replace the 'pretty hopeless stuff' which 'the kids have to read by and large'" (35). Woollatt became a sort of partner in the project; together they edited at least four anthologies specifically for high-school readers (Martindale 17). This collaboration would reflect Souster's long-time efforts to create literary relationships: at the beginning of his career at the end of the Second World War, poetry in Canada was being created almost exclusively in Montreal, leaving Souster, who lived in Toronto and worked at a bank, feeling "isolated" (Davey 8). This isolation spurred him to try to discover and disseminate poetry as widely as possible, thus his impetus for continuing to introduce young readers to the poetry of Canada. While Souster was engaging in the activities of writing and publishing in English during the 1950s, he was also being introduced to poems and poetry written in French, as well as to the art of translation. Through Cid Coreman, Souster began to read contemporary French poets from France, and through Gael Turnbull, poets from Quebec.[15] In a number of letters, Souster discusses his belief that "English-Canadians should make a very determined effort to get to know the work of their fellow French-Canadian poets" (quoted in Godbout, *Traductions* 103), while lamenting his own lack of bilingual capabilities. Much like Scott and Dudek, Souster was attracted to the poems of French Canada because they provided English Canada with elements that their own poetry was lacking. "I begin to feel very strongly that when we can somehow bring the French and English Canadian poets together in some way we're due for some large advances...that great lyrical quality we have somehow missed and which Hébert [sic] has to a great degree" (95). In this regard, Souster shared the same "Make It New" sentiment of Dudek via Pound, and saw French Canadian poetry as a means of making English Canadian poetry new. He also recognized that Hébert was one of those distinct voices that was indeed making it new.

In their proposal document, the editors describe the anthology's uniqueness in two ways: accessibility and organization. As an undated manuscript describes,

> We know of no Canadian anthology of verse presently available that the average reader can understand and enjoy because it relates to him both as a Canadian and to the everyday life about him. Likewise there is no comprehensive anthology of Canadian verse whose contents would appeal to

> the average teen-ager attending high school...It is the only anthology of Canadian verse based on a regional concept, thus giving it added purpose and close unity. (RSP, box 38)

McGraw-Hill Ryerson was the first publishing house to receive the manuscript for the anthology. In a letter dated July 3, 1974, Jane Stinson gives some friendly editorial advice to the editors, "you are overlooking the fact that that there is still ample need to 'teach' both teachers and students about the forces that help to shape Canadian poetry as well as poetry in general" (Souster fonds), leading Souster and Woolatt to include a new section entitled "Preludes and Definitions." This change to the manuscript would not be enough to ensure publication with McGraw-Hill; a later letter, dated October 9, 1974, informs the editors that "we are of the opinion that the school market has almost reached the saturation point in regard to poetry anthologies...we feel that we should not take any more of your time or ours in consideration of your manuscript" (RSP, box 38). No less than four other publishing houses would reject the manuscript, citing cost as an overriding factor, before Academic Press accepted the project.

Despite Souster's extensive knowledge of French Canadian poetry, the editors nonetheless consulted with a fellow expert and translator, David M. Elder. In a letter to McGraw-Hill Ryerson dated September 16, 1974, Woolatt writes, "I neglected to mention while talking to you that we have a special consultant for the Quebec section, Mr. Dave Elder...Besides translating several of the poems he has assisted us in selecting and arranging the material. When we come to prepare study notes for the section we will again be calling on his expertise" ((RSP, box 38). Elder worked with Woolatt at Burlington Central High School, and was an honorary member of the Ontario Modern Languages Teachers Association. Elder was awarded the Order of Canada for his work related to education, and, according to his daughter and fellow translator Jo-Anne Elder, "he not only provided translations, but editing, glossaries, examination questions, etc. to make anthologies useable in actual classroom situations" (personal communication, September 4, 2005). There are a number of his translations in the Souster fonds relating to *Poems of a Snow-Eyed Country*, including a translation of Hébert's poem "Night." Unfortunately, none of Elder's translations would be included in the final edition of the anthology. Initially, there were four different poems by Hébert under consideration for inclusion in the anthology: "Night" translated by Elder, "The Lean Girl" translated by Scott, and "Under the Rain" and "The Little Towns" translated by Glassco. In the end, only "The Little Towns" was included. It is also unclear how much of an influence Elder had on the formation of the section dealing with Quebec, although it is obvious that it was enough of an impact to warrant a mention by the editors when introducing the manuscript to publishers.

In the anthology, Hébert is introduced with "Among the leading poets of this century, the names of Anne Hébert...and Saint-Denys Garneau...are perhaps the most frequently mentioned...They express very sharply much of the stifling, ancestor worshipping attitudes still prevalent among their generation" (46). Her poem "The Little Towns" is paired with her cousin's "Pines Against the Light" in the section "La Belle Province." In closing the section with "Springboards and Bridges," the editors say the following about Hébert's poems and over-all œuvre:

> Reading a poem of Anne Hébert's such as "The Little Towns" is similar to understanding the one by Margaret Atwood ["The Immigrants"]: the real meaning is usually below the surface and most often found in symbols. One of the towns that Hébert could have in mind is her birthplace... Sainte-Catherine-de-Fossambault, north of Quebec City...Hébert is also a novelist; her gothic *Kamouraska* was brilliantly filmed by Claude Jutra and stars Geneviève Bujold. (72–73)

The editors provide high-school students with a simple and common introduction to her poems: symbolism and biography. They also connect Hébert to a relatively well-known English Canadian author, Atwood, as well as signal that she has a movie out based on one of her novels. These attempts to encourage the teenage reader to keep reading (or at least think about) Hébert are obvious, and one would think not ineffective. There is more relative space taken by the editors to promote *Kamouraska* the movie than *Kamouraska* the novel, and even that Hébert is a novelist, not a film-maker; crass, perhaps, but in keeping with their intended audience.

There is virtually no critical reception of any kind for this anthology. One could assume that the relative indifference toward the anthology was because of its intended audience (high-school students) and the still relatively unknown quality of both the editors (Bruce Whiteman, in his biographical note on Souster, written in 1983, observes that "For a major poet and a man whose influence has been wide and sustained, Souster has attracted a surprisingly small amount of critical attention" [239]). The anthologies geared toward a university audience (the Oxford or *Literature in Canada*) received more attention due to other academics reviewing the anthologies for use in their own courses. Compare the reception of Page's anthology, edited by a celebrated poet, or Richler's own anthology, by a controversial figure in Canadian letters, and the reception for Woollatt and Souster's, edited by two lesser-known figures in Canadian literature, and published by a specialty press, to wit. One may also imagine that the subject matter (Canadian poetry) was not as interesting or not seen to be as interesting: Dudek's anthology, which was also geared toward a high-school audience, was much more widely received; he also included modern American poetry within the anthology, and most of the reviewers focused on that part of the anthology, not the inclusion of Canadian modern poetry. This indifference toward Canadian poetry was noted by those reviewing Page's anthology, and accurately predicts the demise or at least the decline of the poetry anthology in Canada. After Barry Callaghan's anthology, which will be dealt with below, there is a fifteen-year lag before another anthology appears that includes Hébert in translation. We can observe this same gap in the publication of French Canadian/Québécois anthologies in translation. In part, it is due to the complex language and identity politics that played out in the country during those fifteen to twenty years. But they also reflect the general disinterest in Canadian poetry in English, from either language group. Regardless, Hébert receives another entry into the academic canon.

LORDS OF WINTER AND LOVE, BARRY CALLAGHAN, 1983

Barry Callaghan published *Lords of Winter and Love: A Book of Canadian Love Poems in English and French* through his own publishing house, Exile Editions, in 1983. Fifty-seven authors are included in the anthology, fourteen from Quebec, whose poems are presented in French and in English translation. Hébert has two poems in the anthology, "The Lean Girl" and "There Is Certainly Someone," both translated by Scott. Callaghan, son of the writer Morley Callaghan, has been an important figure in the Toronto and Canadian literary scene for over forty years. In 1965, Callaghan became an instructor at Atkinson College, York University, teaching contemporary literature. From 1966 to 1971, he was the literary editor of the book-review section of the daily *Toronto Telegram*. He also worked for the CBC, as a host and producer, specializing in documentaries. In 1972, he founded *Exile*, a literary quarterly, and then in 1976, began Exile Editions.[16] Callaghan wanted to battle what he understood to be the current trends in Canadian literary nationalism: "A real writer wants to see himself in relation to writers around the world, he doesn't want to be a hot-house flower, for Christ's sake!" ("Impassioned Exile"). *Exile* published Canadian writers alongside those who Callaghan considered to the best writers from around the world. Callaghan was dedicated to literary excellence, regardless of where it was produced. "If you wrote a book of poetry, well, Lizzie Borden might give you 40 whacks. The fact that you came from Oshawa didn't matter," he wrote ("Impassioned Exile"). This is not to say that Callaghan had no interest in Canadian letters; the subtitle of the interview with *Books in*

Canada is, "If we fail to write in the language of here, there will be no literature of this place" ("Impassioned Exile"). It was in this spirit, the language of here, that Callaghan conceived *Lords of Winter and Love*.

The introduction that Callaghan writes for the anthology provides little background as to the selection of the contents. This is not terribly surprising, however, as Callaghan had little use for introductions, especially of the editorial kind. "It seemed to me that the imaginative writer was being supplanted by scholars or critics, and a whole body of information, and people were more interested in borrowed information than they were in perceiving things with their own eyes and ears" ("Impassioned Exile"). The introduction opens with the quote "We endure the winter, but not in discontent" (ix). Freely quoting from poems that appear in the collection, Callaghan creates a thesis about the language that is used by the poets from Canada to describe the condition of here:

> We are lovers whether we like it or not: ironic, with one foot in the grave, incubating in the gloom, but with visions of planets rotating around a room; or sardonic, believing God loves us like earthworms love wood and catfish love the cut-glass glory of clear water...As lovers, crucified and reborn in our sacks of flesh, we pursue the sacred, are transformed in ancient gardens, in silent rooms, ancestral tombs...Grace and immortality. (ix)

One is struck by the echoes of Hébert's images in this passage (ancient gardens, silent rooms, ancestral tombs). Callaghan liberally uses French expressions in his introduction ("c'est la fin, c'est la fenaison;" "les petits morts," another allusion to Hébert) as further indication that he is trying to write in the language of here, reflecting the influence of both literatures on the language. He viewed Canadian literature as a sum of its two main parts: "There are some very remarkable writers working here now, particularly if you take the French and the English cultures together, as I do" ("Impassioned Exile"). His interest in the French writers of Quebec was prompted by Marie-Claire Blais. "If you look at the first issues of *Exile*, you will see that the writers in them were important to me at that time. In the first issue there was Marie-Claire Blais, who lured me into Quebec" ("Impassioned Exile"). The language of here, for Callaghan, included French, and he included those French poets who measured up to a literary standard and participated in the formation of the language of here. This is also reflected in his choice to include both the French original and English translation; nowhere perhaps is the impact on the other culture more evident than through the translation, which is often done by a fellow poet.

The two Hébert poems included in the anthology are both from *Le Tombeau des rois*, and the translations are from Scott's *St-Denys Garneau & Anne Hébert*.[17] The choice of poems themselves is interesting, given the overall theme of the book: winter and love. Both "The Lean Girl" and "There Is Certainly Someone" deal with the relationships between a man and a woman, although more so with the oppressive and disturbing aspect of love. Both poems, however, present the same sort of image in their conclusions, the image of the woman bound/trapped, but still able to see the wonders of the world around/beyond her. In "The Lean Girl," as it appears in Callaghan's anthology, the last two verses read:

And sometimes
Fastened in your breast,
I half open
My liquid eyes

As strange and childish dreams
Swirl
Like green water. (8)

In "There Is Certainly Someone," we once again get the images of water, eyes, and entrapment:

My two eyes like
Their own pure image of water

Who forgot to erase the beauty of the world
Around me
Forgot to close my hungry eyes
And permitted their wasted passion. (75)

These images at the end of the two poems closely echo one of Callaghan's descriptions of love from the introduction: "We are lovers whether we want to or not: ironic, with one foot in the grave, incubating in the gloom, but with visions of planets rotating around a room" (ix). Irony is one way to describe how Hébert describes love in these two poems, in particular "The Lean Girl," with a lover who has no heart, and another who hangs herself as a gift to him. More strongly, however, is the sense of tragedy in both of the poems in relation to love: in either case, the woman is left alone and isolated, powerless and confused, with only abstract images of the possible worlds outside to keep her company. Perhaps, as

Callaghan puts in his introduction, "We endure the winter," but Hébert's poems show that there is still a great deal of discontent.

Quill & Quire printed a brief review, by Jane Urquhart, of the anthology. In it, she praises how the anthology "demonstrates that love poetry is alive and well in Canada in the post-modern period," but criticizes the overall composition of the anthology: "It is difficult...to determine just what editor Barry Callaghan is attempting to accomplish here...The collection is diminished by the apparent randomness of the selection and irrelevant juxtapositioning" (46). While Urquhart praises a number of poets and poems, she does not make any mention of Hébert or the inclusion of Québécois poets. Although reception is limited, the anthology does speak to the appeal that Hébert holds, included in both popular and more canonical anthologies such as Colombo's or Toye's, and in more independent, smaller anthologies, such as Page's and Callaghan's.

WHO SPEAKS FOR CANADA?, MORTON AND WEINFELD, 1998

In 1998, McClelland & Stewart published *Who Speaks for Canada? Words that Shape a Country*, edited by Desmond Morton and Morton Weinfeld. The book was conceived through McGill University's Canadian ethnic studies program, and then adopted by the McGill Institute for the Study of Canada, in 1994. Both editors are professors at McGill; Morton is a professor of history while Weinfeld is a professor of sociology. The editors' "cheerfully acknowledged the inspiration of Diane Ravitch's *The American Reader*, which captured in words and images the essence of being American" (ix). The two academics received financial support from Citizenship and Immigration Canada, as it was called at the time, and items from the book were used on its website (ix).[18] The anthology includes 130 entries, of which 25 are from French Canada. Hébert is represented by "The Tomb of Kings," translated by Miller, and is presented in both French and English. She is included in "Part Three: 1921–1960" under the heading "Precursor of a New Quebec."

In their preface, the editors explain how the anthology was collected: "From our own different experiences, we assembled prose and poetry, fiction and non-fiction that had spoken to each of us, and, if we found that they spoke powerfully to both of us, they survived" (x). Each editor then wrote their own introduction, reflecting each of their academic disciplines. Morton, son of a Canadian soldier, provides the reader an interesting overview of Canadian history, particularly the history of immigration. Weinfeld takes a more sociological approach to Canada and his own history as the son of Polish Holocaust survivors living in Montreal. While Morton admits that, within his frame of knowledge and reference, "One big block is missing: *le fait québécois*" (xiv). Weinfeld "learned to speak French not in school but working in a hardware store in east-end Montreal" (xvi). He outlines his understanding of the Québécois:

> My generation in Montreal came of age as French nationalism in Quebec emerged onto the streets, on ballots, in classrooms, and later in boardrooms. While I was certainly part of a third solitude [Jewish] in Montreal, I felt then—as I do today—a visceral admiration for the efforts of French Quebeckers to retain their identity in a continental sea of English. That struggle resonated with my understanding of a similar Jewish experience, a concern for survival—"*la survivance*"—whether as a Diaspora minority or in the struggling state of Israel. (xvi)

Both editors, in their respective introductions, address the question of Quebec and its place in Canadian Confederation, as well as the place of Aboriginals and other immigrant/minority groups. Although Hébert is not mentioned directly in the introduction, no author is specifically mentioned, a reflection, perhaps, of the editors' focus on their respective stories and intellectual approaches.

"One of French Canada's most renowned authors" (141) is how the editors introduce Hébert to the reader. The editors provide a brief biographical sketch, and cite the reason why Hébert chose to move to France in 1954 as "the crushing censorship of the Duplessis regime" (141). The editors then explain the title poem from *Le Tombeau des rois*: "It typifies the work of a poet who shuns the lush verbal imagery of her predecessors, seeking a spare modernist form in which each word must carry its own weight, in which the imagination has to work as hard as the poet" (141). Weinfeld explains in an e-mail to this author that Hébert "captured a certain voice at a certain time" and "had a broad reputation," while the poem itself was "moving, full of mystery and power" (personal communication, February 17, 2005). The translation of the poem that is used in the anthology is Miller's, which had first appeared in 1967. The choice of using Miller's translation was simply because it was the one that the editors found, Weinfeld said.

Reaction to the anthology was mixed. While *Maclean's* mentions the appearance of the book, it offers no review, limiting said mention to fifty-one words ("How to Define a Canadian, 101"). An editorial in the *Toronto Star*, by James Stewart, lamenting the decline in young Canadians' knowledge in Canadian history calls for changes in the classroom: "Copies of *Who Speaks for Canada?* by Desmond Morton and Morton Weinfeld, a collection of primary source readings in Canadian history, should also be widely available" (1). Two other mentions of the anthology are interviews with the editors rather than a review of the anthology itself; in *Canadian Jewish News*, Weinfeld talks about how his Jewish heritage influenced his editorial choices, while *Wednesday-Night.com* (Larson) interviews Westmount, Quebec, resident Desmond Morton about editing the anthology. Neither interview dissuades readers from picking up the anthology. That role is left up to W. H. New in an editorial for *Canadian Literature*:

> Unhappily, one of the most well-intentioned of anthologies, *Who Speaks for Canada?*..., sampling Great Paragraphs from the history of Canadian writing, ends up feeling stale, fragmentary, conventional—the identity chestnuts of old journalism and older textbooks—and desperate for a literary perspective. (216)

The lack of critical reception may be a reflection of what New notes at the end of the quote above: who is the audience for this particular collection? Is it literary, historical, sociological, political? All of the above? While important in its aim and scope, the anthology could never succeed at keeping any one potential target group satisfied. Perhaps it is a testament to Hébert's talents as a poet that she was included in an anthology made to appeal across disciplines, potentially, if not practically, exposing her to an entirely different audience from the other anthologies.

POETRY: A POCKET ANTHOLOGY, R. S. GWYNN AND WANDA CAMPBELL, 2004

As you can see from the works listed here, there is a considerable gap in the anthologies devoted to Canadian poetry that include French Canadian works. The final two anthologies dealt with here bring us full circle to where we began: a general poetry anthology for the classroom that included Canadian poetry and a Canadian poetry anthology for a non-Canadian market. First is the Penguin Academics series anthology *Poetry: A Pocket Anthology*, Canadian Edition, published in 2004, with a second edition appearing in 2008.[19] Targeted for the Canadian classroom market, it adds Canadian poets to the popular American edition of the book (currently in its seventh edition). R. S. Gwynn is the editor of the American edition, and numerous other literary anthologies, including of American poetry, drama, and literature. He is a professor of literature at Lamar University, in Texas, as well as a published poet. Wanda Campbell is a literature and creative-writing professor at Acadia University, in Nova Scotia, and was charged with adding the Canadian poets to the Canadian edition.

The anthology is organized chronologically, thus the Canadian poets are interspersed throughout the book according to date of birth. There are fifty-three Canadian poets included in the anthology, with four of them having been translated from French (Émile Nelligan, Hébert, Jacques Godbout, and Herménégilde Chiasson). Of the fifty-three Canadian poets present, only one, Margaret Atwood, is also represented in the standard edition of the anthology. All the Canadian poets (in fact, most of the poets) are represented by only one poem each. Anne Hébert's poem "There Is Certainly Someone," translated by Scott (whose own poetry is also included in the anthology), was selected for the first edition, and "Snow," as also translated by Scott, was substituted for it in the second. In the brief biographical note preceding the contribution, she is described as "one of Quebec's best-known writers...probably best known for her novels, including *Kamouraska*" (248). "There Is Certainly Someone" is highlighted in "Appendix 1—Poems Grouped by Genre, Technique, or Subject," under the category "Death," while the second edition lists "Snow" in the category "Nature—Seasons of the Year."

According to Campbell, she became involved in the project when she proposed another textbook to the publishers and they saw that she had expertise in poetry.[20] Campbell was alone responsible for the Canadian selections, as well as updating some of the international selections, based on Gwyn's original selections. She was interested in "chronological, geographical, and gender representation, as well as minority voices like First Nations writers." Campbell had studied with Fred Cogswell as an undergraduate, and thus was very aware of the rich variety of translations of both Québécois and Acadian poetry. Her decision to change Hébert's selection from "There Is Certainly Someone" to "Snow" was because "it was a nice companion piece to teach alongside Margaret Avison's sonnet 'Snow'...and Stephanie Bolster's poem 'Le Far-West' which responds ekphrastically to the Jean Paul Lemieux painting by the same name." As you can see, Campbell carefully selected the poems so that they informed one another, particularly within the Canadian poetry movements, creating a kind of cohesive narrative, or at least an interconnected one.

According to Campbell, the anthology was well received, and, according to her research, was once used "in almost fifty universities and colleges across the country." There were plans for a third edition, but it was never published, because, "Pearson [Penguin's parent company] decided there just wasn't a sufficient market in Canada, with the incursion of anthologies made to order and a great reliance on online resources."

Once again, we see in this example how Hébert was inserted into the larger narrative of what Canadian literature (in this specific case, poetry) was, and highlighted in important ways; as the anthology was organized chronologically, Hébert's poem is placed in the middle of the modernist movement, alongside African American poet Margaret Walker and Canadian poet P. K. Page. Although somewhat an accident of birth, this nonetheless allows a reader to place Hébert within some of the most important poetry movements of the twentieth century. Unlike Dudek over forty years earlier, Campbell places the Canadian poets alongside more recognizable names in international poetry, contextualizing their poems not as regional or national poetry, but as poetry. However, the anthology is considered here and not in the "world poetry" segment in the next chapter because, like Dudek's anthology, it was meant for Canadian students, thus equally plays a role in national canon formation and literary identity.

MODERN CANADIAN POETS, EVAN JONES AND TODD SWIFT, 2010

Not since Mordecai Richler's *Canadian Writing Today* has there been a collection of Canadian writing targeting a non-Canadian market. In 2010, expat poets and academics Evan Jones and Todd Swift sought to rectify that, editing *Modern Canadian Poets: An Anthology* for Carcanet Press, a publisher based out of Manchester, England. Evan Jones was born in Toronto, completed his PhD at the University of Manchester, and currently lives in Manchester. He was a finalist for the Governor General's Literary Award for Poetry for his first collection of poems, *Nothing Fell Today but Rain*, in 2003. Todd Swift was born in Montreal and received his PhD from the University of East Anglia, Norwich, England. He is currently a lecturer in English literature and creative writing at Kingston University, in London. He edited *Language Acts: Anglo-Québec Poetry, 1976 to the 21st Century*, and has written a number of his own collections of poetry (Jones and Swift i).

In their opening lines of the introduction, Jones and Swift describe the anthology as "introducing readers to thirty-five poets they may never have read before, but will soon find unforgettable" (xiii). In order to accomplish that, the editors spent "five years reading every Canadian poem of the last 100 years" (Swift). The impetus for the anthology came when Swift wrote to the head of Carcanet, Michael Smith, defending Canadian poetry from the claim Smith made in his book, *Lives of the Poets*, that it was "a short street not worth going down" (qtd. in Jones and Swift xiv). In 2004, Swift tracked down Smith at a conference in Norwich and confronted him in front of a crowded lecture hall. Smith then and there offered Smith the opportunity to edit an anthology of Canadian poetry, to be published by Carcanet (McLaren). The editors limited themselves to poets having been born between about 1900 and 1962. They "sought poets within the Canadian tradition who follow similar paths and aspire to those Kleinian [as in

A. M. Klein] standards: individuals as opposed to schools, leaders as opposed to adherents" (Jones and Swift xvii). Most controversially (for many of the critics, at least), they left out many of the biggest names of Canadian letters, such at Atwood, Ondaatje, Malcolm Lowry, and Leonard Cohen.

The editors address the issue of the dual linguistic nature of Canadian literature in their introduction, and the problem of translation:

> This spirit of openness in a poetry anthology which aims to be inclusive must also take into account the dual languages of Canada, often overlooked in English-language Canadian anthologies of the last fifty years. Too few anthologists have endeavoured to include French-Canadian poets, to take up the problematic relationship between French and English in a country whose national literature is based on both languages. In fact, few English-language poets take to translation at all. As this anthology is aimed at a British readership, and it is thus difficult to justify the inclusion of French text, we do not propose to resolve the issue. Instead we have included some of the great poets of Quebec in translation. Among the poems anthologised here are versions of works by Emile Nelligan, Hector de Saint-Denys Garneau, and Robert Melançon. In the case of Anne Hébert, we recognised in the translations of Alan Brown such a significant achievement as to merit her inclusion within the body of Canadian English-language poetry. (xviii)

Anne Hébert is the only French Canadian poet included in the anthology who is explicitly identified in the table of contents; the other poems are listed as part of the larger selections of the poets who translated them (John Glassco, Steven Heighton, Ann Carson, and Eric Ormsby).[21] In other words, to find the works of Saint-Denys Garneau, one would have to know that John Glassco translated him. It is strange that the editors express an awareness the sensitive nature of French-English literary relations and yet simultaneously assimilate the majority of the poems included into the larger English Canadian canon. Certainly, this gives Hébert a privileged position within the anthology, as an equal of sorts to her English Canadian peers. It also emphasizes the translator rather than the poet, but is nonetheless problematic more generally, especially if the anthology is directed to an audience generally not familiar with the politics and, additionally, to the land of Quebec's former colonial rulers, Britain.

The editors introduce Anne Hébert's poetry by citing a selection of her literary accomplishments, but limit themselves to those she earned in Canada. They call Alan Brown "her greatest translator," who was "renowned for his translations of French-Canadian literature" (56), and mention Brown's Canada Council Translation Prize, won in 1974 for *Blackout*, a translation of Hubert Aquin's novel *Trou de mémoire*. As mentioned in Chapter Two, here, there is still some debate as to Brown's "renown," as well his status as a translator of Hébert's. The editors make no mention of their criteria for selecting the translation. Perhaps catering to the British audience, they identify French poet René Char as being "the most apparent influence on Hébert's work," and they continue by pointing out that they "shared an early hermeticism and interest in post-symbolist poetry" (56). The editors also posit Hébert's connections to the surrealist movement, writing that "Hébert was never a surrealist, but like those poets she wrote from the hinterlands of the body and mind, spirit and imagination, her great subjects childhood, loneliness, memory and death" (56). This fits well with their stated goal of chosing poets who break the myth "that to be a Canadian poet is to be part of the country's geography, whereas elsewhere to be a poet is to be part of poetry's history" (xiv). This closely echoes why Scott and others were drawn to Hébert and other French Canadian poets' work; one wonders, then, why more French Canadian poets weren't included. The Hébert poems that the editors selected are "The Closed Room," "Mystery of the Verb," "Snow," "Too Tightly Fitted," and "Captive Gods." The first is from *Le Tombeau des rois*, while the other four are from *Poèmes*.

Reception for the anthology is largely positive, but not uncontroversial. Most of the reviews begin by examining the "meaning" of anthologies, as well as the definition of modern Canadian poetry. But, because the book represents "the most important anthology of Canadian poetry in two decades" (McLaren), it garnered reviews in both major Canadian daily newspapers, the *Globe and Mail* (on two separate occasions) and the *National Post*. Michael Lista, in the *Post*, calls it "a wonderful anthology"; Robert Lecker (who has extensively studied and written about Canadian anthologies) says in *Canadian Literature*, "I like what they have done"; while Jason Guriel, in a collaborative omnibus review of the year's best books published on *Maisonneuve*, states that "in a better world, which is to say an alternate reality, this compact and highly readable anthology would be the book your CanLit course makes you buy" ("Maisy's"). The selections, however, did not impress Jacob McArthur Mooney in the *Globe*, where he criticizes the anthology as being "dishonest and slight." Those same editorial selections, however, are praised by Carmine Starnino on the *Véhicule Press Blog*, where he calls it "a radical break from the present." The reception from the United Kingdom (the book's intended market) is limited; Ian Pople, in the *Manchester Review*, calls the anthology "a lovely book; full of poems that really stand up, and to which you will keep returning."

There are few direct mentions of Hébert (or of the translations) in the reviews. Ingrid Ruthig, in *Northern Poetry Review*, lists Hébert as being one of the "sweet discoveries" a reader will make when reading the anthology. The longest and most critical review of the anthology, by Zachariah Wells in *Contemporary Poetry Review*, does take the editors to task for their choice of only including Hébert's poems as "English-language originals," stating:

> Brown's versions were never intended as English-language originals. The decision to include them, without providing the original French *en face*, is a stupefyingly bling act of cultural colonization, made even worse by the fact that it appears in a *British* book. Swift and Jones give themselves a pat on the back for their "spirit of openness," blithely unaware that the inclusion of one Francophone poet in the midst of 24 Anglophones is not just a bad editorial decision, but an affront to French-Canadian poetry as a whole—a slap in the face that could have been obviated by simply sticking to the stated parameters of their book.

What's most interesting about the critical reception for this anthology, published well into the new media age, is that Swift responded to many of the criticisms on his blog and in the comments section of some of the online versions of the reviews. And while he directly addresses many of the criticisms that Wells outlines in his review, he does not address the issue surrounding how and why the editors chose to frame the translations the way they did within the book.

The anthology itself was a bestseller for Carcanet on both sides of the Atlantic.

The editors say that "the anthology is an introduction for British readers" and that "a nation will always look differently from the outside" (Mierau). We see some of the same debates here that surrounded the Richler anthology some forty years earlier. The editors also revealed that they "spoke with poets and critics, editors of magazines and presses in the UK to see which Canadian poets carried sway...This brought us interestingly, to Klein, to Page, to Avison, to Hébert, to Coles, to Sibum, to Robertson. These names are spoken with awe and wonder in weighty conversations about poetry" (Mierau). If this is true, that Hébert's name is "spoken with awe and wonder" by the literary establishment in the United Kingdom, then her canonization as a Canadian poet would appear to be complete.

CONCLUSION

There are a number of conclusions that can be drawn from looking at how Hébert has been anthologized in and for English Canada. Canadian anthologies are created for as many reasons as there are editors, using as many criteria for selecting both poems and translations. Anthologies in English Canada are also often seen as political tools, informing the reader on how to better understand Canada. To include French Canadian/Québécois poetry in English-language translation only in an anthology of Canadian literature can be said to further an act of cultural assimilation or silencing, and also runs contrary to the reality of how literature is taught in Canada, through language departments (English, French, Spanish, etc.). As the commercial demand for literary anthologies diminishes, the classroom becomes the primary market for the anthology, to be used as a teaching tool. We see in the reviews, particularly those of English Canadian anthologies that include French works in translation, the general non-acknowledgement of the Québécois authors. This could also be explained in part by politics, as well as specialization: Most of the reviewers were specialists in English Canadian literature, not French Canadian. Rather than talk about literature they knew little about, and be accused of misrepresenting the literature, the reviewers stuck to what they knew, which in most cases was English, if not English Canada.

It is worth spending a bit more time on the controversy that surrounded the final anthology, *Modern Canadian Poets*, as it bookends the discussion of the history of canon formation well. In an extended interview with Maurice Mierau in the *Winnipeg Review*, the editors of the anthology address a number of the criticisms levelled against the anthology. But before he begins the interview, Mierau fires a shot across the bow of the Canadian poetry establishment:

> The sad truth is that, in Canada, this anthology appears in a cultural vacuum where critical debate about poetry, and indeed even the simple act of book reviewing, are on life support. In our current climate anything that anyone calls poetry gets published somewhere, almost no one gets read or reviewed, and yet there are more glittering prizes and awards for poetry than ever...Canadian poetry lacks the kind of mainstream that exists in the UK and the US, and therefore any attempt to define a mainstream will arouse heated controversy. Anthologies are attempts to shape literary history, of course, and if Carmine Starnino is right when he wrote recently that *Modern Canadian Poets* "conjures an altered historical outcome for Canadian poetry," it is still an outcome that deserves consideration.

While Penguin discontinued an anthology of international poetry that included Canadians, a British publisher was creating a bestseller made up of many of those same poets. That the Canadian market couldn't support the Penguin anthology (or any other anthology of Canadian poetry) speaks exactly to what Mierau is addressing. While the focus of this study has been on Hébert and her inclusion in these canon-formation-through-anthologization battles, ultimately it would seem that poetry anthologies lost the war.

As for Hébert, there is general agreement as to the role she played in the evolution of French Canadian letters specifically, and literature in Canada in general. While anthologists tend to focus on her earlier poems, *Tombeau des rois* (1953) and *Poèmes* (1960), it is also not surprising, as Hébert's next collection of poems only came out in 1992, *Le jour n'a d'égal que la nuit*. While the personal tastes of the anthologists differ in terms of which translation of which poem to use, each of them sees Hébert in a similar light. Hébert's poems are contextualized in a variety of ways, and made to fit the various central theses of the editors. This adaptation or appropriation of her poetry could be seen elsewhere as a negative; but arguing that this practice is beneficial to her career, looking at the instances of anthologization as a whole, makes more sense. Presenting Hébert to an English Canadian audience in a variety of contexts only adds to her exposure and her appeal, increasing her "capital symbolique." It could also be argued that this versatility is a testament to her skill as a poet: transcending and shifting from one possible means of interpreting and understanding her poems to a multitude. This power to transcend labels serves Hébert well, as her poetry moves past the Canadian borders toward the south, and overseas, as an almost completely different poet.

Notes

1. Raymond Souster's papers at the University of Toronto only date back to 1960; his correspondence with Turnbull only goes as far back as 1960, and none of the files housed at the library date any earlier. There is also no correspondence from Roy among the papers. I would like to thank Patricia Godbout for providing me with the letters from the Turnbull fonds.
2. For a more complete comparison of Glassco's translations of Hébert's poetry, see Godbout's chapter in *Traduction littéraire et sociabilité interculturelle: 1950–1960* (2004).
3. In 1999, Downes released a new collection of her poems and translations from Quebec, entitled *House of Cedars*. The book contains one translation of Anne Hébert's poetry, which had previously appeared in *Ellipse*, in 1993. The book has been excluded from this study because of its relatively few translations overall, but will be addressed in the conclusion.

4. At the time Mezei produced her article, 1986, four other women had translated Hébert's poems for American-published anthologies, which will be discussed in the next chapter.
5. For a detailed outline of this disinterest from English Canada, see Paul Martin's 2013 book *Sanctioned Ignorance: The Politics of Knowledge Production and the Teaching of the Literatures in Canada*.
6. Unless otherwise noted, all information and comments in the section here were taken from an interview conducted by the author at Dr. Sloate's home in Montreal on February 19, 2003.
7. Sloate was the name that Dr. Sloate used for his writing and translating, while Slote was used for his academic endeavours.
8. Although last updated in 1987, *The Annotated Bibliography of Canada's Major Authors*, volume 7, gives an indication of how often Hébert's poems have been included in French-language anthologies.
9. As mentioned previously, Scott's translation of "Ancestral Manor" appears in A. J. M. Smith's third edition of the *Book of Canadian Poetry*, through Gage Publishing in 1957, as well as in Carl F. Klink and R. E. Watters' *Canadian Anthology* (1955 and 1966), as a Scott poem rather than as a translation. In the later anthology's introduction, the editors state that "we have endeavored to indicate the growth and scope of Canadian literature in English" as well as admitting to "excluding the entire roster of our French-speaking authors" (Klink and Watters 1966, xv), and therefore the anthology will not be considered in this study. Underneath the poem in question, it reads "From the French of Anne Hébert" (301), but remains nonetheless under Scott's name. It should also be noted that Smith edited *The Oxford Book of Canadian Verse: In English and French*, published by Oxford University Press in 1960. Although Hébert is present in the collection, she appears in French only, and therefore it is not included in this study either.
10. Barbara Godard and others point to this phenomenon in a special edition of *Voix et Images* (volume 72, 1999).
11. Neither Dudek's nor Scott's archives provide any insight into Dudek's reasoning behind choosing Scott's translation over Miller's. In Scott's archives there is a letter from Macmillan, dated February 26, 1965, asking for permission to use a number of his poems and translations, including "La fille maigre." There is no other mention in either of the archives of the selection.
12. Biographical information on Weaver is taken from Toye's *The Oxford Companion to Canadian Literature*, second edition, 1997. George Woodcock wrote the entry on Robert Weaver. Interestingly, Toye himself does not earn an entry in his own book, nor in the subsequent *Oxford Concise Companion to Canadian Literature* (2001), nor does he appear in W. H. New's subsequent *Encyclopedia of literature in Canada* (Toronto: University of Toronto Press, 2002). The dust jacket on the *Oxford Companion* provides the majority of the biographical information on Toye included here.
13. All biographical information taken from George Woodcock and Rosemary Sullivan's entry in *The Oxford Companion to Canadian Literature*.

14. In an e-mail to the author, Page writes that Scott's translation was the only one of which she was aware (personal communication, March 30, 2005).
15. Patricia Godbout goes into great detail over twenty pages in *Tradution littéraire et sociabilité interculturelle au Canada: 1950–1960* tracing the relationship between Turnbull, Souster, and Corman. Reading the "Editors and Publishers" chapter in Frank Davey's book *Louis Dudek and Raymond Souster* alongside Godbout's account of those same years, one can get a complete picture of the different influences that affected Souster in terms of his views on poetry, Canadian poetry, editing, and publishing.
16. The biographical information has been taken from David O'Rourke's entry to the *Oxford Companion to Canadian Literature* and an interview with *Books in Canada*, 22.5 (1993).
17. The versions that appear in Callaghan's anthology are in fact taken from *St-Denys Garneau & Anne Hébert*, and not *Poems of French Canada*, whose versions are slightly different. It is interesting, because other translations used in the anthology by Scott were taken from *Poems of French Canada*.
18. That material is no longer available online.
19. The Pearson Canada (Penguin's parent company) web catalogue indicates that a new printing of the second edition appeared in 2013, but it is now unavailable
20. All quotations about the process of editing the Canadian edition of the anthology, unless otherwise noted, come from an e-mail correspondence with Wanda Campbell (October 4, 2013).
21. This recalls Scott's translation of "Ancestral Manor" appearing in A. J. M. Smith's third edition of *Book of Canadian Poetry* through Gage Publishing in 1957, as well as in Carl F. Klink and R. E. Watters' *Canadian Anthology* (both 1955 and 1966), as a Scott poem. It is unclear if the editors were aware of these anthologies, but they do mention Smith's other anthology, *The Oxford Book of Canadian Verse: In French and English* as being influential to them in their selections (Jones and Swift xv).

4

Anne Hébert in English Abroad

While the previous chapter was concerned with Anne Hébert and the role she, or her poetry, was made to play in identity and nation-building in Canada, and how that, in turn, created and shaped her image as an author in and for English Canada, this chapter will look at how anthologies *outside* of the Canadian context/nation-building exercise have been involved in this process. If anthologies are indeed narratives, and not necessarily national or territorial narratives, then how does the inclusion of an author into a variety of narratives affect her identity? Additionally, these anthologies outside Canada were typically directed to an American (rather than Canadian) market and targeted different audiences (feminists, francophiles, world literature scholars, rather than "Canadianists"). The importance of anthologies in the United States and beyond is not much different than in Canada. Glen M. Johnson puts the importance of anthologies (written from an American perspective) thusly:

> The anthology may be the means by which the canon reaches the broadest segment of the rising educated class. For professionals of literature, current and apprentice, the anthology is an intersection: it ratifies whatever consensus exists about the canon; it perpetuates that consensus in the act of presenting it and preserves the consensus through assuring that the works are accessible; and it is a forum for changing the consensus through additions, deletions, or changes in format. The dynamic[s] are indeed of the market. (113)

These broader, more general anthologies also risk negating Hébert's specific historical and political context even further than the Canadian identity-building exercise did. Barbara M. Benedict explains, "As anthologies reprint material in different settings and according to different principles, they strip it of its historical and political contexts. Texts become dehistoricized, depoliticized, and hence 'timeless,' immortal, or in other words, eternally contemporary" (6–7). That Hébert is a part of many different canon-building exercises, however, and as problematic as it may be, is nonetheless significant to her image as an author in English.

As stated in the previous chapter's introduction, the analysis of the conditions leading up to Hébert's inclusion in the anthologies in question will be paired with the necessary analysis of the reception of said collections. All of these smaller pieces, so to speak, when assembled give a complete picture of Anne Hébert, poet, as understood in English. Although dealt with in separate chapters, one cannot discount the impact previous anthologies and translations had on the anthologizing process outside of Canada. Any potential exposure of Hébert's poetry to an English-speaking audience increased the likelihood of further translations and inclusion in foreign English-language anthologies.

HÉBERT AS WOMAN WRITER IN THE UNITED STATES

The 1970s in the United States saw a rising interest in women writers and women's writing. At the same time as Hébert was being lauded in Canada as one of the authentic voices of Quebec, she was being discovered in the United States as a voice for women. It is interesting that all of the anthologies considered immediately below had a project of creating a canon, a women's canon, using the traditional and often criticized form of the anthology. But the anthology did provide a number of advantages: access to the classroom, increased visibility, and creating a traditional narrative often associated with collections of this kind. As noted by Lawrence Venuti, "Every stage in the production, circulation and reception of a translation is profoundly marked by its historical moment, tracing a history that is distinct from the history of the foreign text" ("Translation" 800). The following translations and anthologies are marked by the historical moment of the rise of feminism, particularly in the field of literary studies. Separate from the politics of her home country, American feminists discovered Hébert as a voice for women's oppression and potential transcendence. She is thus inserted into a new and, in some ways, larger canon and tradition: that of women's writing. That Hébert was a part of this process of canon formation at its early stages is important in understanding her image as a poet in English.

THE OTHER VOICE, BANKIER ET AL., 1976

In 1976 W. W. Norton published *The Other Voice: Twentieth-Century Women's Poetry in Translation*. The book was edited by six women: Joanna Bankier, Carol Cosman, Doris Earnshaw, Joan Keefe, Deidre Lashgari, and Kathleen Weaver, all of whom were all associated at that time with the comparative literature program at University of California, Berkeley. According to the preface to the anthology,

> In 1970, a group of women, many associated with the Department of Comparative Literature at the University of California, Berkeley, came together to study the work of women writers who had been treated summarily or overlooked in the regular academic curriculum. We soon began to discover excellent women poets from ancient times to the present whose work had not been translated into English. To make this poetry available to the group, original translations were undertaken. In 1971 we began to meet on Sunday nights for poetry readings and translation workshops... Translations presented at these reading-workshops became the core of this anthology, which continued to grow and change over the next three years. (xxiii)

As stated in the introduction, thirty-eight countries and thirty-one languages are represented in the anthology by seventy-seven different poets. Hébert is represented by four poems, all translated by Kathleen Weaver: "Eve" and "Wisdom Has Broken My Arms" from *Poèmes*, and "Night" and "Landscape" from *Le Tombeau des rois*. Hébert is also the only representative from Canada included in the anthology. The anthology is organized thematically: (1) "Being a Woman," (2) "Women and Men," (3) "Meditations," (4) "Speaking for Others," and (5) "Visions." Hébert's "Eve" opens the anthology in the first section, "Being a Woman," while "Wisdom" is included in the "Women and Men" section, and "Night" and "Landscape" are in the "Meditations" section.

In the foreword, Adrienne Rich (who also translated a number of poems in the anthology) writes that this collection of twentieth-century women poets represents "an unearthing [of] our buried cities, our pictographs on the walls of hidden canyons, our anonymous songs, our lost arts and tools, our secret sharings, our inscriptions which are only beginning to be deciphered" (xvii). The idea of limiting the anthology to the twentieth century but at the same time making it broadly based in order to include exclusively poetry in translation originates from the following impetus, says Rich, of the editors:

> Many of the women included here have influenced the poetic traditions and language of their own lands, while remaining unknown to each other. In an age of renewed interest in translation, the women poets of the world have still lacked a real sense of each other's powers. Not just women who write poetry, but the state of poetry itself, and all who look to poetry for greater self-knowledge, have suffered from this ignorance. (xvii–xviii)

The main criterion for selecting the poetry is that it must be "of an extraordinary quality and importance for us today" (1). The editors also explain their decision to group the poems thematically rather than historically or geographically:

> Ultimately, we believe it is important to understand the women poets within the contexts of their respective histories and traditions. At present, with the work of discovery hardly begun, this is only occasionally possible. Therefore we have chosen not to stress distinctions of time and place, but rather to arrange our selections according to recurrent themes that cut across cultural, geographical, and temporal boundaries. (1–2)

The poems were then organized "so that each might benefit from the interplay of echoing and contrasting voices" (2).

As this was the first time that many of these poets had been presented in English, the editors address the issue of translation quite extensively in their introductory sections. Rich acknowledges the inherent difficulties of translating poetry from different languages. "The music, the associative patterns within a language, the way certain words, sounds, meanings conflict and resonate within a poem are, if not lost, anyway transformed, transposed, rescored for a different instrument, in the act of translation" (xx). Rich also reassures the reader that "The translators for this anthology...have sought a natural and translucent English unencumbered by laborious imitations of, say, Russian rhyme-patterns. What we receive are the images, in which we touch our profound common experience" (xx). In their "Note on Translation," the editors remind the reader that "it is important to be aware that these poems in English *are* translations, that they embody a very special kind of literary process. A poetic translation can never reproduce the original poem" (xxv). Citing the difficulties presented by grammatical structure, colloquial expressions and cultural/linguistic allusions, and metric forms, the editors reiterate Rich's assurances that most of the translators "have chosen...to preserve the poetic image of the original poem within a clear and natural English" (xxvi).

Not much is known about Hébert's translator Kathleen Weaver.[1] The biography at the end of the 1976 collection informs the reader that she was born in 1945 (in Polo, Illinois, according to Wikipedia), holds an MA from UC Berkeley in comparative literature, and had previously studied in Paris and Edinburgh. She also taught courses on poetry, women's literature, and film. Her translation experience to that point had been limited to "an anthology of poetry about the coup in Chile, *Chile sí*" (214). One could conclude that Weaver learned, or at least perfected, her French while studying in France. In the anthology, Weaver also translated other poems from French, as well as from Romanian and Portuguese. Her translation interests later shifted toward women poets from Latin America writing in Spanish, such as the Cuban Nancy Moréjon and the Peruvian Magda Portal.

In an article for *Translation Review*, in 1990, Weaver discusses her translations of Portal and how she discovered this poet, a discussion that also provides insight into the research process in creating *The Other Voice*: "I first came across the name Magda Portal sometime in 1975, while doing research for the *Penguin Book of Women Poets* [1979]. On the shelves of the main library of the UC Berkeley, I found *Una esperanza y el mar* (A hope and the sea), 1927" (41). The process of "unearthing" texts for *The Other Voice* (and the subsequent *Penguin Book of Women Poets*, discussed below) likely would have involved a number of trips to the library, wandering through the stacks. The UC Berkeley library, according to its online catalogue, has a copy of Hébert's *Poèmes*, as well as *The Tomb of Kings* translated by Peter Miller, *St-Denys Garneau & Anne Hébert* by F. R. Scott, and *Poems* translated by Alan Brown. The editors, in their biography of Hébert, list Miller's translation, but not Scott's or Brown's (although Brown's was only published the year before of the anthology and may not have been available when the anthology was sent to the publishers). The library database shows that all three books of poetry would have been located in exactly the same area.

Hébert's biography states that the publication of *Le Tombeau des rois* "established her reputation as a French-Canadian poet of major importance" (205). It goes on to describe her as a novelist and short-story writer, as well as having worked in television, theater, and film, mentioning, too, that her novel *Kamouraska* had recently been made into a film. *Poèmes* is not mentioned in the biography, while *Les songes en équilibre* is given an incorrect publication date (1964 rather than 1942). The permissions page, however, states that all four of Hébert's poems used in the anthology were from *Poèmes*, copyright 1960 by Éditions du Seuil, thus confirming that the editors did indeed know the collection.

Hébert's poem "Eve," from *Poèmes*, here translated by Weaver, opens the anthology's "Being a Woman" section. The section is described by the editors in their introduction as being about "the cultural and biological experiences of being a woman" as well as about "the search for identity in figures of myth and legend" (2). "Eve" is cited as being an example of that search for identity, along with Else Lasker-Schüler's "The Voices of Eden" and Sophia de Mello Breyner Andresen's "Sonnet to Eurydice." That Hébert's poem occupies the opening pages of the anthology proper speaks volumes as to the importance and impact the poem could have had on the reader. The poem itself is representative of Hébert's later poems (late 1950s–early 1960s), which were more in the style of prose poems, but no less symbolic than the poems in 1953's *Le Tombeau des rois*.

In the section "Women and Men," the poems "explore different aspects of relationship—fulfillment in love, the desire for independence, and the anguish of conflict and separation. Again and again these poems return to the question of identity, the difficulty of defining oneself as a woman," write the editors (3). While "Wisdom Has Broken My Arms" is not directly mentioned in the introduction, it certainly fits within the overall theme of the quest for identity and the anguish of a love affair, as well as "tension and of bitter conflict" (3). This particular poem is also from *Poèmes*, where it appeared in French, and is written in prose-poem form. The final two poems from Hébert are included in the section "Meditations." This section contains poems "in which states of feeling are projected through images of nature and the cycle of seasonal change. These are poems of solitude, often of sadness" (4). "Landscape" is singled out by the editors for how it portrays water, "an image of the decay of memory and the loss of childhood" (4). While "Night" is not directly mentioned, the poem once again fits within the overall theme, using the image of water as "a metaphor for female stasis and silence" (4). Both these poems originally appeared in French in Hébert's earlier collection, *Le Tombeau des rois*, and are shorter, sparser, and more compact than the other Hébert poems in the anthology.

Reaction to the anthology is generally positive. In her brief review in *Library Journal*, Suzanne Juhasz calls the anthology a "major achievement" and anticipates the impact that the anthology may have: "How we have been granted access to the poetry of women from the rest of our world: this collection expands and enriches our understanding of the matter and range of women's poetry" ("Sensibility" 205). Sally Rosenbluth, in the *University of Windsor Review*, problematizes the choice of a women-only poetry anthology: "I would suggest that a book like this one may well prove self-defeating...For these poems need no such limiting feminist appellation: they are poetry, pure and simple, and some of them very good indeed" (93). She concludes her review by stating that "The feminist movement ought to be grateful: sexual equality, when it comes, will have its basis in that—in our common humanity and nothing else" (95). *Choice* commends the editors and concludes that the anthology has "merit enough to deserve inclusion in every high school, college and university library." (Rev. of *Other* 675). Gerard Grealish, in *Best Seller*, on the other hand, comments that "A cliché is a cliché—if translations cannot rise above them, are they worth it?" (21) In *Parnassus*, Gloria Bowles provides not only a review but also a more in-depth analysis of the anthology and its contents. She is the lone reviewer to mention Hébert (identifying her as Canadian), and looks at "Eve" in regards to how Hébert rewrites myth and integrates the women's perspective: "The conscious contemporary woman poet is the sum total of the women she has known through her poems" (336). Bowles concludes by stating that "*The Other Voice* not only adds to our knowledge of literature by women; it reminds us that the history of twentieth-century poetry is an *international* history" (338). Hébert, through her inclusion in this anthology, is thus made a part of this "international history" of poetry.

THE PENGUIN BOOK OF WOMEN POETS, COSMAN ET AL., 1979

In 1979, Viking Press published *The Penguin Book of Women Poets*, edited by Carol Cosman, Joan Keefe, and Kathleen Weaver.[2] This project was again realized by the Berkeley group, as the three other editors of *The Other Voice*, Joanna Bankier, Doris Earnshaw, and Deirdre Lashgari, are listed as consulting editors. This anthology, which takes a historical perspective on women poets beginning from ancient Egypt, includes poets who wrote in English. Over two hundred individual authors are featured, each represented by a small selection of her poems. The anthology was in the works when *The Other Voice* was published, as Weaver's biographical note in the earlier anthology would indicate: "co-editor of a historical survey of women poets" (214). The Penguin anthology is divided into four historical sections, "The Ancient World," "The Middle Period," "The Renaissance and its Contemporaries," and "The Twentieth Century: Moderns and Contemporaries," which is by far the largest section. Each poet has an accompanying biography and brief historical context preceding the selected poems. Hébert is represented in the twentieth-century section by two poems, again translated by Kathleen Weaver, "The Tomb of Kings" from *Le Tombeau des rois* and "Spring over the City" from *Poèmes*. Hébert is identified as representing "French Canada," and is the only such representative.

In their relatively brief preface, the editors explain their selection process: "first, the desire to present a cross-cultural panorama by representing as many literatures as possible; second, the desire to be representative with respect to each literature; third and most important, the concern for literary excellence, against which the other factors were weighed" (32). The editors, reflecting their background in comparative literature, consciously attempt to encourage a comparative analysis of the poems: "[The poems'] collection into a single anthology must inevitably remove them from their immediate contexts, but the comparative view to be gained by the presentation in English of poetry from so many different languages and cultures is illuminating" (31). The editors' views on translation remain unchanged between the two anthologies. "Necessity, then, provided the opportunity to present diverse translations, which, while conveying the sense of the originals, succeed as readable, often extremely fine poems in English, " they write in the second anthology (31–32). The editors also address the criticisms of the first anthology. They address the issue of a women-only anthology and acknowledge the divergent views: "It does not come as a surprise that even today some women poets will not allow their work to appear in anthologies devoted exclusively to women" (30). The editors also directly contradict one of Adrienne Rich's more militant statements from her foreword to *The Other Voice*. Rich wrote that "[*The Other Voice*] reinforces my sense that women of whatever class, nation or race share a common sensibility" (Bankier xviii). But the editors of *Women Poets* conclude their preface with, "We hope that this book is presented in a way that permits each poem to be appreciated for its particular merits and each poet to speak in her own voice" (33). The singular voice from the previous anthology is replaced by a multitude of voices.

Preceding Hébert's poems is a brief biographical note, which is more complete and accurate than the one in *The Other Voice*. Her education in Canada is outlined, "She received, at her father's insistence, a rigorous education in the French tradition" (356), as well as that she lived in France. *Les Songes en équilibre* is given the correct publication date (1942). It is interesting to note that once again, even though one of the two poems included in the anthology is from *Poèmes*, that collection is not mentioned in the biographical note, nor are any titles of her novels or short stories. The collection is properly cited in the copyright acknowledgement section at the end of the book (as is the Musson Book Company for both poems). It is also mentioned in the biographical note that Hébert "has received the highest literary honors of French Canada" (356). While not entirely accurate, as she had won Canada's highest literary honour, the biography in this anthology is more accurate than the biography included in *The Other Voice*.

The anthology includes ""The Tomb of Kings" and "Spring over the City," taken from *Poèmes*, both translated here again by Weaver. "Spring over the City" is reflective of the longer, more prose-like style of Hébert's later poems of that period. But, we can see the various hands that helped shape Weaver's translation of "The Tomb of Kings," by far Hébert's most famous poem, although this marked the first time it had been included in an American anthology. At the end of Weaver's translation of "The Tomb of Kings," she leaves the following translator's note: "I am indebted to the interchange between Anne Hébert and F. R. Scott on the subject of Mr Scott's translation of this poem in *Tamarack Review*, August 1962" (358). It is unclear how Weaver discovered the dialogue (which had by then appeared as a book, *Dialogue sur la traduction*), although Scott does acknowledge Hébert's input into the translations in the translator's note in *St-Denys Garneau & Anne Hébert*, which was available in the Berkeley library. Weaver did, however, consider a great number of the recommendations, and even improved the poem in certain areas, using the feedback Scott received from Hébert. The chart below compares Weaver's translation with Scott's "Version Two," the version that Weaver would have had access to in *Tamarack Review* (Scott's third version was exclusive to *Dialogue sur la traduction*, although neither version appears in *St-Denys Garneau & Anne Hébert*, which I have included in column three). Underlined are those sections in Weaver's translated poems in which she recreates the poem according to Hébert's suggestions; highlighted are those that would seem to be taken from Scott's version in *St-Denys Garneau & Anne Hébert*; in bold are those sections that improve on Scott's version, as per Hébert's suggestions; and italicized are those sections where Weaver chose to ignore Hébert, going so far as to change the poem.

Weaver	**Scott "Version Two"**	**Scott *St-Denys Garneau...***
I have my heart on my fist Like a blind falcon	I bear my heart on my fist Like a blind falcon.	I have my heart on my fist Like a blind falcon.
Taciturn bird gripping my fingers Lamp swollen with wine and blood, I descend Towards the tomb of the kings Astonished Barely born	The taciturn bird held on my fingers A swollen lamp of wine and blood I go down Toward the tomb of kings Astonished Scarcely born	The taciturn bird gripping my fingers A swollen lamp of wine and blood I go down Toward the tombs of the kings Astonished Scarcely born
What thread of Ariadne *Leads me through muted labyrinths* The echoing steps **are swallowed** as they fall	What Ariadne-thread leads me Along the muted labyrinths? The echo of my steps fades away as they fall	What Ariadne-thread leads me Along the muted labyrinths? The echo of my steps fades away as they fall

Weaver	Scott "Version Two"	Scott St-*Denys Garneau...*
(In what dream Was this child tied by her ankle Like a fascinated slave?) The maker of the dream **Draws** on the thread *And the naked footfalls come* *One by one* Like the first drops of rain In the hold of the well	(In what dream Was this child tied by her ankle Like a fascinated slave?) The maker of the dream Presses on the cord, Then come the naked steps One by one Like the first drops of rain In the bottom of the well	(In what dream Was this child tied by her ankle Like a fascinated slave?) The maker of the dream Presses on the cord, Drawing the naked steps One by one Like the first drops of rain In the bottom of the well
Already the odour stirs in swollen storms **Sweats under door-sills** Of secret, round chambers, There, where **curtained** beds are **raised.**	Already the odour stirs in swollen storms Seeps under the edges of the doors Of chambers secret and round, Where the closed beds are laid out.	Already the odour stirs in swollen storms Seeps under the edges of the doors Of chambers secret and round, Where the closed beds are laid out.
The **still desire of reclining kings** *Leads me* I **see**, astonished, On the black bones gleam Blue **inlaid** stones.	The motionless desire of the recumbent dead draws me I behold with astonishment Encrusted upon black bones The blue stones gleaming	The motionless desire of the recumbent dead lures me. I behold with astonishment Encrusted upon black bones The blue stones gleaming
A few tragedies, patiently wrought, Laid on the breast of kings *Are offered me* *In the guise of jewels* With no regrets, no tears.	A few tragedies patiently wrought Lying on the breasts of kings As if they were jewels Are offered me Without tears or regrets.	A few tragedies patiently wrought Lying on the breasts of kings As if they were jewels Are offered me Without tears or regrets.

Weaver	**Scott "Version Two"**	**Scott *St-Denys Garneau...***
In a single line arrayed: Smoke of incense, the cake of dried rice And my flesh, **trembling**: **Obedient, ritual** offering.	In a single rank arrayed: The smoke of incense, the cake of dried rice, And my flesh, which trembles: A ceremonial and submissive offering.	In a single rank arrayed: The smoke of incense, the cake of dried rice, And my flesh, which trembles: A ceremonial and submissive offering.
Gold mask on my absent face Violet flowers for eyes, Love's shadow paints me with **small, sure strokes**; And this bird I have breathes And *cries* strangely.	A gold mask on my absent face Violet flowers for eyes, The shade of love paints me in small sharp strokes; And this bird I have breathes And complains strangely.	A gold mask on my absent face Violet flowers for eyes, The shade of love paints me in small sharp strokes; And this bird I have breathes And complains strangely.
A long shudder Like wind that **lifts** from tree to tree *Moves* the seven great ebony pharaohs In their solemn, ornate **encasings**.	A long tremor Like a wind rising, from tree to tree, Shakes the seven tall ebony Pharaohs In their stately and ornate cases.	A long tremor Like a wind rising, from tree to tree, Shakes the seven tall ebony Pharaohs In their stately and ornate cases.
It is only the profundity of death that persists, Simulating the **last** torment Seeking its appeasement And its eternity In a light clicking of bracelets Vain hoops, alien games Circling the sacrificed flesh.	It is only the profundity of death which persists, Simulating the ultimate torment Seeking its appeasement And its eternity In a faint tinkle of bracelets Vain rings, alien games Around the sacrificed flesh.	It is only the profundity of death which persists, Simulating the ultimate torment Seeking its appeasement And its eternity In a faint tinkle of bracelets Vain rings, alien games Around the sacrificed flesh.

Weaver	Scott "Version Two"	Scott *St-Denys Garneau...*
Avid for the fraternal source of evil in me	Greedy for the fraternal source of evil in me	Greedy for the fraternal source of evil in me
They lay me down and drink:	They lay me down and drink me;	They lay me down and drink me;
Seven times I know the **vise** of bones	Seven times I know the tight grip of the bones	Seven times I know the tight grip of the bones
And the dry hand that seeks my heart to break it.	And the dry hand seeking my heart to break it.	And the dry hand seeking my heart to break it.
Livid, **gorged** with the horrible dream	Livid and satiated with the horrible dream	Livid and satiated with the horrible dream
My limbs **unlocked**	My limbs untied	My limbs freed
And the dead, thrust out of me, assassinated,	And the dead out of me, assassinated,	And the dead thrust out of me, assassinated,
What **faint glint** of dawn strays here?	What glimmer of dawn strays in here?	What glimmer of dawn strays in here?
Why then does this bird shiver	Wherefore does this bird quiver	Wherefore does this bird quiver
And turn toward morning	And turn toward morning	And turn toward morning
Its blinded eyes?	Its burst pupils?	Its blinded eyes?

Weaver has taken into consideration both of Scott's versions of the poems, as well as adding her own improvements. Note how Weaver eliminates pronouns and conjunctions in most instances, preserving Hébert's economy of language, something that Scott does not do. In only two instances does Weaver directly contradict what Hébert suggests to Scott in *Dialogue*. Lines 17–18 in the original version read "Et viennent les pas nus / Un à un" and Hébert insists that that particular inversion be preserved (Hébert and Scott 61). Weaver chooses to maintain the more natural sounding English "And the naked footfalls come / One by one" (357), much as Scott had in his original translation for *Dialogue*. In lines 45–46, Hébert explains, "Les pharaons sont remués par le vent qui passe. Il ne s'agit pas de dérangement intérieur, moral. Ils bougent comme de grands arbres que le vent agite en passant" (Hébert and Scott 74; The pharaos are moved by the passing wind. It is not an internal, moral displacement. They move like large trees swaying in the wind). Weaver chooses to use to the word "moves," which is less suggestive than Scott's original "troubles," but which still carries the double implication of both physical and moral disturbance. Outside of these two examples, the other significant changes that conflict with the original poem are Weaver's choices to break lines apart. Overall, Weaver's example provides valuable insight in how a translator can incorporate existing translations with her own style, creating a unique translation.

Reactions to this anthology are mixed. Suzanne Juhasz calls the anthology "the most ambitious collection to date in the ongoing search for poetry by women" in her review for *Library Journal*, but adds that "to read the book is a tantalizing but frustrating and strangely disappointing experience. The one or two poems by each writer don't make much of a statement...I find that the collection tells me less about women poets of the world than I thought it might" (Rev. of *Penguin* 633). Joyce Carol Oates, in a considerably longer review in the *New Republic*, indicates that the editors may be victim of their own ambition: "One's spirits sag at the very *thought*: hundreds of poems by more women poets than I cared to count, arranged in chronological order...A dizzying profusion, necessarily uneven" (28). Oates describes the effects of reading the final section of the anthology as "being approximately that of a train ride at high speed through an exotic and varied landscape. So promising are some of the sights, though blurred, that one fully intends to return—which is perhaps an anthology's primary reason for being" (29). While Hébert is not mentioned directly in either of the reviews, one would probably be inclined to conclude that the reviewers simply had too many authors to reference. Also, given that the reviewers are both American, it is not surprising that they choose to focus on those women writers who are already part of the English canon, and thus well known (Oates mentions Dickinson, Plath, Stein, and the like), or sufficiently exotic and unknown to warrant a mention (for Oates, early Chinese poetry, medieval *trobairitz*, etc.). Nonetheless, from the reviews, a reader would not be discouraged from buying either anthology. While they most likely would not have been directly drawn to Hébert via the reviews, her exposure would certainly have been increased simply through her inclusion in the anthology.

A BOOK OF WOMEN POETS FROM ANTIQUITY TO NOW, ALIKI AND WILLIS BARNSTONE, 1980

In 1980 Schocken Books published *A Book of Women Poets from Antiquity to Now*, edited by Aliki Barnstone and her father, Willis Barnstone.[3] Divided first by language of origin, then by country of origin, and finally historically, the anthology includes 311 women poets. Each poet is represented by significant selections of her poetry, and is accompanied by a brief biography and selected bibliography. Anne Hébert is listed under French, Canada, and nine of her poems are included, representing the different stages of her career as a poet—five from *Le Tombeau des rois* ("The Great Fountains," "The Skinny Girl," "Our Hands in the Garden," "The Tomb of Kings," "Life in the Castle"), two from *Poèmes* ("Bread Is Born," "Alchemy of the Day"), and two uncollected poems ("Crown of Happiness," "The Offended") that would eventually appear in the original French in *Jour n'a d'égal que la nuit*. This fulfills one of the goals of the editors, as expressed in the introduction, to "give the reader a notion of the scope of key poets" (ix). Four different translators were used: Maxine Kumin for "Bread Is Born," Alfred Poulin Jr. for "Alchemy of the Day" and "Our Hands in the Garden," while Aliki and Willis Barnstone collaborated on "The Tomb of Kings," with the elder Barnstone providing translations of the rest. Willis Barnstone is a distinguished professor at Indiana University, a Guggenheim fellow, and has been nominated for a Pulitzer Prize in poetry on several occasions. He has also translated extensively from Spanish, ancient Greek, Portuguese, and Chinese. He is credited with translating, alone or in collaboration, 276 of the 788 poems in the anthology. Aliki Barnstone is currently professor of English in the creative writing program at the University of Missouri, Columbia, but was previously professor of English at the University of Nevada, Las Vegas, as well as a distinguished poet and translator in her own right.[4] Maxine Kumin is a Pulitzer Prize–winning poet who provided a number of translations from French for the anthology.

Work on the anthology began in early 1977, with the following announcement in the "Wanted" section of the literary newsletter *Coda*:

> Aliki and Willis Barnstone are looking for poems translated from foreign women poets (European, Asian, African, etc.) for an anthology they are editing for Schocken Books. Please send translations with a stamped, self-addressed envelope to Aliki and Willis Barnstone, Indiana University, Bloomington, Indiana 47401. ("For Anthologies" 23)

Kumin, however, was already sending Willis Barnstone some of her translations from the French in March 1977 (Maxine Kumin, March 11, 1977, Barnstone MSS), indicating that the anthology had been in the works even earlier than 1977. In a letter dated April 5, 1978, Sonia Raiziss Giop recommended Hébert for inclusion and pointed Willis Barnstone to the *The Other Voice* anthology (Sonia Raiziss Giop, April 5, 1978, Barnstone MSS). Willis Barnstone knew Hébert from his research for an earlier anthology, *Modern European Poetry* (1967), and felt that she was and remained the best Canadian poet in either language (personal communication, October 14, 2005). At that time, the most complete selection of Hébert's poems in English was Alan Brown's *Poems*, which Barnstone "hated," as he recounted. For Barnstone, the translated poem had to be beautiful in English, he said, or as he has put differently elsewhere, "Fidelity to the quality of the original, presumably a good poem if worth translating, is foremost. If the new poem is not a good poem, the translation is a betrayal" ("ABC's" 35). Through his work as a poet and translator, Barnstone was friends with Alfred Poulin Jr., and knew of his upcoming translations of Hébert's poetry for the *Quarterly Review of Literature*. Two of the poems translated by Poulin had appeared previously, in the anthology *The Contemporary World Poets* (1976), which will be dealt with later in this chapter. Unfortunately for Barnstone, the rights holder for Hébert's poetry in English (General Publishing) would not permit him to use the new translations. He appealed directly to the author and received the following reply from Hébert, in a letter dated August 26, 1979, from Paris,

> *De retour à Paris, après un séjour au Canada, je retrouve une lettre des Éditions du Seuil, ainsi qu'une copie de votre lettre du 25 juillet.*
>
> *Pour ma part je serais très heureuse que mes poèmes soient publiés dans "A Book of women poets from antiquity to now." J'écris dans ce sens à mon éditeur de General Publishing.*
>
> *Dans l'espoir que tous les problèmes soient réglés entre vous et General Publishing, veuillez agréer, Monsieur, l'expression de mes meilleurs sentiments.* (Anne Hébert, August 26, 1979, Barnstone MSS; Upon returning to Paris, after a stay in Canada, I found this letter from Éditions du Seuil, as well as a copy of your letter from July 25th.
>
> I would be very happy to see my poems published in "A Book of women poets from antiquity to now." I am expressing this right now in writing to my editor at General Publishing.
>
> In the hope that the problems between you and General Publishing will be solved, Yours, sincerely.)

And thus the "new" translations were included in the anthology. Despite all this hard work to receive proper copyright permission, the acknowledgements section lists "The Alchemy of Day" and "Our Hands in the Garden" as being taken from "*Eve* by Anne Hébert" (*A Book of Women Poets* 582), a non-existent publication. The selection of the poems follows the observation outlined in the critical biography for Hébert preceding the poems: "[Hébert's] most common subject is a woman in a bizarre domestic setting, repressed and sad. The scene appears normal, but on closer inspection it takes on a surreal, even hallucinatory quality" (229). "Bread Is Born" takes one of the most common and mundane "female" tasks, baking, and creates a truly surreal setting, while the other poems follow suit with similar results.

For the most part, the translations follow Barnstone's own guidelines for good poetry translations. Concerned with sound and rhythm, he writes, "Sound is an essential element in an original poem. In a translated poem sound is also essential" ("Sound" 162). In his "ABC's of Translations," Barnstone states "Freedom is permitted. Freedom to make errors is not. Freedom and errors are not the same" (35–36). Take, for example, this verse from Kumin's translation of "Bread Is Born." The original French reads as

> J'entends battre contre la porte, lâches et soumises, milles bêtes aigres au pelage terne, au yeux aveugles; toute une meute servile qui mâchonne des mots comme des herbes depuis les aubes les plus vieilles. (*Œuvre* 67)

Kumin's translation reads as

> what I hear are a thousand blind and bitter animals thumping against the door, a servile pack of hounds, slack and submissive in their mangy pelts, who've been chomping on words like grass since the dawn of time. (*A Book of Women Poets* 230)

The poem lends itself to a freer translation due to the prose-like structure, and Kumin takes advantage of this freedom by moving the images around in the verse. In so doing, she recreates sound patterns from the original French. Hébert uses the "m" sound in the verse (*mille, meute, mâchonne, mots*), while Kumin uses both a "b" sound (*blind, bitter*) and an "s" sound (*servile, slack, submissive*). In the Barnstones' translation of "The Tomb of Kings," they manage to recreate a line in translation that had stumped previous translators. The line "Ce n'est que la profoundeur de la mort qui persiste" becomes "It's only the depth of death that survives" (239).

Critical reaction to the anthology is generally quite positive. The critique from *Library Journal* calls the collection "essential for libraries" (Judd 1639), while *School Library Journal* says the anthology "is more ambitious than the recent *Penguin Book of Women Poets*" as well as more accessibly organized (Chapin 162). But the real coup for the anthology is a featured review in *Time* magazine, which spans two pages, complete with illustrations and extensive quotes from the collections. And, referring to the two previous anthologies studied above, critic Patricia Blake states "In scope and in quality of translation, [the work of the Barnstones] surpasses such previous efforts as the *Penguin Book of Women Poets* and *The Other Voice: Twentieth-Century Women's Poetry in Translation*" (85). Hébert merits a special mention by Blake, who notes that "There are scores of surprising talents such as the French Canadian Anne Hébert, 64, and the American Ruth Stone, 65, who are among the most personal, powerful and sensuous of the contemporary poets represented" (85). The review appears in late 1980. In 1981, *Time* would introduce new features to its books section, including an "Editor's Choice" list. Starting in the January 12, 1981, edition and running weekly until the March 9, 1981, edition, *A Book of Women Poets from Antiquity to Now* is listed as an "Editor's Choice" selection.[5] The mainstream attention this anthology attracted is likely the result of both the quality of the anthology and the increasing interest in women writers and poets.

There are a number of similarities between the Barnstone anthology and *The Poetry of French Canada in Translation* by John Glassco. All three editors were respected poets and translators in their own right before embarking on what can be described as a tremendous undertaking. All three sought to create landmark anthologies celebrating the poetry of a group previously ignored or marginalized. The three editors sought the best poets to include and the best translators to use for their respective anthologies. All three were very active in the poetic community, and thus had a vast network of knowledgeable people at their disposal to consult. All three subscribe to the idea of using an "informant," as put by Willis Barnstone, or consulting someone who is more familiar with the original text while translating ("ABC's" 35). The three translators also have very similar ideas regarding the translation of poetry. And finally, the three created (or helped create) what would become seminal anthologies, building on and expanding the work that came before. Their similar approaches guaranteed a certain degree of success for their respective anthologies as well as increased exposure to a new audience for Hébert.

SINUOUS LACES, JANIS L. PALLISTER, 1986

In 1986, Janis L. Pallister, through Presse Orphique, published *Sinuous Laces: A Sampler of French Canadian Women Poets*. The collection contains selections from sixteen French Canadian women poets, all translated by Pallister. Hébert is represented by eight poems: three poems each from *Les Songes en équilibre* ("Music," "Sea-Front," "Two Hands") and *Le Tombeau des rois* ("The Voice of the Bird," "Certainly Someone," "The Tomb of the Kings"), one from *Poèmes* ("Eve"), and one uncollected poem ("Ballad of a Dying Child"). The collection also includes notes on each of the authors. Pallister was a distinguished professor emeritus of Romance languages at Bowling Green State University, and was a poet in her own right. Pallister translated poetry from French, Catalan, Spanish, German, and Italian. In 2001, she edited a collection of essays on Anne Hébert, *The Art and Genius of Anne Hébert*. In her forward to that collection, Pallister writes that Hébert "is a major literary figure of the twentieth century" (11), and praises her "poetic style," whose "beauty and originality...are more easily experienced than described" (12).

In her notes on the poets, Pallister offers little more than basic biographical information, and mentions only a few of Hébert's other publications, though Hébert's bio contains additional commentary as compared with the other poets in the collection. One such comment reads, "Her poem entitled Eve is one of the most famous by any French Canadian poet" (*Sinuous Laces* 52). Looking at the anthologies studied here, as well as the critical work regarding Hébert's poetry, one does not find "Eve" receiving any sort of excessive attention. While Hébert is the first poet featured in the small anthology, Pallister provides a dubious introduction at best; for example, in her translation of "The Tomb of Kings," Pallister translates the lines "Et cet oiseau que j'ai / respire" as "The bird that I've inhaled."[6]

LONGMAN ANTHOLOGY OF WORLD LITERATURE BY WOMEN: 1875–1975, ARKIN AND SHOLLAR, 1989

The *Longman Anthology of World Literature by Women: 1875–1975* was published in 1989 after years of hard work by editors Marian Arkin and Barbara Shollar. Better known for their books on language arts and tutoring, both worked in the City University of New York (CUNY) system and were noted feminists and women's studies advocates. The anthology includes over three hundred women authors; over twenty-one from Canada, with seven from Quebec. It includes not only short stories and poetry, but also essays, speeches, journalistic writing, letter, diaries, and oral works. Each author receives a brief biographical introduction and each country also receives a short essay contextualizing women writers in that particular country's evolution. The dates for the anthology were selected because it was "the period we see as the first vigorous flowering of women's writing on an international scale," (Arkin and Shollar xl). Anne Hébert is represented by the poems "Castle-Life," "There Is Certainly Someone," and "Eve," all translated by Fred Cogswell. The anthology includes the title of the works in the original language, but only the English translation of the complete work is provided.

Arkin and Shollar did not work alone in compiling the anthology; twenty-one other academics were included on a "Board of Advisors," divided by geographic boundaries. Gillian Norma Davies was the advisor for "Francophone Canada." Davies was born in England, taught at the University of New Brunswick, Fredericton, and has written extensively on Québécoise and Acadian writers. This may also explain why Cogswell's translations were selected over the other available ones, as Davies and Cogswell would have been colleagues (Cogswell was a professor of English at UNB). The biography of Hébert (it is unclear who wrote it) calls her "the founder of modern Quebec poetry" (571). At this point, Hébert was still living "in exile" in France, and the editors also point to how private Hébert kept about her life. They also make the connection between Hébert and the Hexagone poets in Quebec, associated with the publishing house Editions de l'Hexagone. The editors also decided to focus on her novels and plays in the biography, rather than her poetry, even though they choose to include three of her poems and none of her prose. They do however draw the connections between the symbols and themes that traverse all of Hébert's writing, concluding, "It is a Gothic vision distinguished by its mordant social satire" (572).

In the essay at the end of the anthology by Davies entitled "Francophone Canada," Hébert is discussed alongside Gabrielle Roy, Marie-Claire Blais, and others as being part of the generation of woman writers who were beginning to challenge the subjects of Quebec literature more generally: "romantic love, Catholicism, the family, the land" (1104). "Castle Life" and "There Is Some One, To Be Sure" are both from *Le Tombeau des rois*, while "Eve" is from the later *Poèmes*. These three poems illustrate well how Hébert has been contextualized by the editors. Both "Castle Life" and "There is Some One" critique "the sterility of the *haute bourgeoisie*" of Quebec, as well as the sexism and oppression women faced. "Eve" evokes and inverts the Catholicism that dominated Quebec for so many years, but also works to "create a distinctly female mythology" (xxxv) as described by the editors in their introduction. "Eve" fits within the editors observation that "woman artists have made use of traditional mythological figures...but they also have created new texts for these legendary figures" (xxxv). The inclusion of "Eve" inserts Hébert into the larger corpus of international woman writers, connecting her to a larger tradition and practice.

Cogswell's translations are stark and moving, but unfortunately the layout leaves much to be desired, especially with the poem "Eve." The poems are presented in two narrow columns on the page. This is not a problem for the first two poems, which are written in Hébert's free-verse style of shorter lines. But "Eve" is a later poem, where each verse is one long sentence that usually runs over two lines, but sometimes up to four. There is a full blank line between each verse in the original French (and in the Cogswell translation as it appears in his collections). But because of the way the page is set up in the *Longman Anthology*, the spacing is ruined; there isn't a full line of space between the verses, and for some of the verses, the final word is placed right-hand justified immediately under the line that preceded it. For example, in the original French, the following verses appear as

> Contre la mort, contre la rage, nous te porterons scapulaires de plumes et d'os broyés
>
> Femme couchée, grande fourmilière sous le mélèze, terre antique criblée d'amants (*Ouevres poétique* 88)

In the *Longman Anthology*, the translated verse appears as

> We will wear you against death and against
> wrath,
> scapulars of feathers and shattered bones
>
> Recumbent woman, great anthill under the
> larch,
> ancient riddled by lovers (573)

Visually, the poem takes on a new dimension, emphasizing words that were never meant to be emphasized in the original.

Reviews for the anthology appeared in the *Women's Review of Books*, *Women's Studies International Forum*, and *Ariel*. Shirley Geok-Lin Lim generally praises the anthology, but questions the dominance of American and British writers in the anthology.[7] Diana M. A. Relke strongly recommends the anthology, too, and notes, "I think the Canadian choices are defensible, and certainly none of the selections is a 'bad' one" (130). Annette Bennington McElhiney praises the anthology, stating, "This anthology challenges readers, both casual and academic, at the same time it provides them with a matchless breadth and diversity of international women writers" (375). But perhaps the lasting impact of the anthology is providing English translations of many different international women writers, to be used in research and teaching. For example, Diane Engber used selections from the anthology in the development of her course on postcolonial women's writing. She chronicles the evolution of the course in her article "Evolving a Course on Postcolonial Writings by Women." While she doesn't directly praise the book, by adopting the book for her class, she implicitly endorses the book.

Obviously, the number of poetry anthologies from the United States that included Hébert is much smaller than in Canada. But, although the sample is small, the impact is no less important: Hébert is firmly established as an important member of the international canon of women writers. The Penguin anthology brings along with it the name Penguin, as well as the weight of its influence; the Barnstone anthology carries the importance and influence of one of the first families of American poetry and translation; and while Pallister's anthology is smaller, it is no less significant because it represents another market where Hébert is being introduced. And by being included in one of the first anthologies of international women's writing, Hébert is introduced in women's studies and women's literature classes. The importance that academia, particularly modern language and comparative literature programs, played in the introduction of Hébert's poetry to a more mainstream audience should not be ignored either. Not only were these professors/editors teaching women poets, including Hébert, to their students, but they were also providing the tools necessary to allow instructors across the country to introduce themselves and their students to Hébert's poetry. The field of women's studies was also growing rapidly during this period, creating an appetite for these types of anthologies. While limiting in a certain sense, these anthologies of women poets provided important exposure for Hébert in a market that may not have been otherwise introduced to her works.

It is not, however, unproblematic. Cynthia G. Franklin offers a criticism about these kinds of women's anthologies, stating that they promoted "white middle-class models of community based on women's sameness" and reiterates "feminist models of community in the early 1980s privileged women's similarities" (11). We see this kind of "sameness" promoted in the prologues and explanatory materials found within the anthologies, which frame Hébert in a very specific way. It marginalizes or even nullifies (echoing Benedict) the very specific socio-cultural environment from where the poetry originated, emphasized in Hébert specifically by Popovic and others. The bridge-building or identity-building exercise that took place in Canada is replaced with community building within the emerging women's studies and feminist community.

An interesting and explicit exclusion of Hébert in an anothlogy of women poets in translation is Domna C. Stanton's *The Defiant Muse* (1986). Stanton explains:

> The present anthology of French feminist poetry does not include those three contemporary authors [Hébert, Simone Weil, Marguerite Clerbaut]. That discrepancy, however, should not simply be ascribed to the partialness or incompleteness of every anthology. Rather, it reflects the partiality, the particular ideological point of view of this editor who, like all editors, determines by the texts selected for inclusion what image of a poetic tradition is created. (xvii)

Staton is actively pushing against this image of *la poésie féminine* and toward a more "feminist bias" (xviii). It is fascinating to read this introduction, because

Hébert is excluded as a result of her canonical status, while her poetry does, in fact, meet the requirements set forth by the editor, such as "exlud[ing] poems that privilege [K]*inder*, [K]*irche*, [K]*üche*, extol conjugal bliss, passively bemoan seduction and abandonment, and seek escape into transcendent saintliness or the beauty of flora and fauna" (xviii). Hébert's status, then, within the femine/feminist canon is contested and contentious.

HÉBERT AS FRENCH POET

While Hébert was primarily known in English as a French Canadian/Québécoise poet, she lived a great deal of her life in France, while winning a number of literary awards and enjoying great critical and commercial success in her adopted country. Her popularity in France, as well as France's tendency to assimilate the best writing from former colonies into its own canon, was not lost on editors of anthologies that dealt with French or European poetry in translation. As stated, Willis Barnstone had considered Hébert for his anthology of European poets in translation, although one would imagine she was excluded because she was not, in fact, European. This inclusion into a wholly new and different canon exposes Hébert to another audience who may not have otherwise discovered her poetry, adding further pieces to her image as a poet in English.

ANTHOLOGY OF CONTEMPORARY FRENCH POETRY, G. D. MARTIN, 1972

In 1972, Graham Dunstan Martin edited the *Anthology of Contemporary French Poetry*, published by the University of Edinburgh Press as part of its Bilingual Library collection.[8] The aim of the Bilingual Library series was to "aid those who have a wide-ranging and adventurous interest in literature to jump the hurdles of language" as well as provide translations that are "good literature worth publishing in [their] own right," as per the preface (v–vi). Martin also produced all of the translations for the anthology, which consisted of works from thirty-six French poets from France, Canada, and North Africa. In his introduction, Martin says he focused on what he considers "the most interesting new figures in French poetry of the 1950s and 1960s," and therefore favoured "younger and lesser known [poets]," primarily from the surrealist movement (1). He identifies "Canadian poet Fernand Ouellette" as one of the more influential poets of the surrealist movement (2), and while he does not mention Hébert directly, he does address the situation with French Canadian poetry and his criteria for selecting poets from outside of France:

> In Canada too, where there are also serious public dilemmas, and where poetry has now come of age, the best work seems to me still to be inward-looking. I have included two coloured and two French Canadian poets, but practically none of their poems given here could be said to involve a possible political theme. (11)

Although many would argue that there is a very strong political undercurrent to Hébert's poetry, the statement does reveal Martin's leaning toward the universal in his selection for the anthology. Martin also included a biographical sketch of each author in the back of the anthology, and called Hébert "perhaps French Canada's finest poet," pointing to her poems' "hard metallic quality, their compression, and the painful quality of much of the imagery" (202). This view of Hébert's poetry is reflected in Martin's translations of her poems.

Martin taught French at the University of Edinburgh from 1965 to 2000, where he also wrote and translated poetry. In a letter dated February 23, 2004, Martin explains his choice to include Hébert in his anthology:

> I chose Anne Hébert...because she is a true poet, writing poems that, often, seem like excerpts from an evil fairy-tale and which, always, provides that authentic shiver down the spine which, according to Robert Graves, is the sign of true poetry. I should add that I was delighted to find her, since the French poetry of France is strangely lacking in female poets of the first rank (though I am less familiar with the present situation). The only other woman poet in my anthology is Joyce Mansour, a rather sinister writer, of Egyptian origin, associated with the Surrealists. I found no other women poets from the period who were, in my opinion, of that quality.... You will notice however, that, in my anthology, AH has as many poems as anybody else, namely 8 (with the exception of Jean Follain, who has 9. But his poems are very short and he has only 6 pages, whereas she has ten.) I obviously thought very highly of her back in 1969–70, and of course I still do. She has a marvelous gift for imagery. (Personal communication)

This passage is illustrative of Martin's attitudes toward poetry for a number of reasons. Martin reiterates his emphasis in the selection for the anthology, and how Hébert exemplified this standard. Martin tried to include as many women poets as possible, but, in French, not many were "of that quality" at that time. Quality of the poetry trumped all other considerations, including national origin. Certainly Martin maneuvered the various politics of creating an anthology on his own, according to his letter, as the press left Martin to make all of his own decisions: "I was entirely free to do what I wanted, how to translate it and so forth...the Publishing House of the University simply trusted me." As for his philosophy of translation, Martin explains, "My approach always was and is: I am a poet, I understand poetry. I'm going to create a poem here [in translation]. A translation of a poem is not a translation if it's not a poem." Again, this would reflect his universal view of poetry, extended to translation.

The critical response to the anthology is fairly extensive, and comes from both sides of the Atlantic.[9] In the United States, a brief review in *Choice* praises "the inclusion of French-Canadian poets" and recommends the anthology "to all libraries" (Rev. of *Anthology* 1596). Tatiana Greene reviews the anthology for *French Review* and calls Martin's translations "beautiful" (Martin archives). She calls the anthology "most useful to readers interested in modern French poetry," and says that Martin "has done us all a great service." In the United Kingdom, *Forum for Modern Language Studies* briefly reviews the book and calls it "a good introduction to the field" while making "a welcome case for Meaning." S. I. Lockerbie reviews the anthology for *Lines Review* and praises the book extensively: "No other anthology from the English-speaking world can match the up-to-date panorama that is thus presented, while in France itself only a handful can compare, and, arguably, all but one of these are less well edited." The translations are "of a high quality," while "the professional expertise of a linguist is always evident... linked to the felicitous touch of someone whom one guesses to be a poet—or strongly attracted—to poetry himself." Ian Revie, for *Scottish International*, writes that "in most cases Mr. Martin has succeeded in catching the tone of the original very successfully...which makes this volume an extremely interesting." Martin's anthology even warranted a review from the French journal *La Quinzaine*, where Jean-Pierre Attal writes, "G. D. Martin a des qualitiés de traducteur...assez exceptionnellement réunies chez un même homme...les poètes choisis sont en général excellents et assez représentatifs des tendances actuelles de la poésie française." The *Times Literary Supplement* points to the anthology's inclusion of "some French-language poets from outside France" ("Between Words" 360) while commending the translation and selection. While none of the reviewers point directly to Hébert's poetry, many of them direct the readers' attention to the somewhat unique inclusion of francophonie poets in the anthology. This would lead readers to Hébert's poetry, and introduce a possibly new and different audience to her works.

MODERN VERSE TRANSLATIONS FROM FRENCH, D. B. ASPINWALL, 1981

In 1981, Dorothy Brown Aspinwall edited *Modern Verse Translations from French*, published by Todd & Honeywell. Aspinwall was emeritus professor of European languages and literature at the University of Hawaii. The anthology is bilingual in its format, and Aspinwall translates thirty-six poets, including eight from French Canada. Hébert is represented by four poems: "Seascape" from *Songes en équilibre*; "Presence," which is uncollected but first appeared in 1944; and "Our Hands in the Garden" and "There Is Certainly Someone," both from *Le Tombeau des rois*. Aspinwall explains her criteria for selecting the poets in a brief preface, stating that "All [poets] were chosen without regard for their standing with critics.... Their poems were selected because of the universality of themes: beauty, love, fear, death, life" (ix). Of Hébert, she writes, "Her suffering and her constant meditation are the wellsprings of her lyricism" (89). Aspinwall also briefly addresses the issue of translation in her preface: "Every effort has been made to render the thought, the style, and the music as faithfully as possible" (ix). There appears to be no critical reception for the anthology.

20TH-CENTURY FRENCH POEMS, STEPHEN ROMER, 2002

In 2002, thirty years after the Martin anthology, poet and translator Stephen Romer edited *20th-Century French Poems*, published by Faber and Faber, London. The collection, according to the back cover, sought to provide "around 200 poems which provide an ideal introduction and guide to the extraordinary diversity of poetry in French in the last century." Anne Hébert is one of only seven women poets included in the anthology, the only representative from Quebec, and one of only three poets from "la francophonie." The poems included by Hébert are "The Offended," "Cities Setting Out," "Love," and "Rain," which are all from *Day Has No Equal but Night*, translated by Alfred Poulin Jr.

In his preface, Romer, who is maître de conférences in the English department at Université de Tours, states that he wanted to offer "something like a prolonged wine-tasting," while his focus on the "quality of the translation has been a sovereign concern" (xv). He also expresses that "I feel it is not the business of the anthologist to impose a single dogmatic line upon the reader" (xvi). What he does provide, however, is a "series of notes for the curious" in an introduction that groups smaller collections of the poets together and provides a context for their inclusion and relation to one another. Hébert is grouped with Aimé Césaire and Léopold Sédar Senghor as representatives of "la Francophonie." Hébert receives the longest description, as her poetry is perhaps not as well known to audiences as the work of Césaire and Senghor:

> As far as *poésie Québécois* is concerned, I have chosen the magnificent poet Anne Hébert to represent this fiercely independent-minded and linguistically beleaguered province. The psalmodic verse-form adopted in her collection *Le jour n'a d'égal que la nuit* (1992) is at times reminiscent of Saint-John Perse, with its celebration of the foundation of an unnamed city and its people: but there is also what has been called a 'ritualization of the feminine' in Hébert's work, and this is visible in the rhapsodic symbiosis she effects between landscape and the female body in poems like 'Love' and 'Rain.' (xxxviii)

He goes on to connect French Canadian poetry to Baudelaire and Rimbaud "in their poetry of revolt." Romer, more so than any of the anthologists writing an introduction to Hébert's work, connects her poetry to both the land (Quebec) and the body (female), as well as to important French poets. He does not mention her work as a novelist, something that most of the other introductions mention. Instead, we are pointed directly to a relatively recent collection of her poems, framed in a way that leaves it open to multiple and a multitude of interpretations.

The anthology was well received and was reviewed in high-profile publications like *The Guardian* and the *Times Literary Supplement*. Alistair Elliot, in his review in TLS, praises the translations, but wonders about some of the selections of the poems themselves, calling it "eccentric" (26). Adam Phillips, in his review in *The Guardian*, calls the book "a fabulous anthology" as well as "endlessly intriguing and accessible." Patrick Quinn, in *PN Review*, criticizes that Romer "leaves the reader happily oblivious to the political and historical contexts in which the poems were written" (147), which is exactly the case with Hébert, where the political situation in Quebec is only obliquely referenced. Quinn does, ultimately, recommend the anthology, as does the review in *Signals* magazine (AP). Hébert only warrants a mention in the TLS review, and only to note that she and her fellow francophonie poets are included. Nonetheless, this well-received anthology would expose Hébert's work to a different audience, particularly given the paucity of women poets included in French poetry anthologies (more on that below).

THE YALE ANTHOLOGY OF TWENTIETH-CENTURY FRENCH POETRY, MARY ANN CAWS, 2004

We come now to the most recent and perhaps most prestigious inclusion for Hébert's poetry. Respected academic and translator Mary Ann Caws edited, for Yale University Press, an anthology of over one hundred poets from the twentieth century who wrote in French. On the inside cover, the anthology is indeed heavily touted—"Not since the publication of Paul Auster's *The Random House Book of French Poetry* (1984) has there been a significant and widely read anthology of modern French poetry in the English-speaking world."[10] Caws is a distinguished professor of English, French, and comparative literature at the Graduate School, CUNY. She has written extensively on the French surrealists, as well as translated numerous works of poetry and criticism.[11] She includes two poems by Anne Hébert, "I Am Earth and Water" and "Earth at Its Origin." Noted poet and translator Marilyn Hacker[12] (winner of the PEN Award for Poetry in Translation in 2009) provided the translation of "I Am Earth and Water," while Hacker translated "Earth at Its Origin." All the poems in the volume are presented with the French on the left and English translation on the right. In total, there are four French Canadian poets represented in the anthology.

Caws divides the anthology chronologically and places Hébert in the "1931–1945: Prewar and War Poetry" section. The decision was to organize the poets according to when they were born, not when they published (Caws xxviii). That Hébert is included in this category is strange; she was born in 1916 and only her first collection of poems, *Les songes en équilibre* (1942), was published within that time frame. The poems selected are from her later *Poèmes* (1960) and *Le jour n'a d'égal que la nuit* (1992), although "Original Earth" (as it is translated in this anthology) is part of the "Poèmes Anciens 1961–1980" section of the collection. She does, however, fit into part of Caws' description of the period, which she describes as follows:

> The influx of Francophone writers from Algeria, Haiti, Martinique, the Maghreb, Canada, and other countries increased during this period, as did their influence...During the years surrounding the war, the frontiers of French poetic establishment finally began to open to what we might think of as a great otherness—woman poets and poets from other lands. That spirit of generosity become [sic] increasingly felt. (261)

That Hébert had been awarded the Prix David in Quebec in 1943 (as was Rina Lasnier, who is not included in the anthology) perhaps qualifies her for inclusion in this period. Caws highlights *Les Songes en équilibre* in her brief biographical introduction to Hébert, noting it "was immediately popular" (321). There is some irony to Caws emphasizing this first collection of Hébert's poetry, as Hébert refused to see it ever reprinted or republished. Earlier in the introduction to the anthology proper, Hébert is described as one of the "successors of the famous École de literature de Montréal" (xxviii), along with Gaston Miron (who is included in the anthology). In the biographical note, Caws identifies the themes of Hébert's poetry as "exploring the themes of escape from what she perceived as the stultifying weight of Quebecois society and tradition" (321). The two poems well represent this idea of escape, in particular through love and friendship.

Because the anthology is so important, it understandably received much attention. The cover of the book is filled with advance accolades from various important scholars and authors, as is the book's web page at Yale University Press. Of course, it also received its fair share of criticism, including critiques that it does not include enough Belgian poets (McGuinness), that it does not distinguish enough between French and francophone poets (Palattella, Turner), and that the anthology focuses too much on the major names of French poetry while ignoring the "discrete voices of small press poets" (Slater) or, of course, which poems are selected to represent individual poets (all of them). But these are the same arguments that one finds repeatedly when curating an anthology of any kind. Often, Caws is commended for including more women and francophone (as opposed to French) poets than proceeding anthologies of French poetry (most notably in Piette, 136–37). McGuinness, writing in TLS, praises the anthology generally, stating that it "feels compressed without being reductive, ample without being aimless" (18). *Translation and Literature* has a lengthy review, focusing unsurprisingly on the quality of the translations and concludes that it is "happily, more hit than miss" (Piette 136), while noting that "[Caws'] versions of Hébert are very fine" (141).

There is an important consideration that bears discussing here: the thirty-year gap between major anthologies of French poetry in translation that included Anne Hébert. The issue is partly because of her position as a poet from la francophonie, but also because she is a woman. Most anthologies of French poetry, in translation or in the original French, do not include many women poets, if any, which would explain in part why Romer would assume Césaire and Senghor were better known than Hébert. Very little research or writing has been done in this area, but according to a rough count done by Jonathan Wonham, of the poets included in anthologies of French poetry, only 7 percent are women.[13] The editors of the majority of the anthologies also happen to be men. Even more recent anthologies of French poetry put out by one of the most important publishing houses in France (Gallimard) contain virtually no women. It is no surprise, then, that Hébert would not appear in many anthologies of French poetry in translation as she (along with many, many other fine women poets) do not appear in anthologies in French. That an author as celebrated as Hébert was in France and could still be excluded from French anthologies reflects an underlying sexism in the literary systems in France.

Alongside that, what is interesting about these anthologies of French poetry that feature Hébert is the way that many of the editors choose to introduce the anthology and their selection criteria; that is, the universality that they feel Hébert represents. This can be seen as an important moment in the evolution of Hébert's image as a poet, but also as an important consideration in the reasons *why* she was included when few women were. While she starts as a provincial writer, then expands to an identity tied into her nationality and/or gender, she is now introduced to readers as a poet that transcends these labels. While language is still used as a category, it begins to push the boundaries previously set up to identify Hébert as a poet, which eventually even leads to a certain transcendence away from linguistic considerations.

HÉBERT AS POET

If the 1960s could loosely be categorized as the time when Hébert was being introduced as a Quebec poet, the 1970s as a Canadian poet, and the 1980s as a woman poet, the 1990s saw the introduction of Hébert as, simply, a poet. After multiple incarnations, so to speak, as French Canadian, Québécoise, Canadian, woman, and French, Hébert is finally accepted into the broader literary canon called World Poetry or, more broadly, World Literature. David Damrosh defines world literature as the following:

1. World literature is an elliptical refraction of national literatures.
2. World literature is writing that gains in translation.
3. World literature is not a set canon of texts but a mode of reading: a form of detached engagement with world beyond our own place and time. (281)

It is enlightening to read Damrosh's definition after encountering so many different refractions and reflections, translations, and readings of Hébert's poetry. Also, one might be resistant to Damrosh's ultimately optimistic view of world literature after reading so many negative criticisms of the "misreading" and "misframings" of Hébert's poetry to serve various political and aesthetic aims. But Damrosh didn't see these distortions as losses necessarily: "As it moves into the sphere of world literature, far from inevitably suffering a loss of authenticity or essence, a work can gain in many ways...a literary work *manifests* differently abroad than it does at home" (6). It's worth remembering this potential as Hébert is further rewritten into a new and wider canon.

This move into a larger canonical framework can hardly come as a great surprise after analyzing how Hébert had been introduced and received in a great majority of the anthologies, regardless of their respective political bents. Almost all identify a "universal" quality to her poetry, pointing the reader beyond the limiting central thesis of the anthology in question. Her poetic voice has transcended the categories imposed by the anthologies, illustrated in both her flexibility to be included in multiple canons and her subsequent entry into the world poetry canon.

THE CONTEMPORARY WORLD POETS, DONALD JUNKINS, 1976

Four of Hébert's poems appear in translation in 1976 in *The Contemporary World Poets*, edited by Donald Junkins and published by Harcourt Brace Jovanovich. Hébert appears under the entry "Canada" and is the only poet included there from either official language. The selected poems are "The Thin Girl," "Alchemy of Day," and "Our Hands in the Garden" translated by Alfred Poulin Jr., and "Bread Is Born" translated by Maxine Kumin. Junkins is a professor emeritus in English at the University of Massachusetts, Amherst, as well as a poet of some renown.

In his preface, Junkins outlines his aim in selecting poets for his anthology, "We want not mere poetry, but the best poems," while making this particular selection of poetry "originate in a world we recognize as our own" (v). Junkins looked for "the best translations of the best poems of the best world poets, 1930–1970" (xxxi). As for what qualifies as the best translations, Junkins explains:

> Excellent translations of poetry must be inventive rather than duplicative: the artistic skills and awareness giving rise to the original poem should be matched in the translation, not by a language expert duplicating the literal meanings of the original text, but by someone skilled in language who reinvents in a new poem the meanings and effects of the original. The poet-translator must not merely substitute the familiar poetic qualities of the original language, but should expand the available poetic qualities of English in the way that all first-rate original poems do...The translation

is more than a translation in the old sense; it is a new and exciting English poem. (xxviii)

While it remains unclear how Junkins discovered Hébert's poetry, he leaves clues as to perhaps how he came to know it. Both Norman Shapiro (who had just recently translated *Kamouraska* into English) and Alfred Poulin Jr. are specifically thanked by the editor for their "special assistance" (vi). Junkins also mentions that he owes "special thanks to the poets who did new translations for this collection" (vii), and mentions Maxine Kumin, who apparently translated "Bread Is Born" especially for this anthology.

The anthology is organized alphabetically by country of origin, placing Hébert near the beginning. Each author's poetry is preceded by a brief biographical sketch and what Junkins describes as "[my] own feelings and ideas as I loved in and around the poems...[that] may encourage the readers to open their own storehouses of perceptions and sensations to the poems" (vi). In his biography of Hébert, Junkins points to the influence of her father and the symbolist and surrealists on her writing, as well as listing her three collections of poetry published to date. As for his own feelings and ideas, he writes:

> The poems of Anne Hébert bring us to our own senses: rare touchings, colors, smells, pain. Domestic visions enshroud great things, and a thin voice breaks the silence like a snapping whip. Anne Hébert chooses subjects like an archeologist familiar with old terrain, and her poems lay delicate fingers on the extraordinary. Inert things come alive, and we are summoned closer to the fragmented parts of our unfamiliar selves. (26)

The four poems selected certainly reflect Junkins' impressions. Two ("The Thin Girl" and "Our Hands in the Garden") are taken from *Le Tombeau des rois*, while the other two are from *Poèmes*.

In *Choice*, the reviewer states that the "Junkins anthology has a fine sweeping range of poets" and that "there has been careful consideration of translations into English" (Rev. of *Contemporary* 811). While not pointing to Hébert directly, the review does recommend that the anthology "should be considered a priority purchase for all academic libraries," as "many of these poets will be heard from at length in the future; several almost certainly will win the Nobel Prize for literature" (811). Meanwhile, *American Poetry Review* published a particularly scathing review of the anthology, attacking in particular both the selection of poets and the poetry chosen to represent them. Hébert gets a passing, indirect reference, as regards the view that Junkins is an anglo phobe of sorts: "In this direction,

Junkins is dogged to the bitter end. Canada has only one entry; it should be noted that she's a *French* Canadian" (Young 19). Vernon Young, the reviewer, does not recommend the anthology, and quotes a friend who wrote that Junkins "doesn't really like poetry at all" (19).

While it is almost twenty years before Hébert appears again in an anthology of world poetry, the importance of her inclusion in this anthology should not be overlooked. While it is unclear as to whether Willis Barnstone would have known of Hébert before reading this anthology, it was the anthology used by Barnstone for some of the versions of Hébert's translations included in his anthology (Barnstone MSS). As well, a large publisher such as Harcourt Brace Jovanovich would have ensured a certain degree of exposure for the anthology, including considerable promotion and distribution. As Junkins clearly set his selection criteria for the anthology, Hébert is placed squarely in the tradition of poetic "excellence," placing her in a privileged position within the poetic canon, and within the Canadian poetic canon, as she is the lone entry from Canada, regardless of language.

THE AGE OF KOESTLER, NICOLAS P. KOGON, 1994

The next anthology to include Hébert appeared in 1994, *The Age of Koestler*, edited by Nicolas P. Kogon and published by Practices of the Wind, of Kalamazoo, Michigan. Anne Hébert was represented by her poem "Christmas," translated by Jan Pallister from *Le jour n'a d'égal que la nuit*. The anthology consists of "more than a thousand pages of both original poetry and translations, and prints both English and foreign texts from 17 languages including Afrikaans, Finnish and Frisian" (Dana 28). As explained by the editor, "the unifying theme of the anthology is the spirit of Arthur Koestler" (Kogon 28), the Hungarian-born British author best known for his anti-Stalinist novel *Darkness at Noon* (1940) and his political activism, which was highly critical of the Soviet regime. Kogon describes the author as a "revolutionary, a scientific determinist, a psychologist, a mystic, and a futurist," as well as a writer whose deep divisions "reflect the deep split in the twentieth century itself" (28). Inspired by the man, Kogon spent nine years working on this project "without a cent of foundation money, without a financial angel of any kind, without a graduate degree, without the support of a university...I created this anthology for the love of it" (29).

The anthology is divided into twenty-eight sections; Hébert's poem is in section 22, entitled "Tears of Our Exile." Each section begins with explanatory and translator notes in regards to the poems that will follow, while the original foreign-language poems appear in a large appendix. Each contributor and translator also receives a brief biographical note at the end of the collection. Hébert is mentioned as "one of the leading French-Canadian poets" as well as the author of *Kamouraska* (1033). Pallister writes that her translation "is freer... than I usually give" (680).[14] The structure of the original French poem (free verse) lends itself to a freer translation. Pallister is fairly direct, however, in her translation and quite accurate. She chooses to change the word order in some verses in order to maintain the poem's flow in English. Overall, the translation is quite successful and maintains its haunting quality in English.

There is little critical reaction to this anthology, but it is another example of an anthologist presenting Hébert as a poet, alongside other "great" poets from across time and from around the world. As Robert Dana states, this anthology was conceived and produced because of Kogon's "love of literature" (29). That the anthology was published represents a feat. That Hébert was included is testament to her appeal to the editor and his hope that Hébert would speak to his readers in the same was as she had obviously spoken to him.

WORLD POETRY, KATHLEEN WASHBURN ET AL., 1998

Finally, in 1998, Norton and Book-of-the-Month Club published an anthology entitled *World Poetry: An Anthology of Verse from Antiquity to Our Time*, edited by Kathleen Washburn, John S. Smith, and Clifton Fadiman. The aim of the anthology was to provide "poems [that] are intended to be read for pleasure, not to score points. According to the editors, the anthology was to represent "a landmark of multiculturalism...by nature...rather than because it has been cut to fit an ideological pattern" (xv). Hébert's poem "The Tomb of Kings" appeared in part VIII, "The Twentieth Century," under the subheading "French Poetry in Canada," alongside "Watteau, A Dream" by Émile Nelligan. The translation was done by Alfred Poulin Jr., and had previously appeared in his book *Anne Hébert: Selected Poems*. By its inclusion, Hébert's poem had the ability to "surprise and delight the common reader" as well as the capacity to survive "in Darwinian fashion...the survival of the finest" (xv). There exists, in this context, a double choice of sorts on the part of the editors: Not only were the poems judged as poems, but also as translations. In that regard, the translations were "intended to be read as good English" (xxi). Thus, through her inclusion in this anthology, Hébert's poem was immortalized as being one of the world's "finest" through Poulin's translation.

The anthology was an update of the influential 1928 anthology of the same name, edited by Mark Van Doren. The release of the 1998 version saw reviews published in *TLS*, *New Republic*, *Times Educational Supplement*, *Christian Science Monitor*, *Library Journal*, and *Translation and Literature*. The reviews were generally positive, and Washburn became known for her work editing the anthology.[15] As a Book-of-the-Month Club title, the anthology was guaranteed a great deal of exposure. And while Anne Hébert is not singled out in either the introduction to the anthology or in any of the reviews, her inclusion in the anthology nonetheless would have exposed her to a number of potential readers who might not otherwise have been introduced to her writing. As a number of the reviewers mentioned, the anthology was "condusive to browsing" (Muratori 75), and would allow a reader to discover Hébert amongst the best poets of all time.

CONCLUSION

The breadth and the depth of Anne Hébert's inclusion in various anthologies outside of Canada is an important development in terms of her image as a poet. All of her appearances in English, either in anthologies or in collections, reinforced one another in terms of Hébert's ascent to the global canon. Whether it be fellow translators collectively recommending Hébert to each other, or industrious editors scouring library shelves in search of that elusive poet, her poetry had the power to inspire these people to include her and thus disseminate her poetry to a larger audience. Each inclusion in an anthology, large or small, each review that mentions Hébert or even recommends the anthology adds another frame, another shade to her image as a poet for the English-speaking world.

A word or two is necessary here to note where Hébert is not present, however, how she is still largely peripheral to the centre of the world literature (and even women's literature) canon. A quick survey of the anthologies of world literature from the big academic publishers (Norton, Longman under Pearson, and Bedford) shows that Anne Hébert does not appear in either poetry or fiction. Nor is she included in the *The Norton Anthology of Literature by Women*. Cambridge has just published *Twentieth-Century French Poetry: A Critical Anthology* and Anne Hébert isn't included. The Longman anthology analyzed here is out of print. Clearly, despite Hébert's growing literary reputation, she has hit a ceiling of sorts.

This is not necessarily a negative; in fact, the majority of great world authors are excluded from the main anthologies, due to space, cost, and other considerations. In her essay, "The Poetry and Prose of Recovery Work," anthologist Karen L. Kilcup, looking to recover lost or previously overlooked authors, observes: "my publisher urged me to include at least a few familiar texts that would entice people to buy my first collection.... The power exerted by presses and publishers over the recovery process represents an important element in the economics of recovery work" (177–78). In Canada, Hébert was well known and thus not a part of the recovery process, having been one of the first poets from French Canada to be included in anthologies of that nature. But Hébert is less known internationally and therefore would be considered a "recovery" author—lesser known and less likely to be included—in that context. As Cary Nelson, another anthologist, put it: "Critics can revive a poet's reputation, but the only sure way to keep a poem alive is to anthologize it...anthologies shape our memory of poetic history" (182). Her inclusion in the recent *Yale Anthology of Twentieth Century French Poetry* does position Hébert in a more central role in the contemporary collective memory of poetic history.

Notes

1. A number of attempts to contact Kathleen Weaver through her publishers and UC Berkeley have been unsuccessful, although she now has a Wikipedia page (en.wikipedia.org/wiki/Kathleen_Weaver). Attempts have also been made to contact the other editors of the anthology, with no success.
2. The anthology was reissued in 1985.
3. A revised edition was published in 1992, with an expanded section on American women poets. Comparing the two editions, nothing regarding Hébert was changed.
4. Biographical information taken from www.alikibarnstone.com/Aliki_Barnstone/Bio.html.
5. Taken from www.time.com/time/archive.
6. It is not terribly surprising, then, that Hébert refused to allow Pallister to produce and publish a complete collection of her poetry in English. In a draft e-mail dated August 20, 2001, Pallister wrote to Robert Harvey asking him for his assistance in obtaining permission: "Je vous écris pour vous dire que j'ai bien l'idée qu'il est temps de réunir toutes les poésies d'Anne Hébert dans un seul volume, et que vous êtes à mon avis la personne qui pourrait réaliser un tel projet." (I'm writing to you because I think that it's time to bring together all of Anne Hébert's poems in one volume, and in my opinion you are the person who could make such a project happen.) Another issue in Pallister's quest to publish the complete poems is Hébert's refusal to see her early poetry, *Les Songes en équilibre*, republished in any form. Finally, the relationship between Poulin and Hébert may have influenced Hébert's decision to not allow permission to translate to another translator. I would like to thank Janis Pallister for sharing the e-mail with me.
7. In a subsequent issue of the *Women's Review of Books*, Schollar addresses the criticism that there were not enough non-anglophone women included in the anthology: "When Longman first considered publishing a textbook for women's literature courses, they insisted on making a survey...when the time came for the editors to sign the contract with Longman, the publisher's demand with regard to the content was that 35 percent of the book be devoted to British and American literature. This was the only demand put into writing and made legally binding" (4).
8. The anthology is listed in the Library of Congress as being published by the University of Texas Press, Austin, for distribution in the US. Included in the anthology are the

poems "Vie de château," "Il y a certainement quelqu'un," "Les grandes fontaines," "Un bruit de soie," and "Nos mains au jardin," from *Le Tombeau des rois*, as well as "Un mur à peine" from *Poèmes*, and the then still uncollected poems, "Couronne de félicité" and "Les offensés".

9. I would like to extend my thanks to Graham Dunstan Martin for sending me copies of the reviews for his anthology from his private archives. All the review quotations that follow here were taken from these copies.
10. Clearly, given its absence in this study, Auster's anthology did not include Anne Hébert. It should be noted that he only included one woman poet in his anthology.
11. Biographical and bibliographical information on Mary Ann Caws comes from her personal website, www.maryanncaws.com.
12. Biographical information on Marilyn Hacker has been taken from her Wikipedia page.
13. It should be noted that his research also showed that Canada, by far, did the best in terms of the representation of women poets in anthologies, at 45 percent.
14. While Pallister's other translations are outside the scope of this study, one wonders how she could translate Hébert any "freer" than in her collection *Sinuous Laces*.
15. The headline for her obituary in the *New York Times* reads "Katherine Washburn, 57, Editor Known for Poetry Anthology" (Saxon B9).

Conclusion: The Narrative of Anne Hébert's Poetry in English

Lawrence Venuti, in his article "Translation, History and Narrative" (2004), examines the various ways the history of translation has been shaped, and what kind of narrative these histories create: romance or tragedy. The narrative of the history of the translation of Anne Hébert could be considered a romance. A romance because of the love and affection most translators and editors of her poetry have shown; a romance because of the parallels between how Hébert is understood in French and how she is understood in English; but a romance mostly because Hébert is finally being understood in the way that she had fought to be: as a poet. She often claimed not to be a nationalist or a feminist, but a humanist—sentiments she reiterates in the final interview before her death, in 2000: "Les êtres vivants, qu'ils soient d'origine québécoise, française ou espagnole, m'attirent et me passionnent. Je tâche d'atteindre en chacun d'eux ce qu'il y a d'humain et d'unique. Je cherche leur âme solitaire et cachée sous les apparences extérieures d'une caste ou d'une nationalité" (Gosselin 9; I am drawn to and passionate about all human beings, be they from Quebec, France, or Spain. I take on the task of finding in each one what is human and unique. I seek out their unique soul, hidden beneath the external appearances of caste or nationality). Although Hébert's poetry was translated (and manipulated) to a certain degree so as to fit the agenda of a particular translator or editor, each of these individual manifestations helped to create the image of the author and poet she strove to be.

Each instance of translation, each anthology, each mention of her poetry in English thus becomes a small part of the whole. Our understanding of that whole is re-informed and re-evaluated as more and more instances of Hébert in English occur. The narrative is far from complete. Helen Vendler, in her review of the Washburn et al. *World Poetry*, writes, "And one is grateful to the competent translators: even though their work will age and be unsuitable, perhaps, in fifty years, they are renewing literature for half a century" (35). We can only hope that Hébert's poetry will continue to inspire translators, and that her poems will continue to be translated and "manipulated" by the men and women in the middle for years to come.

POWER DYNAMICS WITHIN THE NARRATIVE

Patricia Godbout, in the conclusion to her book *Traduction littéraire et sociabilité interculturelle au Canada (1950–1960)*, states "Nous avons cherché à préciser les *circonstances* de leur [the translators] action: leur environnement concret (milieu de travail, etc.), le contexte entourant la naissance de telle revue ou de tel livre, les particularités d'un événement donné" (225; We attempted to specify the circumstances of their [the translators'] action: their concrete environment (work milieu), the context surrounding the genesis of such and such a journal or book, the particulars of a given event). The goal of this study is similar: to examine the circumstances and events surrounding the translation and publication of Hébert in English. I sought to discover how these anthologies and translations were conceived, and why; how they were produced, and why; and how they were received, and why. Examining the dynamics of each context, each individual translation/publication teaches us a great deal about the power of the translator and, to a lesser extent, the editor and how it has evolved over the past half-century.

One immediately notices the difference in attitude between translators F. R. Scott and Alan Brown in their dealings with Hébert. While Scott grants Hébert a great deal of authority and accepts her suggestions graciously, Brown does not, and chooses to disregard many of her suggestions regarding his translations. Scott's case is also fascinating because even though he grants a great deal of authority to Hébert, he nonetheless consolidates his power over the translations by buying the rights to his translations from her, going so far as to offer to oversee her image in English. Scott would appear not to be satisfied with the role of "manipulator" or "rewriter" in the middle, to recall Levefere's terms, but instead sought to become more of an original creator.

Other individuals would exert their power over Hébert's image through the paratextual materials included with their translations. The most obvious examples are the introductions and biographies included within the various collections and anthologies discussed. Do these extra-textual materials identify or point the reader to a nationalist interpretation of Hébert's poetry, or connect her with the broader French symbolist tradition? Is she identified exclusively through gender, nationality, or language? Are her other novels or novellas mentioned in the biographical information? This framing takes place above and beyond the translations themselves, and the selection of poems to be included. In isolation, each instance of Hébert's translation into English remains a distinct and partial picture of her poetry. The translators and editors have the power to present Hébert to their audience, to shape their expectations and frame of reference.

They may rely on external authorities to justify their selections, but, nonetheless, they choose to present Hébert according to their own aims and agendas.

The power relationship becomes more complex the more players there are in any given production of a translation. This complex structure of power and authority is highlighted in the case of *Canadian Writing Today*, edited by Mordecai Richler. Richler ultimately held the power to edit and produce his version of the anthology, but not without others trying to assert their own power over his decisions. Initially, the editor at Penguin did not want to include Hébert's poem "A Manor Life" and Scott did not want his translation of the poem published. This is an interesting situation, as Scott exerted his own power over his translations by being sole owner of the copyright, and also taking into consideration his well-known literary relationship with Hébert. Richler was free to choose another translation of the same poem (Miller had produced a version), but insisted on Scott's. Even more interesting is Richler's framing of the anthology and, thus, Hébert's poem—although housed in a nationalist and, therefore, political anthology, his introduction makes clear Richler's preference for universal criteria for evaluating writing. But this criteria comes into question with the selection immediately preceding Hébert's poem: Pierre Elliott Trudeau's political essay on French Quebec. Neither a work of art nor apolitical, this essay undercuts Richler's own claims to a universal standards for writing. What was Richler's endgame in his selections for the anthology? The extra-textual material, archives, and introduction provide conflicting answers, further highlighting the complexity involving the power of the editor; by placing Hébert's poem immediately after Trudeau's essay, Richler politicizes her poem, something he claims to have sought to avoid.

As time passes, Hébert also slowly relinquishes some of her authority over the translations; although she corresponds with Poulin late in her literary career, she nonetheless allows him more freedom in his translations, albeit not to the extent of what is translated and how it is presented. However, Hébert continues to have an influence on translations of her work, even posthumously—translators have to address *Dialogue sur la traduction* in any translation of her poetry, as well as the letter[s] and conversations included in this study. The letters in the *Dialogue* and here are now a part of the public discourse surrounding Hébert's poetry and translation, and thus Hébert's words have become a part of what Diaz-Diocaretz calls the extra-textual materials, or a part of Hébert's larger œuvre. Translators are confronted with the question of what to do with *Dialogue* and this study: to either take Hébert's advice or to wilfully resist what she has said about the translation of her work. We see that consideration in the discussions that translators have had about her work; some, like Weaver, choose to use the letters, while others, like Sloat, while not translating "The Tomb of Kings," would nonetheless choose not to consider such materials. This study introduces her letters to Brown and Alfred Poulin Jr. to a wider audience, making the negotiations even more complex for the translator. Thus, if a translator were to truly consider all extra-textual materials in order to fully understand the author's "personality," the letters discussed in this work must be dealt with. By leaving behind these various records of her thoughts on the translations of her work, Hébert has ensured that her views will have a lasting impact; they will remain present.

Conversely, we also notice that the translators become less interested in the author's authority over the poems as time passes. While in their correspondence Louis Dudek points Peter Miller to the importance of consulting and bowing to the authority of the original author whenever possible, later translators (Brown, Barnstone, Downes) assert their independence and autonomy from the authority of the author. This is reflected as well in the evolution of the theories of translation. As translators become more aware of their role as manipulator, they seek to assert that power over the original text, as seen in the writings of theorists like Levine ("subversive"), Venuti ("foreignizing") and Godard ("Womanhandling"). Other forms of authority thus take the place of the author, such as current theories, poetics, and the demands of the target audience. As pointed out by Tymoczko and Gentzler, "as Madison Avenue tightened its grip on the United States and the world and pioneered techniques for using mass communications for cultural control, practicing translators began consciously to calibrate their translation techniques to achieve effects they wished to produce in their audience" (xii). This is where introductions, prefaces, afterwords, and notes become important in understanding the project of each translator and editor. Disagree as many will on the validity of each translator's and editor's selection of sources of privileged authority, his or her consistency in applying said sources can be evaluated.

POET VS. TRANSLATOR

One of the most striking features of almost all the translators of Hébert's poetry is their capacity, their reputation, as authors and poets themselves. This creates an interesting internal tension, not only between the poet and the translator during the process of translation, but also concerning their shifting attitudes toward translation more generally. Hébert captured the attention of many a translator only briefly, and one wonders if that is a result of the translator/poet losing interest in the author or translation in general. Scott never translated again after *Poems of French Canada* (and had not translated much in the years leading up to its publication). There are a number of complex reasons behind Scott's abandonment of translation, one of which was his disappointment over the political situation evolving in Canada at that time. Moreover, given his reaction to Richler's request to include him as a translator in *Canadian Writing Today*, and not as a poet in his own right, one has to wonder if he was not concerned that his legacy as a translator would overshadow his legacy as a poet.

We can see a different kind of evolution in John Glassco's attitude toward translation. When looking at his reasons for refusing to translate Hébert's *Poèmes*, they appear on the surface to be a rebuff of Hébert's poetry: "The work [*Poèmes*] is unsympathetic to me...translation reveals in the most merciless way their instrinsic intellectual and semantic emptiness" (JGF, container 8, file 17). But they also represent a profound shift in Glassco's overall attitude toward translation. Compare the comments above with previous comments in regards to translation from his earlier article, "The Opaque Medium"—

> Why then, it may be asked, make translations of poetry at all? If the result is a loss, a depreciation, a betrayal, surely the expense of effort, the dizzying labour of trying to transmute essence of that most incommensurable thing, a poem, might better be applied elsewhere...But is not this question only another and insidious way to asking why poetry itself should be written? The poet, as Saint-Denys-Garneau found, is aware sooner or later that in pursuing his vocation he is exposing, deprecating and betraying himself, and finally failing to express the reality of his experience, but this does not stop him from writing poetry. In the same way, the devoted translator of poetry will not be balked: he is possessed by the necessity of making a *translation*—in the older, religious sense of a conveyance or assumption, as of Enoch or Elijah—of the vision of reality he has received from a poem, and of communicating his experience to those of another tongue and when he wholly succeeds, as he sometimes does, the sense of achievement is that of poetic creation itself. At the worst, he has made a bridge of sorts. (28)

The hope that translation held for Glassco has seemingly disappeared. It should be noted that Glassco gave up translating, not only of Hébert, but all translation. It is unclear when and how Glassco's attitude toward the possibility of translating poetry shifted, and when this possibility became an impossibility. Brian Busby, in his biography of Glassco, speculates:

> The long exhaustive struggle to get *The Poetry of French Canada in Translation* into print, the hostile reception, the accusations of exclusion, and the "québecisme" may have contributed to a lessening in interest on Glassco's part.... However, Sheila Fischman sees a much more simple reason for the

> decline in his interest: "He had had very strict standards. He was adorably inflexible. I suspect that he had run out of poems that he'd wanted to translate or that he thought he should translate." (239)

Was, perhaps, the poet in Glassco reasserting itself, or was this a more pernicious pessimism that extended beyond translation and into his attitude toward poetry in general? Glassco's final collection of poetry, *Montreal*, was published in 1973, and his final collection of translations of Saint-Denys Garneau appeared in 1975. Between 1975 and his death, in 1981, Glassco stopped producing writings of any kind. Abandoning Hébert would appear to reflect a more general abandonment of poetry.

There are any number of reasons why these poet/translators never translated Hébert again after their initial contact with her poems. G. V. Downes, as described on the back cover of her latest book, *House of Cedars* (1999), "is known as a poet of restraint and precision. She has chosen to publish very little, but what she has published has left an enduring mark on Canadian literature." This is her first collection of poems since *Out of the Violent Dark* (1978) and contains one translation of Hébert's poetry ("A Cage for the Sun"), which had previously appeared in a special issue of *Ellipse*, in 1993, where twenty-one translators, including Downes, were invited to translate the same poem. The translation of Hébert's poem, as well as other translations of other poets, are obscured within the overall collection, thereby privileging the voice of the poet over the voice of the translator.

Of the other poet/translators, Fred Cogswell would appear to have lost interest in the Quebec poets, but not in translation itself. Geographic proximity would have favoured his shift toward Acadian poets, as evidenced by the collection *Unfinished Dreams*, an anthology of Acadian poetry in translation that he co-edited and co-translated from the French with Jo-Anne Elder. Willis Barnstone has turned his attention to translating Sappho's poems and the Bible into English, as well as concentrating on his own poetry. One also wonders if he translated Hébert out of necessity, specifically for his anthology. Alfred Poulin Jr. died before having the chance to translate more of Hébert's poetry.

Sometimes the decision of whom to translate comes down to cold economic concerns. Peter Miller gave up writing and translating poetry soon after the publication of *The Tomb of Kings*, even leaving Contact Press all together, due to his financial situation and recent marriage (CPR, box 2, file 7). Many of the other translators (Slote, Brown, Tostevin) were specifically commissioned to translate Hébert and there appears to be little evidence that they would have translated her poetry otherwise. Kathleen Weaver chose to focus her translation efforts on

Spanish-speaking women poets, perhaps in part because of the demands of the American market. Her translations of Hébert, much like Barnstone's, were to a certain extent out of necessity, and out of the multitude of poets she translated for the two anthologies, the Latin-American women poets perhaps stood out to her more than Hébert's verse.

Another shift is from translation-as-passion projects (Roy, Scott, Miller, Cogswell, Glassco) to translations-as-commissions (Brown, Tostevin, Sloate), particularly in Canada. This shift represents the change in how translations were funded. Introduced in 1971, translation grants had a huge impact on the output of literary translations published in Canada. But, as Ray Ellenwood points out,

> In the first place, the system of payment through the publisher to the translator has been criticized because it does not recognize that translators usually know more about the books and authors in the source language than do publishers. Also, the present method of payment affects the kind of works translated. Since it is based on word count, the current rate being 10 cents per word, it means that anyone who depends to any extent on literary translation for a living can ill afford to translate poetry. But no amount of argument or complaint has brought any change in these policies. (83)[1]

We can begin to also see why Hébert's poetry (and poetry in general) was largely abandoned for novels: There was more money to be made. But with the power of funding in the hands of publishers rather than translators, it is the publishers who initiate the translations rather than the translators themselves.

Thus, unlike Hébert's later novels, all of which were translated by Sheila Fischman, her poetry has not yet found an "official" translator. A number of other, non-economic factors have played into that lack: the voice of the individual poet overwhelming the voice of the translator, economic or other forms of necessity, the relatively long time between collections of poetry by Hébert (by the time *Le jour n'a d'égal que la nuit* came out, in 1990, most of her original translators were deceased), politics, and so on. So although there emerged no single figure to translate Hébert's poetry (who would, by extension, have tremendous control over her poetic image in English), her poetry nonetheless continues to inspire new generations of translators. While her last collection of poetry, *Poèmes pour la main gauche*, remains untranslated into English for the moment, one imagines that it is only a matter of time before a new, young translator "discovers" the power of Hébert's poetry and embarks on the journey to recreate her poetry in English, like so many other translators before.

ARCHIVES AND THE FUTURE OF TRANSLATION STUDIES

Many of the conclusions and insights gathered in this study would have been impossible without the use of archival resources. For example, we would not know the extent of Scott's power over Hébert's translations without examining the archives. Or the extent of Louis Dudek's influence on Peter Miller's translations; or Glassco's process for editing *The Poetry of French Canada in Translation*; or indeed Barnstone's reasons for translating much of Hébert's poetry himself. The list goes on. What the archives reveal about the process, the politics, and the choices each translator and editor makes is invaluable in understanding the complex mediating force that is translation. In the case of Hébert, we see the multitude of forces that worked on her image as an author in English, through translators, editors, mentors, colleagues, and friends. The process is as revealing as the final product, and the process of translating and anthologizing Hébert in English would not have been complete without the archival resources.

Archives reveal the translator as both an individual with personal preferences, biases, aesthetic values, politics, and so forth, but also as a member of a larger community of translators, authors, editors, readers, and compatriots. How his/her community influences the translator can also be discovered through archives. As Diaz-Diocaretz put it: "In this act of interpretation [translation], the translator's *persona* (the writing-self assumed in the text), the empirical person (individual concrete circumstances, private and cultural presuppositions), and the psycho-social factors external to the work, determine distinct relations in the interplay between [source text] and [receptor text]" (36). Archives can go a long way to illuminating these factors that "may account to a certain extent for the textual strategies chosen, which will in turn affect the receivers response in the [receptor text]" (36). In particular, the personal becomes an interesting factor in possibly influencing the translator. Case in point, during the production of *The Poetry of French Canada in Translation*, Glassco's wife's mental health was slowly deteriorating. His letters to his closest friends (Scott, Smith), after discussing the progress of the anthology, would contain a update concerning his wife's health. While it is unclear, Glassco's turn away from poetry may have been influenced by the fact that he eventually had to have his wife committed.

This is not to say that the archives are infallible. Or the researcher within the archives, either. Jocelyn Hallman elaborates:

> The literary archive is a space of transaction. In this space, the producers, arrangers, describers and interpreters of texts exchange ideas about words and collaborate in the production of literary meaning. As they

> perform these tasks, authors, archivists and readers transact in an archival space that is at once physical and discursive. The materiality of the archives works alongside the discourses that surround and inhabit it, and the spatial relationship between the physical and the discursive within this space is characterized by extremes of proximity and distance to a literary text. (205)

In my own research, I suffered from having too narrow a focus when approaching certain archives, such as my own ignorance of Glassco's eventual turn away from translating Hébert's poetry, as the letters fell outside of my focus on the making of his anthology. As well, if you were to just focus on one particular translator and their involvement in Glassco's anthology, you would not get a complete picture of the possible implications; for example, if only the letters between Miller and Glassco were consulted, it would remain unclear as to why none of Miller's translations of Hébert were included in the anthology. It is only through consulting all the letters concerning the anthology that you get a complete picture of Glassco's attitude toward all of the translators and their translations. My unfamiliarity with American translators and translation led me to also remain ignorant of much of what may be found in Poulin's or Barnstone's archive, and I was forced to focus on just his translations of Hébert's poetry. At the same time, the archives can be overwhelming: how to limit what letters or what parts of the archive to consult? Looking at Poulin's archives or Scott's archives, there are volumes and volumes of letters and manuscripts to go through in order to find what you are looking for, or perhaps find something you never considered.

But archives, much like more traditional publication, are human productions and, thus, mediated. Individuals can choose which letters and manuscripts are included for public consultation, thus altering what can be known about them. Limits on access to archives can also alter our perception of an author. F. R. Scott has archives housed at Queen's University that will only be accessible to the public in 2035, fifty years after his death. Authors can also neglect to recognize the possible importance of drafts and different versions of their translations, as illustrated in the case of Cogswell, who used the other side of pages containing old drafts of poems for letters and other drafts, thereby confusing the organization of his archives. The introduction of electronic means of communication and preservation (or lack thereof) of letters and drafts are also challenging to future research; Janis Pallister's e-mails were sent to me in a format that made accessing them challenging due to incompatibility between e-mail platforms, as well as her early drafts of the translations, which were done in a now obsolete word processing program, rendering them virtually unreadable. The e-mails I received from many of the editors and translators now only exist because I bothered to print them out, as my e-mail address and thus digital recards of the correspondences has long since disappeared.

There also needs to be someone who is interested in housing the archives, and believes that they have some value to current and future researchers.[2] In the case of Hébert, many of the people involved in the translations of her poetry were poets of some renown, and their archives were considered valuable. But others, such as academics who edited anthologies or lesser-known translators, might not have their records and archives preserved somewhere. Thanks to the efforts of Breon Mitchell at Indiana University, translator archives in the United States are being collected for future researchers, archives that may not have been preserved otherwise. The archives themselves, even if they are housed and preserved, also need to be carefully organized and catalogued. When I first visited the BOA-Poulin archives, the papers were not well-organized, documented, and sorted, which meant that I didn't find the long and rich correspondences between Poulin and Hébert. During the intervening years, they were more properly organized with a finding aid, allowing me to include the letters in this study. And sometimes, life simply gets in the way of good record-keeping. Hébert's personal archives at the Université de Sherbrooke are relatively sparse, in part because of all of her moves to and around Paris and back to Quebec, but also because of a fire and a flood that affected her personal belongings while in Paris.

The archival materials available do provide a rich resource for the field of translation studies, in terms of either understanding the manipulation or writing the narrative, among others, that remains largely untapped. In Canada alone, the archives of Glassco, Miller, and Brown contain letters and drafts of translations only briefly dealt with in this study. Elsewhere, the Poulin and Barnstone manuscripts can reveal much about translation politics external to those in Canada. The perspective adapted for the purpose of this study was to select an author and work from there, but the opposite is equally possible, if perhaps even more manageable: starting from the perspective of the translator or editor and working forward from there. Hébert was but one of many authors translated by each translator, and but one of the many poets included in the anthologies.

THE STORY OF ANNE HÉBERT AND THE STORY OF?

It is difficult to compare Hébert's case in English to any other author or poet writing in French from Québec. Often, Hébert is grouped together in "the three sisters" of Quebec writing, with Gabrielle Roy (who is not from Quebec) and Marie-Claire Blais, the three authors who are the most translated into English from Quebec. Both other authors are novelists, and only Roy, with *The Tin Flute*, achieved the kind of popularity outside of English Canada that Hébert reached, while Blais was widely known in English for her novel *A Season in the Life of Emmanuel*. But their appeal in English, despite a high number of translations available, would seem to remain limited primarily to these two novels. A comparative study on the translation and reception of these three author's novels, along with Hébert's poetry in English, would be essential in order to fully understand the differences in how each author is perceived in English. On the poetry side, Hébert's success could be compared to Émile Nelligan's; he is included in the anthology *World Poetry*, along with Hébert as the two representatives of Quebec/French Canada. But Nelligan never reached the same level of recognition in English as Hébert. As a poet, Nelligan never published a novel like *Kamouraska* that propelled him to literary fame in English, and his literary career was quite short, as he died young. It will be interesting to see the impact that the recent publication of a selection of Nicole Brossard's poetry in English translation, by the University of California Press (*Nicole Brossard: Selections*, 2010), will have on her visibility in English.

The question remains: Is there something about Hébert that lead her to such a large number of translations, translators, and published instances in English? Why has Hébert transcended to the level of universal author? If we use the literary critic Pascale Casanova's criteria for achieving "littérarité," then certainly she has reached that status. Casanova identifies Paris as being the "capital de l'univers littéraire"(41) [universal capital of the literary world (34)] or the "lieu transnational dont les seuls impératifs sont ceux de l'art et de la littérature" (49) [a transnational realm whose sole imperatives are those of art and literature (29)]; in other words, the place where an author must achieve greatness in order to be a part of the universal. Hébert certainly fits that criteria; in fact, she follows the same path as many authors identified by Casanova—fleeing the repression of Quebec in the 1950s, Hébert sought (and achieved) artistic freedom and recognition in Paris. Casanova goes on to differentiate between "les écrivains nationaux (ceux qui se réfèrent à la définition nationale ou 'populaire' de la littérature)" and "les écrivains internationaux (ceux qui ont recours au modèle autonome de la littérature)" (157) ["national writers (who embody a national or popular definition of literature)" and "international writers (who uphold an autonomous conception of literature)" (108)]. It is clear also that Hébert fits into this second category of international writer; she certainly did not fit into what was considered popular, or at least acceptable, in Quebec when she began writing, and statements that she has made, some repeated in this study, further reinforce her commitment to a more universalist notion of literature, or at least a less nationalistic one.

So if Hébert has already achieved universal status, or status as a world author according to Casanova's criteria, why even bother looking at her translations into English? Casanova provides an answer: "La traduction est la grande instance de consécration spécifique de l'univers littéraire...elle est une forme de reconnaissance littéraire" (133; Translation is the foremost example of a particular type of consecration in the literary world... Its true nature as a form of literary recognition). In this case, Casanova is talking primarily about translations in French. But in her preface to the English translation of *The World Republic of Letters*, she states:

> Translation...is one of the principal means by which texts circulate in the literary world. And so I am pleased that this book...should be itself internationalized through translation into English. In this way its hypotheses will be able to be scrutinized in a practical fashion, and its propositions debated at a truly transnational level, by the various actors in international literary space. (xiii)

Casanova acknowledges the central position English has achieved in the distribution of, in this case, ideas, but also literature. Paris may be the pole around which world literature is judged, but English is the language to assure transnational attention. The English translations of Hébert's work are important to understanding her larger journey in world literature.

Put another way, why has Anne Hébert's poetry been translated so often into English? I would argue that it comes down to means and opportunity, not to mention timing, for the translators who worked on her poems. If we look at when her poems began to appear in English, it reflected the beginning of a cultural awakening in both English and French Canada. F. R. Scott's project was both political and personal, in his goals to create bridges between French and English Canada, as well as invigorating what he saw as stagnant English Canadian poetry. This project, as shown in Chapter One, would have a lasting impact on how French Canadian poetry, particularly Hébert's, was translated and understood in English Canada. The rise in both Canadian and Quebec nationalism fuelled more translators, and provided much-needed funds to support publishing these translations, both as an identity-building and bridge-building exercise. The public equally had an appetite for these translations, making them commercially viable, and more likely to be repeated. Hébert was by now both locally and internationally renowned, and when the project of building a canon of women poets came about, Hébert would seem like a logical choice for those creating the anthologies, not to mention the opportunity to introduce a poet of her stature to an American audience, as in the case of Poulin or even Pallister. Again, the market was hungry for such books, which made them an economically smart choice on the part of the publishers paying for the projects.

But there would seem to be something else to her attraction to translators. Why so many different translations? Indeed, Hébert's poems are deceptively simple in their form and composition, and yet provide a challenging project for any willing translator. But something that returned over and over again was the sentiment expressed by many of the translators of how Hébert's poetry touched them in a way that compelled them to pick up a pen and translate. Each translator, regardless of sex, nationality, or political project, found something in the poems that communicated to them on a very basic, yet complex, level. Her ability to appeal to many different groups of people, but mainly *poets*, would seem to imply that there is something universal to her poetry, something that communicates to the reader almost immediately. Anne Hébert's poetry is beautiful and haunting, skilfully crafted and moving, even (in the words of many of her translators) inspiring. This is perhaps the best way to describe the journey of Hébert's poetry into English: The poetry itself inspired that journey.

Certainly, in the history of literature, there exist authors whose poems have been translated repeatedly over sustained periods of time, but the history of post-colonial and post-settler colony literature is relatively short, along with the list of poets who have transcended their marginal status either because of language, country of birth, gender, or a combination of the three. To find a contemporary situation comparable to Hébert's, we will need to look beyond Canadian borders. Latin American poets such as Pablo Neruda and Octavio Paz have inspired a great number of translators to endeavour to translate their words. Others exist, and as our anthologies and our classrooms open up to literatures beyond the traditional Western canon, we will hopefully discover more poets and poetry that deserves the kind of romance with translators, editors, and poets that Hébert's did.

FOUND THROUGH TRANSLATION: A POET

It is through translation—although mediated, manipulated, and imperfect—that for many the poet Anne Hébert is discovered. Although F. R. Scott may have initiated much that came after, and may have created some of the most enduring images of Hébert in English, it is the poet herself and her poetry that link all of the editors and translators studied here. It is through translation that Hébert's reputation is expanded and celebrated, her poetry perpetuated. Her popularity in French in both Canada and in Europe is not to be discounted or dismissed as an unimportant factor in her transition into English, and, thus, into the global canon, but it is overshadowed in many instances by the English translators and editors who chose to celebrate her achievement. This romantic narrative, this love affair between the translators and editors and Hébert in individual instances, could be considered tragic due to the many mistakes, misunderstandings, and manipulations, but in the end the goal of Hébert to be seen as simply a poet is largely achieved.

Notes

1. The rate is now, generally, twenty-five cents a word.
2. I would be remiss not to mention the recent cuts to Archives Canada, given that so much of my research took place there. Not only does there need to be a desire to preserve the archives, but the funding to properly house the archives and make them accessible to researchers and others.

Bibliography

Archives and Research Centres

Alan Brown fonds, Special Collections, University of Calgary [MsC 220].

Barnstone MSS, Lilly Library, Indiana University.

Blackfish Press fonds, National Archives of Canada, Ottawa [LMS-0116].

Fonds Anne-Hébert, Université de Sherbrooke.

Contact Press records, S. Thomas Fisher Rare Book Library, University of Toronto [MS Coll 00069].

Fiddlehead/Cogswell Papers, Archives and Special Collections, University of New Brunswick [UA RG83].

Fonds Anne-Hébert, Universté de Sherbrooke [P25].

Francis Reginald Scott fonds, National Archives of Canada, Ottawa [R5822-3-X-E].

Gael Turnbull fonds, National Archives of Canada, Ottawa [R11823-0-2-E].

Graham Dunstan Martin archives, private.

John Glassco fonds, National Archives, Ottawa [R4070-0-8-E].

Louis Dudek fonds, National Archives of Canada, Ottawa [R11726-0-5-E].

Mordecai Richler fonds, Special Collections, University of Calgary [MsC 36, 285, 319, 332].

P. K. Page fonds, National Archives of Canada, Ottawa [R2411-0-2-E].

A. Poulin papers and BOA Editions records, Beinecke Rare Book and Manuscript Library, Yale [YCAL MSS 635].

Raymond Souster Papers, S. Thomas Fisher Rare Book Library, University of Toronto [MS Coll 00203].

References

AP. Rev. of *20th-Century French Poems*, edited by Stephen Romer. *Signals*, 1, 2004.

Aquin, Hubert. *The Antiphonary*. Translated by Alan Brown. Toronto: Anansi, 1973.

Arkin, Marian, and Barbara Shollar, editors. *Longman Anthology of World Literature by Women: 1875–1975*. New York: Longman, 1989.

Aspinwall, Dorothy Brown, editor and translator. *Modern Verse Translations from French*. Great Neck, NY: Todd & Honeywell, 1981.

L'Archevêque-Duguay, Jeanne. "'Les Songes en équilibre': Poèmes par Mlle Anne Hébert." Rev. of *Les Songes en équilibre* by Anne Hébert. *Le Devoir*, 10 Mar. 1942, p. 10.

Aubert, Rosemary. Rev. of *To Say The Least*, ed. P. K. Page. *Quill and Quire*, vol. 46, no. 3, 1980, pp. 62–63.

Balakian, Anna. Rev. of *Selected Poems by Anne Hébert*, translated by Alfred Poulin Jr. *Translation Review*, no. 32/33, 1990, pp. 53–54.

Bankier, Joanna, et al., editors. *The Other Voice: Twentieth Century Women's Poetry in Translation*. New York: Norton, 1976.

Barbour, Douglas. "John Robert Colombo." *Canadian Writers since 1960: First Series*. Edited W. H. New. Dictionary of Literary Biography, vol. 53. Detroit: Bruccoli Clark, 1986, pp. 142–47.

——. "Re: Viewing: Giving and Receiving in Canadian Poetry, or The Role of Reviewing in the Reception of Poetry in English Canada in the 20th Century." *Problems of Literary Reception/Problèmes de reception littéraires*, edited by E. D. Blodgett and Al Purdy. Edmonton: Research Institute for Comparative Literature, University of Alberta, 1988, pp. 49–60.

——. "John Robert Colombo." *The Oxford Companion to Canadian Literature*. Second edition. Edited by Eugene Benson and William Toye. Toronto: Oxford UP, 1997, pp. 226–28.

Barnstone, Aliki, and Willis Barnstone, editors. *A Book of Women Poets from Antiquity to Now*. New York: Schocken, 1980.

Barnstone, Willis. "The ABC's of Translation." *Translation Review*, no. 2, 1978, pp. 35–36.

——. "Sound in Translation." *Northwest Review*, vol. 21, no. 2/3, 1983, pp. 162–68.

Barrett, Amy. "L'esprit de la vie." Rev. of *Esprit de Corps: Québec Poetry of the Late Twentieth Century in Translation*, edited by Louise Blouin et al. *Quill & Quire*, vol. 63, no. 5, 1997, p. 35.

Barthes, Roland. "The Death of the Author." *Modern Criticism and Theory: A Reader*. Second edition. Edited by David Lodge and Nigel Wood. London: Longman, 2000, pp. 146–50.

Beaudoin, Réjean, and André Lamontagne. "Un demi-siècle de reception critique de la literature québécois au Canada anglais: 1939–1989." *Canadian Literature*, no. 175, 2002, pp. 19–43.

Benedict, Barbara M. *Making the Modern Reader: Cultural Mediation in Early Modern Literary Anthologies*. Princeton: Princeton UP, 1996.

Bennett, Donna. "Conflicted Vision: A Consideration of Canon and Genre in English-Canadian Literature." *Canadian Canons: Essays in Literary Value*. Ed. Robert Lecker. Toronto: UTP, 1991.

Bergeron, Leandre. "Une heureuse initiative." Rev. of *St-Denys Garneau and Anne Hébert*, ed. and translated by F. R. Scott. *Canadian Literature*, no. 18, 1963, pp. 75–76.

"Between Words and Things." Rev. of *French Poetry Today*, edited by Simon Watson Taylor and Edward Lucie Smith, and *Anthology of Contemporary French Poetry*, edited by Graham Dunstan Martin. *Times Literary Supplement*, 12 Mar. 1972, p. 360.

Blake, Patricia. "A Room of Their Own." Rev. of *A Book of Women Poets from Antiquity to Now*, edited by Aliki and Willis Barnstone. *Time*, vol. 116, no. 25, 1980, pp. 84–85.

Blodgett, E. D. "Towards a Model of Literary Translation in Canada." *TTR: Traduction, Terminologie, Rédaction*, vol. 4, no. 2, 1991, pp. 189–206.

Blodgett, E. D., and Jacques Brault. *Transfigurations*. Saint-Hippolyte, QC: Noroît; Toronto: Buschek, 1998.

Blouin, Louise, and Bernard Pozier, editors. *Poètes québécois: Anthologie*. Trois-Rivières: Écrits des Forges, 1996.

Blouin, Louise, et al., editors. *Esprit de Corps: Québec Poetry of the Late Twentieth Century in Translation*. Winnipeg: The Muses' Company; Trois-Rivières: Écrits des Forges, 1997.

"Book Reflects Canadian Experience." Rev. of *Who Speaks for Canada?*, edited by Desmond Morton and Morton Weinfeld. *Canadian Jewish News*, vol. 28, no. 47, 1998, p. 24.

Bouchard, Denis. *Une lecture d'Anne Hébert: La recherché d'une mythologie*. Montreal: HMH, 1977.

Bourbonnais, Nicole. "Femme Métonymique, femme métaphorique: La poésie d'Anne Hébert et de Renée Vivien." *Atlantis*, vol. 11, no. 2, 1986, pp. 108–14.

Bowles, Gloria. "Becoming Other than Other." *Parnassus: Poetry in Review*, vol. 6, no. 1, 1977, pp. 331–38.

Brochu, André. *Anne Hébert: Le secret de vie et de mort*. Ottawa: Les Presses de l'Université d'Ottawa, 2000.

Busby, Brian. *A Gentleman of Pleasure: One Life of John Glassco. Poet, Memorist, Translator, and Pornographer*. Montréal: McGill-Queens UP, 2011.

Callaghan, Barry. "Mordecai is Back in Town." Rev. of *Canadian Writing Today*, edited by Mordecai Richler. *Toronto Telegram* 10 Oct. 1970, p. 30.

——, editor. *Lords of Winter and Love: A Book of Canadian Love Poems in English and French*. Toronto: Exile, 1983.

——. "The Impassioned Exile of Barry Callaghan." *Books in Canada*, vol. 22, no. 5, 1993, pp. 9–13.

Campbell, Chad. "Interview With Evan Jones." *Maisonneuve.org*. 30 Nov 2012.

"Can. Lit." Rev. of *Canadian Writing Today*, ed. Mordecai Richler. *Times Literary Supplement*, Nov 30 1970, p. 1279.

Capperdoni, Alessandra. "Acts of Passage: Women Writing Translation in Canada." TTR, vol. 20, no. 1, 2007, pp. 245–79.

Carrier, Jean-Guy. "The One-Eyed Ambassadors." Rev. of *Voices from Quebec*, edited by Philip Stratford and Michael Thomas; *Poems of French Canada*, translated by F. R. Scott; and *The Poetry of Modern Quebec*, edited and translated by Fred Cogswell. *Books in Canada*, vol. 6, no. 8, 1977, pp. 22–23.

Casanova, Pascale. *La République Modiale des Lettres*. Paris: Seuil, 1999.

——. *The World Republic of Letters*. Translated by M. B. DeBevoise. Cambridge, MA: Harvard UP, 2004.

Caws, Mary Ann, editor. *The Yale Anthology of Twentieth-Century French Poetry*. New Haven, CT: Yale UP, 2004.

Cellard, Karine. "Sur quelques classiques de l'anthologie québécoise." *Voix et images*, vol. 35, no. 2, 2010, pp. 43–55.

Chapin, Nancy. Rev. of *A Book of Women Poets from Antiquity to Now*, edited by Aliki and Willis Barnstone. *School Library Journal*, no. 27, 1981, p. 162.

Cloutier, Pierre. "Fred Cogswell, *A Second Hundred Poems of Modern Quebec*." Rev. of *A Second Hundred Poems of Modern Quebec*, translated by Fred Cogswell. *Quarry*, vol. 22, no. 2, 1973, pp. 74–75.

Cogswell, Fred, editor and translator. *One Hundred Poems of Modern Quebec*. Fredericton, NB: Fiddlehead, 1970.

——, editor and translator. *A Second Hundred Poems of Modern Quebec*. Fredericton, NB: Fiddlehead, 1971.

——. Rev. of *New: American & Canadian Poetry Magazine* and *The Poetry of French Canada in Translation*, edited John Glassco. *Fiddlehead*, no. 88, 1971, pp. 103–4.

——, editor and translator. *The Poetry of Modern Quebec*. Montreal: Harvest House, 1976.

——. "Strange Capture." *Ellipse*, no. 50, 1993, pp. 14–15.

Cogswell, Fred, and Jo-Anne Elder, editors and translators. *Unfinished Dreams: Contemporary Poetry of Acadie*. Fredericton, NB: Goose Lane, 1990.

Collie, Joanne. "Anne Hébert's *Écriture Féminine*." *British Journal of Canadian Studies*, vol. 3, no. 2, 1988, pp. 285–92.

Colombo, John Robert, editor. *How Do I Love Thee: Sixty Poets of Canada (and Quebec) Select and Introduce Their Favorite Poems from Their Own Work*. Edmonton: Hurtig, 1970.

——, editor. *The Poets of Canada*. Edmonton: Hurtig, 1978.

——, editor and translator. *Selected Translations*. Windsor, ON: Black Moss, 1982.

Cosman, Carol, et al., editors. *The Penguin Book of Women Poets*. New York: Viking, 1979.

Cunningham, John Herbert. Rev. of *French Symbolist Poetry* and *The Yale Anthology of Twentieth-Century French Poetry*. *Raintaxi Review of Books*, Winter, 2008/2009.

Dafoe, Christopher. "Struggling to Support the Muse." Rev. of *To Say the Least*, edited by P. K. Page. *The Vancouver Sun*, 1 Dec. 1979, p. D7.

Damrosch, David. *What is World Literature?* Princeton: Princeton UP, 2003.

Dana, Robert. "Flower Offerings in the Morning." *Poets and Writers*, vol. 26, no. 2, 1998, pp. 28–33.

Davey, Frank. *Louis Dudek & Raymond Souster*. Vancouver: Douglas and McIntyre, 1980.

Daymond, Douglas, and Leslie Monkman, editors. *Literature in Canada*. Vol. 2. Toronto: Gage, 1978.

Deslisle, Jean. Rev. of *Dialogue sur la traduction*, by Anne Hébert and Frank Scott. *Meta*, vol. 20, no. 3, 1975, pp. 228–29.

Diaz-Diocaretz, Myriam. *Translating Poetic Discourse: Questions on Feminist Strategies in Adrienne Rich*. Critical Theory 2. Amsterdam/Philadelphia: John Benjamins, 1985.

Diepeveen, Leonard. "When Did Modernism Begin? Formulating Boundaries in the Modern Anthology." *English Studies in Canada*, vol. 30, no. 1, 2004, pp. 137–56.

Dixon, Michael. "Anthologies: Protocol or Bullram?" Rev. of *The Poets of Canada*, edited by John Robert Colombo; *Fifteen Canadian Poets Plus Five*, edited by Gary Geddes and Phyllis Bruce; and *Literature in Canada*, edited by Douglas Daymond and Leslie Monkman. *Essays on Canadian Writing*, no. 16, 1979/80, pp. 248–52.

Djwa, Sandra. *The Politics of the Imagination: A Life of F. R. Scott*. Toronto: McClelland & Stewart, 1987.

Djwa, Sandra, and R. St. J. Macdonald. *On F. R. Scott: Essays on his Contributions to Law, Literature, and Politics*. Montreal: McGill-Queen's UP, 1983.

Downes, G. V. "Is the Muse Bilingual?" *Meta*, vol. 14, no. 4, 1969, pp. 195–99.

——. *When We Lie Together: Poems from Quebec and Poems by G. V. Downes*. Vancouver: Klanak, 1973.

——. "Hébert in English." Rev. of *Poems by Anne Hébert*, translated by Alan Brown. *Canadian Literature*, no. 71, 1976, pp. 87–89.

Downes, Gwladys. *Out of the Violent Dark*. Victoria, BC: Sono Nis, 1978.

——. "Women Poets in Quebec Society." *The Malahat Review*, no. 63, 1982, pp. 100–110.

——. *House of Cedars*. Victoria: Ekstasis, 1999.

Dudek, Louis, editor. *Poetry of Our Time*. Toronto: MacMillan, 1964.

——. "Ann Hebert Translated: Some Thoughts On Dual Literature in Canada." *Montreal Gazette*, 29 Apr, 1967, p, I9.

Dudek, Louis, and Michael Gnarowski, editors. *The Making of Modern Poetry in Canada*. Toronto: Ryerson, 1967.

Ellenwood, Ray. "Government Funding: the effect on writers, translators and their associations." *Questions of funding, publishing and distribution/Questions d'édition et de diffusion*, edited by I. S. MacLaren and Claudine Potvin. Edmonton: Research Institute for Comparative Literature, University of Alberta, 1989, pp. 77–84.

Elliot, Alistair. "Valériy et cie." Rev. of *20th Century French Poems*, edited by Stephen Romer. *Times Literary Supplement*, 5178, 2002, p. 26.

Émond, Maurice. *Le récit québécois comme fil d'Ariane*. Québec: Nota Bene, 2000.
Engber, Diane. "Evolving a Course on Postcolonial Writings by Women." *NWSA Journal*, vol. 8, no. 1, 1996, pp. 157–70.
Even-Zohar, Itamar. "The Position of Translated Literature within the Literary Polysystem." *Translation and Literature*, edited by James S. Holmes et al. Leuven, Belgium: Acco, 1978, pp. 117–27
——. "Polysystem Theory." *Poetics Today*, vol. 1, 1979, pp. 287–310
Everett, Jane, editor. *In Translation: The Gabrielle Roy-Joyce Marshall Correspondence*. Toronto: U Toronto P, 2005.
——. "Grabrielle Roy traduite." *Gabrielle Roy traduite*, edited by Claude La Charité. Quebec: Nota bene, 2006, p. 15–67.
——. "Anthologies et anthologisations." *Voix et images*, vol. 35, no. 2, 2010, pp. 57–72.
Everett, Janet, and Sophie Marcotte. "De l'anthologie." *Voix et images*, vol. 35, no. 2, 2010, pp. 7–15.
"For Anthologies." *Coda*, vol. 4, no. 3, 1977, p. 23.
Ferry, Anne. *Tradition and the Individual Poem: An Inquiry into Anthologies*. Stanford: Standford UP, 2001.
Francis, Wynne. "20th Century Poets In a New Anthology." Rev. of *Poetry of Our Time*, edited by Louis Dudek. *Montreal Star*, 2 Apr. 1966, supplement 8.
Franklin, Cynthia G. *Writing Women's Communities: The Politics and Poetics of Contemporary Milti-genre Anthologies*. Madison: U Wisconsin P, 1997
Fraser, Keath. "Richler's Canadiana." Rev. of *Canadian Writing Today*, edited by Mordecai Richler. *Canadian Literature*, no. 48, 1971, pp. 89–91.
French, William. "Books and Bookmen." Rev. of *Canadian Writing Today*, edited by Mordecai Richler. *Globe and Mail*, 19 Sept. 1970, p. 18.
——. "Books and Bookmen." Rev. of *To Say the Least*, edited by P. K. Page. *Globe and Mail*, 23 Oct. 1979, p. 13.
Garant, France Nazaire. *Ève et le cheval de grève: Contribution à l'étude de l'imaginaire d'Anne Hébert*. Québec: CRELIQ, 1988.
Garneau, Saint-Denys, and Anne Hébert. *St-Denys Garneau & Anne Hébert*. Translated by F. R. Scott. Vancouver: Klanak, 1962.
Genette, Gerard. *Paratexts: Thresholds of Interpretation*. Translated by Jane E. Lewin. New York, Cambridge UP, 1997.
Gentzler, Edwin. "Translation, Poststructuralism, and Power," *Translation and Power*, edited by Maria Tymoczko and Edwin Gentzler. Amhest: U Massachusetts P, 2002, pp. 195–218.
Glassco, John. "The Opaque Medium." *Meta*, vol. 14, no. 1, 1969, pp. 27–30.
——, editor. *The Poetry of French Canada in Translation*. Toronto: Oxford UP, 1970.
Glenn, Lori Nelson. "Context for the CWILA numbers." *Canadian Women in the Literary Arts*. www.cwila.com.

Gnarowski, Michael. "Introduction to Dudek, l'essentiel." *Louis Dudek: Essays on his Works*, edited by George Hildebrand. Toronto: Guernica, 2001.

Godard, Barbara. "Poems. Anne Hébert." Rev. of *Poems*, translated by Alan Brown. *Waves*, vol. 4, no. 2, 1976, pp. 13–16.

——. Rev. of *Literature in Canada*, edited by Douglas Daymond and Leslie Monkman. *Quill & Quire*, vol. 45, no. 1, 1979, pp. 31–32.

——. "Translations" Rev. of *Anne Hébert: Selected Poems*, translated by Alfred Poulin Jr. et al. *University of Toronto Quarterly*, vol. 59, no. 1, 1989, pp. 84–110

——. "Translating (With) the Speculum." TTR, vol. 4, no. 2, 1991, pp. 85–121.

——, editor. *Collaboration in the Feminine: Writings on Women and Culture from Tessera*. Toronto: Second Story, 1994.

——. "Une littérature en devenir: la réécriture textuelle et le dynamisme du champs littéraire. Les écrivaines québécoises au Canada anglais." *Voix et images*, no. 72, 1999, pp. 495–527.

——. "A Literature in the Making: Rewriting and the Dynamism of the Cultural Field. Quebec Women Writers in English Canada." *Ilha do Desterro*, no. 42, 2002, pp. 49–102.

Godbout, Jacques, and John Robert Colombo, editors. *Poésie/Poetry 64*. Montréal: Éditions du Jour; Toronto: Ryerson, 1963.

Godbout, Patricia. *Traduction littéraire et sociabilité interculturelle au Canada (1950–1960)*. Ottawa: U Ottawa P, 2004.

——. "L'espace du *Dialogue sur la traduction* entre Anne Hébert et Frank Scott." *Cahiers Anne Hébert*, no. 9, 2010, pp. 85–96.

——. "La dialogisme chez Anne Hébert." *Cahiers Anne Hébert*, no. 10, 2011, pp. 56–69.

Gosselin, Michel. "Entrevue avec Anne Hébert." *Cahiers Anne Hébert*, no. 2, 2000, pp. 5–12.

Granbois, Alain. *Selected Poems*. Translated by Peter Miller. Toronto: Contact, 1964.

Grealish, Gerald. Rev. of *The Other Voice: Twentieth Century Women's Poetry in Translation*, edited by Joanna Bankier et al. *Best Seller*, no. 37, 1977, pp. 21.

Grosskurth, Phyllis. "A Troubled Apologia, a Gesture of Hope." Rev. of *Canadian Writing Today*, edited by Mordecai Richler. *Saturday Night*, Oct. 1970, pp. 33–34.

Guy, Chantal. "Anne Hébert, l'édition ultime." *La Presse*, 16 Feb. 2013.

Gwynn, R. S., and Wanda Campbell, editors. *Poetry: A Pocket Anthology*. Canadian Edition. Penguin Academics Series. Toronto: Pearson Education, 2004.

Haeck, Philippe. "Naissance de la poésie moderne au Québec." *Études françaises*, vol. 9, no. 2, 1973, pp. 95–113.

Hallman, Jocelyn. "Tilting *He Drown She in the Sea*: The Archive as Paratext." *Archival Narratives for Canada: Re-Telling Stories in a Changing Landscape*, edited by Kathleen Garay and Christl Verduyn. Blackpoint, NS: Fernwood, 2011, pp. 205–21.

Harvey, Robert. "La modernité comme travail du sujet chez Anne Hébert." *Les cahiers Anne Hébert*, no. 2, 2000, pp. 27–43.

Hayward, Annette and André Lamontagne. "Le Canada anglais: une invention québécoise?" *Voix et images*, no. 72, 1999, pp. 460–79.

Hébert, Anne. *Les songes en équilibre*. Montréal: Éditions de l'Arbre, 1942.

——. *Le Torrent*. Montréal: Beauchemin, 1950.

——. *Le Tombeau des rois*. Québec: Institut littéraire du Québec, 1953.

——. *Les Chambres de bois*. Paris: Éditions du Seuil, 1958.

——. *Poèmes*. Paris: Seuil, 1960.

——. *The Tomb of Kings*. Translated by Peter Miller. Toronto: Contact, 1967.

——. *Kamouraska*. Paris: Seuil, 1970.

——. *The Torrent: Novellas and Short Stories*. Translated by Gwendolyn Moore. Montreal: Harvest House, 1973.

——. *Kamouraska*. Translated by Norman Shapiro. Don Mills, Ont: PaperJacks, 1974.

——. *The Silent Rooms*. Translated by Kathy Mezei. Don Mills, Ont: Musson, 1974.

——. *Les Enfants du sabbat*. Paris: Éditions du Seuil, 1975.

——. *Poems by Anne Hébert*. Translated by Alan Brown. Don Mills: Musson, 1975.

——. *Children of the Black Sabbath*. Translated by Carol Dunlop-Hébert. Don Mills, Ont: Musson, 1977.

——. *Héloïse*. Paris: Éditions du Seuil, 1980.

——. *Les Fous de Bassan*. Paris: Éditions du Seuil, 1982.

——. *Héloïse*. Translated by Sheila Fischman. Toronto: Stoddart, 1982. Toronto: General, 1983.

——. *In the Shadow of the Wind*. Translated by Sheila Fischman. Toronto: General, 1984.

——. *Anne Hébert: Selected Poems*. Translated by Alfred Poulin, Jr. Brockport, NY: BOA, 1987.

——. *Le Premier jardin*. Paris: Éditions du Seuil, 1988.

——. *The First Garden*. Translated by Sheila Fischman. Toronto: Anansi, 1990.

——. *Le jour n'a d'égal que la nuit*. Montréal: Boréal/Seuil, 1992.

——. *Œuvre poétique: 1950–1990*. Montréal: Boréal, 1993.

——. *The Burden of Dreams*. Translated by Sheila Fischman. Toronto: Anansi, 1994.

——. *Day Has No Equal but Night*. Translated by Alfred Poulin Jr. Brockport, NY: BOA, 1994.

——. *Aurélien, Clara, Mademoiselle et le Lieutenant anglais*. Paris: Éditions du Seuil, 1995.

——. *Poèmes pour la main gauche*. Montréal: Boréal, 1997.

——. *Day has no equal but the night*. Translated by Lola Lemire Tostevin. Toronto: Anansi, 1997.

——. *Est-ce que je te dérange?* Paris: Éditions du Seuil, 1998.

——. *Am I disturbing you?* Translated by Sheila Fischman. Toronto: Anansi, 1999.

——. *Un habit de lumière*. Paris: Éditions du Seuil, 1999.

——. *A Suit of Light*. Translated by Sheila Fischman. Toronto: Anansi, 2000.

Hébert, Anne, and Frank Scott. *Dialogue sur la traduction*. Montréal: Bibliothèque québécoise, 2000.

Helwig, David. "Economic Fictions." Rev. of *Canadian Writing Today*, edited by Mordecai Richler. *Books in Canada*, vol. 1, no. 1, 1971, pp. 89–91.

Hewson, Lance, and Jacky Martin. *Redefining Translation: The Variational Approach*. London: Routledge, 1991.

Hoeksema, Thomas. "The Translator's Voice: An Interview with Willis Barnstone." *Translation Review*, no. 6, 1980, pp. 8–12.

Holland, Patrick. Rev. of *The Poetry of Modern Quebec: An Anthology*, editor and translator. Fred Cogswell. *Canadian Book Review Annual* 1976. Dean Tudor et al., editors. Toronto: Peter Martin, 1977, p. 191.

Homel, David, and Sherry Simon, editors. *Mapping Literature: The Art and Politics of Translation*. Montréal: Véhicule, 1988.

Holmes, James S. *Translated! Papers on Literary Translation and Translation Studies*. Approaches to Translation Studies, vol. 7. Amsterdam: Rodpi, 1988.

"How to Define a Canadian, 101." *Maclean's*, vol. 112, no. 3, 1999, p. 13.

Hughes, Siân. "Silk Lining." Rev. of *World Poetry: An Anthology of Verse from Antiquity to Our Time*, edited by Katherine Washburn et al. *Times Educational Supplement*, no. 4268, 1998, pp. 8–9.

Hutchman, Laurence. "Interview with Fred Cogswell." *Ellipse*, no. 68, 2002, pp. 60–71.

Irvine, Dean J. "Translation Incorporation." Rev. of *Esprit de Corps: Québec Poetry of the Late Twentieth Century*, edited by Louise Blouin et al., and *Body Inc,: A Theory of Translation Poetics*, by Pamela Banting. *Canadian Literature*, no. 159, 1998, pp. 169–71.

Jones, D. G. Rev. of *Poems*, by Anne Hébert, translated by Alan Brown. *Queen's Quarterly*, vol. 85, no. 1, 1978, pp. 151–52.

——. "F. R. Scott as Translator." *On F. R. Scott: Essays on His Contribution to Law, Literature, and Politics*, edited by Sandra Djwa and R. St J. Macdonald. Kingston: McGill-Queen's UP, 1983, pp. 160–64.

Jones, Evan, and Todd Swift, editors. *Modern Canadian Poets: An Anthology of Poems in English*. Manchester: Carcanet, 2010.

Johnson, Glen M. "The Teaching Anthology and the Canon of American Literature: Some Notes on Theory in Practice." *The Hospitable Canon: Essays on Literary Play, Scholarly Choice, and Popular Pressures*, edited by Virgil Nemoianu and Robert Royal. Philadelphia: Benjamins, 1991, pp. 111–35.

Judd, Inge. Rev. of *A Book of Women Poets from Antiquity to Now*, edited by Aliki and Willis Barnstone. *Library Journal*, no. 105, 1980, p. 1639.

Juhasz, Suzanne. "A sensibility 'complex, subversive, and heterodox." Rev. of *The Other Voice*, edited by Joanna Bankier et al. *Library Journal*, no. 102, 1977, p. 205.

——. Rev. of *The Penguin Book of Women Poets*, edited by Carol Cosman et al. *Library Journal*, no. 104, 1979, p. 633.

Junkins, Donald, editor. *The Contemporary World Poets*. New York: Harcourt Brace Jovanovich, 1976.

Kelly, Darlene. "Gabrielle Roy and Translator Harry Lorin Binsse: How Their Disputes Shaped The Texts." *Canadian Literature*, no. 187, 2005, pp. 87–102.

Kelly, Peggy. "Anthologies and the Canonization Process: A Case Study of the English-Canadian Literary Field, 1920–1950." *Studies in Canadian Literature*, vol. 25, no. 1, 2000, pp. 73–94.

Kells, Kathleen. "From the First 'Eve' to the New 'Eve': Anne Hébert's Rehabilitation of the Malevolent Female Archetype." *Studies in Canadian Literature*, vol. 14, no. 1, 1989, pp. 99–107.

Kilcup, Karen. "The Poetry and Prose of Recovery Work." *On Anthologies: Politics and Pedagogy*, edited by Jeffrey R. Di Leo. Lincoln: U Nebraska P, 2004, pp. 112–138.

Kiss, Iren *et al*. "The Writer as Translator/The Translator as Writer." *Mapping Literature: The Art and Politics of Translation*, edited by David Homel and Sherry Simon. Montreal: Véhicule, 1988, pp. 15–26.

Klink, Carl F., and R. E. Watters. *Canadian Anthology*. Toronto: Gage, 1955, 1966.

Kogon, Nicolas P. *The Age of Koestler*. Kalamazoo, MI: Practices of the Wind, 1994.

Koustas, Jane. "Quebec Literature in Translation: Loaded Canon." *Quebec Studies*, no. 23, 1997, pp. 29–42.

——. "Translations." Rev. of *Day Has No Equal but the Night*, translated by Lola Lemire Tostevin et al. *University of Toronto Quarterly*, vol. 68, no. 1, 1988/89, pp. 328–44.

Lacoste, Liliane. "Transgressions sexuelles et textuelles dans la poésie d'Anne Hébert." RLA, no. 6, 1994, pp. 116–19.

Lacôte, René. *Anne Hébert*. Paris: Seghers, 1969.

Lamontagne, Marie-Andrée. "Tout Anne Hébert." *Le Devoir*, 23 Feb. 2013.

Lane, M. Travis. "'Heart on Fist': Three Translations." Rev. of *Anne Hébert: Selected Poems*, translated by Alfred Poulin Jr. et al. *Fiddlehead*, no. 164, 1990, pp. 97–103.

Lane-Mercier, Gillian. "Philip Stratford: The Comparatist as Smuggler." *Writing Between the Lines:Portraits of Canadian Anglophone Translators*, edited by Agnes Whitfield. Waterloo, ON: Wilfred Laurier UP, 2006, pp. 75–105.

Larson, Wayne. Rev. of *Who Speaks for Canada*, edited by Desmond Morton and Morton Weinfeld.

Lecker, Robert. *Making it Real: The Canonization of English-Canadian Literature*. Concord, ON: Anansi, 1995.

——. *English-Canadian Literary Anthologies: An Enumerative Bibliography*. Teeswater, ON: Reference, 1997.

——. Rev. of *Modern Canadian Poets* and *Pith & Wry: Canadian Poetry*. *Canadian Literature*. Canlit.ca.

Lecker, Robert, and Jack David, editors. *The Annotated Bibliography of Canada's Major Authors*. Vol. 7. Toronto: ECW, 1979, 1987.

Le Grand, Albert. *Anne Hébert: De l'exil au royaume*. Montréal: Presses de l'Université de Montréal, 1967.

L'Heureux, J. M. "Translating French-Canadian Poetry." Rev. of *The Poetry of French Canada in Translation*, edited by John Glassco, and *One Hundred Poems of Modern Quebec*, edited and translated by Fred Cogswell. *Canadian Forum*, vol. 50, no. 3, 1970, pp. 182–83.

Lefevere, André. *Translation, Rewriting and the Manipulation of Literary Fame*. London: Routledge, 1992.

Lemieux, Pierre-Hervé. "Le Tombeau des rois." *Dictionnaire des œuvres Littéraires du Québec*. Tome III. Montréal: Fides, 1978, pp. 1001–1006.

Levenson, Christopher. "Ironic Fairness and Other Qualities." Rev. of *To Say the Least*, edited by P. K. Page et al. *CV/II*, vol. 5, no. 3, 1981, 24–25.

Lianeri, Alexandra. "On Defining Norms and Laws: A Western Discourse on Translation Production?" In Workshop Conference: Translations and Translation Theories East and West, Papers from Workshop 1: Basic Issues In The Intercultural Study Of Translation. University College London, 9–10 July 2001. www.soas.ac.uk/Literatures/satranslations/Lianeri.pdf. Accessed 15 July 2006.

Lim, Shirley Geok-Lin. "Welcome Presences, Unwelcome Absences." *The Women's Review of Books*, vol. 7, no. 10/11, 1990, pp. 15–16.

Lista, Michael. "Michael Lista on Poetry: It's Our Critics, Not Our Poets, Who Don't Get It." *National Post*, 26 Nov. 2010. arts.nationalpost.com.

Lynes, Jeanette. "Gwladys Downes." *Canadian Writers, 1920–1959*. Second series. Dictionary of Literary Biography, vol. 88, edited by W. H. New. Detroit, London: Bruccoli Clark Layman, 1989, pp. 42–44.

"Maisy's Best Books of 2011." *Maisonneuve*. maisonneuve.org. 4 Jan 2012.

Major, Jean-Louis. *Anne Hébert et le miracle de la parole*. Montréal: Presses de l'Université de Montréal, 1976.

Melançon, Robert. "Beneficial Resistance." *Mapping Literature: The Art and Politics of Translation*, edited by David Homel and Sherry Simon. Montreal: Véhicule, 1988, pp. 20–23.

Marchand, Pierre. "À propos de la traduction du 'Tombeau des rois.'" *Meta*, vol. 21, no. 2, 1976, pp. 155–60.

Marcotte, Gilles. "'Le Tombeau des Rois.'" Rev. of *Le Tombeau des rois*, by Anne Hébert. *Le Devoir*, 9 May 1953.

Marshall, Joyce. "The Writer Escaping Herself." *Mapping Literature: The Art and Politics of Translation*, edited by David Homel and Sherry Simon. Montréal: Véhicule, 1988, pp. 18–19.

Martin, Graham Dunstan, editor. *Anthology of Contemporary French Poetry*. Edinburgh: Edinburgh UP, 1972.

Martin, Paul. "Re: Producing Culture(s): The Politics of Knowledge Production and the Teaching of the Literatures of Canada." Diss. University of Alberta, 2001.

——. *Sanctioned Ignorance: The Politics of Knowledge Production and the Teaching of the Literatures of Canada*. Edmonton: U Alberta P, 2013.

Martindale, Sheila. "Richard Wollatt." *Canadian Author and Bookman*, vol. 67, no. 4, 1992, p. 17.

Maugey, Axel. *Poésie et société au Québec (1937–1970)*. Québec: Presses de l'Université Laval, 1972.

McGann, Jerome. *The Textual Condition*. Princeton: Princeton UP, 1991.

McGuinness, Patrick. "Not Many Belgians." *Times Educational* Supplement, no. 5332, 2005, p. 18.

McElhiney, Annette Bennington. Rev. of *Longman Anthology of World Literature by Women: 1875–1975*. *Women's Studies International Forum*, vol. 14, no. 4, 1991, p. 375.

McLaren, Leah. "Rescuing Canadian Poetry from International Obscurity." *Globe and Mail*. globeandmail.com. 24 Nov 2010.

Merler, Grazia. "Vita Nova." Rev. of *Le Jour n'a d'égal que la nuit* by Anne Hébert. *Canadian Literature*, no. 140, 1994, pp. 110–11.

Mezei, Kathy. "*Poems of French Canada* translated by F. R. Scott." Rev. of *Poems of French Canada*, translated by F. R. Scott. *Canadian Literature*, no. 79, 1978, pp. 103–106.

——. "A Bridge of Sorts: The Translation of Quebec Literature into English." *The Yearbook of English Studies*, no. 15, 1985, pp. 201–26.

——. "The Question of Gender in Translation: Examples from Denise Boucher and Anne Hébert: A Corollary to Evelyne Voldeng's Trans lata latus (*Tessera*, Number 1)." *Canadian Fiction Magazine*, no. 57, 1986, pp. 136–41.

——. *Bibliography of Criticism on English and French Literary Translations in Canada*. Ottawa: U Ottawa P, 1988.

——. "Speak White: Translation as a Vehicle of Assimilation in Quebec." *Culture in Transit: Translating the Literature of Quebec*, edited by Sherry Simon. Montreal: Véhicule, 1995, pp. 133–48.

Mierau, Maurice. "'Modern Canadian Poets': An Interview with the Editors." *Winnipeg Review*, no. 2, 2011. Nov 26 2013.

Mooney, Jacob McArthur. Rev. of *Modern Canadian Poets*. *Globe and Mail*, 8 Apr. 2011. Globeandmail.com.

Morgan, Edwin. Rev. of *World Poetry: An Anthology of Verse from Antiquity to Our Time*, edited by Katherine Washburn et al. *Translation and Literature*, vol. 8, no. 2, 1999, pp. 273–76.

Moritz, Albert. "Hébert with Anglo-Saxon Flair." Rev. of *Poems by Anne Hébert*, translated by Alfred Poulin Jr. *Books in Canada*, vol. 9, no. 9, 1980, p. 20.

Morton, Desmond, and Morton Weinfeld, editors. *Who Speaks for Canada?: Words That Shape a Country*. Toronto: McClelland & Stewart, 1998.

Muratori, Fred. Rev. of *World Poetry: An Anthology of Verse from Antiquity to Our Time*, edited by Katherine Washburn et al. *Library Journal*, no. 123, 1998, p. 75.

Murray, Rona. "Four Women Poets." Rev. of *Out of the Violent Dark*, by Gwladys Downes et al. *Event*, vol. 11, no. 1, 1982, pp. 152–57.

Nelson, Cary. "The Economic Challenges to Anthologies." *On Anthologies: Politics and Pedagogy*, edited by Jeffrey R. Di Leo. Lincoln: U Nebraska P, 2004, pp. 170–185.

New, W. H. "Contradicting 1998." *Canadian Literature*, no. 163, 1999, pp. 212–20.

Oates, Joyce Carol. Rev. of *The Penguin Book of Women Poets*, edited by Joanna Bankier et al. *The New Republic*, no. 108, 1979, pp. 28–30.

O'Connor, John J. "Translations." Rev. of *The Poetry of Modern Quebec: An Anthology*, edited and translated by Fred Cogswell et al. *University of Toronto Quarterly*, vol. 46, no. 4, 1977, pp. 399–415.

——. "Translations." Rev. of *Voices from Quebec, et al*. *University of Toronto Quarterly*, vol. 47, no. 4, 1978, pp. 381–395.

——. "Translations." Rev. of *Anne Hébert: Poems*, translated by Alfred Poulin Jr. et al. *University of Toronto Quarterly*, vol. 50, no. 4, 1981, pp. 75–97.

O'Driscoll, Dennis. "Going a-roving." Rev. of *World Poetry: An Anthology of Verse from Antiquity to Our Time*, edited by Katherine Washburn et al. *Times Literary Supplement*, 12 June 1998, p. 24.

O'Driscoll, Michael, and Edward Bishop. "Archiving 'Archiving,'" *English Studies in Canada*, vol. 30, no. 1, 2004, pp. 1–16.

Ondaatje, Michael. *La Danse Eliminatoire*. Translated by Lola Lemire Tostevin. London, ON: Brick, 1991.

O'Rourke, David. "Barry Callaghan." *The Oxford Companion to Canadian Literature*. Second edition. Edited by Eugene Benson and William Toye. Toronto: Oxford UP, 1997, p. 163.

Pagé, Pierre. *Anne Hébert*. Montréal: Fides, 1965.

Page, P. K. *To Say The Least: Canadian Poets from A to Z*. Toronto: Press Porcépic, 1979.

Palattella, John. "The Illusion of Inclusion." *The Nation*, 27 Dec. 2004, pp. 34–37.

Pallister, Janis, editor. *Sinuous Laces: A Sampler of French Canadian Women Poets*. Bowling Green, OH: Presse Orphique, 1986.

Pallister, Janis L. "Thanatos and Logos in the Poetry of Anne Hébert." *The Art and Genius of Anne Hébert: Essays on Her Works: Night and Day Are One.* Edited by Janis L. Pallister. Madison, NJ: Fairleigh Dickinson UP, 2001, pp. 139–45.

Paustian, Shirley I. *Teacher's Handbook to the Oxford Anthology of Canadian Literature.* Toronto: Oxford UP, 1982.

Paz, Octavio. *The Sun Stone.* Translated by Peter Miller. Toronto: Contact, 1963.

Piette, Adam. Rev. of *The Yale Anthology of Twentieth-Century Poetry. Translation and Literature*, vol. 15, no. 1, 2006, pp. 136–142.

Phillips, Adam. "In Praise of the cul-de-sac." Rev. of *20th-Century French Poems*, edited Stephen Romer. *The Guardian*, 7 June 2002.

Pople, Ian. Rev. of *Modern Canadian Poets. The Manchester Review*, 12 Dec 2010. themanchesterreview.co.uk.

Popovic, Pierre. *La contradiction du poème: poésie et discours social au Québec de 1948–1953.* Montreal: Balzac, 1992.

Quinn, Patrick. "French Connection." Rev. of *20th-Century French Poems*, edited by Stephen Romer. *PN Review*, no. 147, 2002, pp. 74–75.

Relke, Diana M. A. Rev. of *Longman Anthology of World Literature by Women. Ariel*, vol. 23, no. 2, 1992, pp. 128–30.

Rev. of *Anthology of Contemporary French Poetry*, edited by Graham Dunstan Martin. *Choice*, no. 10, 1973, p. 1596.

Rev. of *The Contemporary World Poets*, edited by Donald Junkins. *Choice*, no. 13, 1976, p. 811.

Rev. of *The Other Voice: Twentieth Century Women's Poetry in Translation*, edited by Carol Cosman et al. *Choice*, no. 14, 1977, p. 675.

Richler, Mordecai, editor. *Canadian Writing Today.* Harmondsworth: Penguin, 1970.

Richmond, John. "Behind the Times with Canadian Writing." Rev. of *Canadian Writing Today*, edited by Mordecai Richler. *Montreal Star*, 12 Sept, 1970, p. 72.

Rièse, Laure. Rev. of *Twelve Modern French-Canadian Poets*, edited and translated by G. R. Roy. *Canadian Forum*, no. 38, 1959, p. 286.

Robert, Guy. *La poétique du songe: Introduction à l'œuvre d'Anne Hébert.* Montréal: AGEUM, 1962.

Roht, Toivo. "The Problems and Work of Translators." Rev. of *The Tomb of Kings*, translated by Peter Miller et al. *Culture*, vol. 29, no. 3, 1968, pp. 254–59.

Romer, Stephen, editor. *20th-Century French Poems.* London: Faber and Faber, 2002.

Rose, Marilyn Gaddis. "Hébert's "Le Tombeau des Rois" (1953): A Modernist Manifesto." *Translation Perspectives*, no. 3, 1987, pp. 32–39.

——. Rev. of *Selected Poems by Anne Hébert*, translated by Alfred Pouline Jr. *Québec Studies* no. 8, 1989, pp. 132–33.

Rosenbluth, Sally. Rev. of *The Other Voice: Twentieth Century Women's Poetry in Translation*, edited by Joanna Bankier et al. *The University of Windsor Review*, vol. 13, no. 1, 1977, pp. 93–95.

Roy, Gabrielle. *The Tin Flute*. Translated by Alan Brown. Toronto: McClelland & Stewart, 1980.

Roy, G. R. editor. *Twelve Modern French Canadian Poets*. Toronto: Ryerson, 1958.

Roy, G. Ross, and Michael Gnarowski. "Canadian Poetry: A Supplemental Bibliography." *Culture*, no. 25, 1964, pp. 160–70.

Roy, Lucille. *Entre la lumière et l'ombre: L'univers poétique d'Anne Hébert*. Sherbrooke: Editions Naaman, 1984.

Rubin, Merle. "Universe of Verse in One Volume of Collected Poetry." Rev. of *World Poetry: An Anthology of Verse from Antiquity to Our Time*, edited by Katherine Washburn et al. *Christian Science Monitor*, vol. 90, no. 167, 1998, p. B8.

Russell, Delbert W. *Anne Hébert*. Boston: Twayne, 1983.

Ruthig, Ingrid. Rev. of *Modern Canadian Poets*. *Northern Poetry Review*. northernpoetry review.com.

Saxon, Wolfgang. "Katherine Washburn, 57, Editor Known for Poetry Anthology." *New York Times*, 14 Mar. 2000, p. B9.

Scott, Chris. "Oxon Drawn Bandwagon." Rev. of *The Oxford Anthology of Canadian Literature*, edited by Robert Weaver and William Toye. *Books in Canada*, vol. 2, no. 2, 1973, pp. 5–6.

Shaw, Mary Lewis. *The Cambridge Introduction to French Poetry*. Cambridge: Cambridge UP, 2003.

Shollar, Barbara et. al. "Letters." *The Women's Review of Books*, vol. 8, no. 3, 1990, pp. 4–5.

Shouldice, Larry. "Anne Hébert Translated." Rev. of *Poems by Anne Hébert*, translated by Alan Brown. *Matrix*, vol. 2, no. 1, 1976, pp. 22–23.

Simon, Sherry. "Volontés des savoir: Les prefaces aux traductions canadiennes." *Prefaces and Literary Manifestoes/Préfaces et manifestes littéraires*, edited by E. D. Blodgett and A. G. Purdy. Edmonton: Research Institute for Comparative Literature, U Alberta, 1990, pp. 98–110.

——. "Introduction." *Culture in Transit: Translating the Literature of Quebec*, edited by Sherry Simon. Montréal: Véhicule, 1995, pp. 7–15.

——. *Translating Montreal: Episodes in the Life of a Divided City*. Montréal and Kingston: McGill-Queen's UP, 2006.

Skelton, Robin. "Canadian Poetry?" Rev. of *St-Denis Garneau & Anne Hébert*, translated by F. R. Scott, et al. *Tamarack Review*, no. 28, 1963, pp. 71–82.

Slater, Howard. "The Dishonour of Poets." *Mute*, vol. 1, no. 29, 2000.

Slote, Daniel. "Literary Translation. A Few Remarks." Rev. *Poems by Anne Hébert*, translated by Alan Brown. *Meta*, vol. 21, no. 2, 1976, pp. 165–68.

——. "Translating Rimbaud's 'Illuminations': Games with Words." *Meta*, vol. 23, no. 1, 1978, pp. 86–96.

——. "Comment on Sharma." *Meta*, vol. 39, no. 2, 1994, pp. 313–15.

Smart, Patricia. "La poésie d'Anne Hébert: Une perspective féministe." *L'autre lecture: La critique au féminin et les textes québécois*." Tome 1. Ed. Lori Saint-Martin. Montréal: XYZ éditeur, 1992.

——. *Écrire dans la maison du père*. Montréal: Québec/Amérique, 1988.

——. *Writing in the Father's House: The Emergence of the Feminine in the Quebec Literary Tradition*. Toronto: U Toronto P, 1991.

Smith, A. J. M., editor. *The Book of Canadian Poetry*. 3rd ed. Toronto: Gage, 1957.

——, editor. *The Oxford Book of Canadian Verse: In English and French*. Toronto: Oxford UP, 1960.

Smith, Donald. *L'écrivain devant son œuvre*. Montréal: Québec/Amérique, 1983.

Smith, Martha Nell. "The Human Touch Software of the Highest Order: Revisiting Editing as Interpretation." *Textual Cultures: Texts, Contexts, Interpretation*, vol. 2, no. 1, 2007, pp. 1–15.

Stanton, Domna C., editor. *The Defiant Muse: French Feminist Poems from the Middle Ages to the Present*. New York: The Feminist Press, 1986.

Starnino, Carmine. "The Death of Modern Canadian Poetry." *The Véhicule Press Blog*. Véhicule Press. 8 Apr. 2011.

Stevens, Peter. *The McGill Movement*. Toronto: Ryerson, 1969.

Stewart, James. "Our Students Need the 'Sun of History'; Immersed in a sea of American culture, many here are growing up without a grand idea of what it means to be Canadian." *Toronto Star*, 10 Mar. 2000, p. 1.

Stratford, Philip. "French-Canadian Literature in Translation." *Meta*, vol. 13, no. 4, 1968, pp. 180–187,

——. "Circle, Straight Line, Ellipse." Rev. of *Poetry of French Canada in Translation*, edited by John Glassco, and *One Hundred Poems of Modern Quebec*, by Fred Cogswell. *Canadian Literature*, no. 49, 1971, pp. 88–91.

——. *All the Polarities: Comparative Studies in Contemporary Canadian Novels in French and English*. Toronto: ECW Press, 1986.

Stratford, Philip, and Michael Thomas, editors. *Voices from Québec: An Anthology of Translations*. Toronto: Van Nostrand Reinhold, 1977.

Sugars, Cynthia. "Reading Between the Poles: The 'English' French-Canadian Canon." *Changing Representations of Minorities East and West*, edited by Larry E. Smith and John Rieder. Honolulu: College of Languages, Linguistics and Literature, University of Hawaii, with East-West Center, 1996, pp. 113–30.

Swift, Todd. "Zach Tough." *Eyewear*. 23 Apr. 2012. toddswift.blogspot.com.

Sypnowich, Peter. “Canadian Writing Today is Yesterday’s News.” Rev. of *Canadian Writing Today*, edited by Mordecai Richler. *Toronto Daily Star*, 25 Aug. 1970, p. 24.

Tostevin, Lola Lemire. *The Colour of Her Speech*. Toronto: Coach House, 1982.

——. *Gyno Text*. Toronto: Underwhich, 1983.

——. *Frog Moon*. Dunvegan, ON: Cormerant, 1994.

——. *Subject to Criticism*. Stratford, ON: Mercury, 1995.

Tougas, Gérald. Rev. of *St-Denys Garneau and Anne Hébert*, translated by F. R. Scott. *Queen’s Quarterly*, vol. 70, no. 3, 1963, pp. 449–50.

Trehearne, Brian. *The Montreal Forties: Modernist Poetry in Transition*. Toronto: U Toronto P, 1999.

Turner, Alison. “Anthologizing Postcolonial Francophone Literature.” *Inquire*, vol. 1, no. 1, 2011.

Tymoczko, Maria, and Edwin Gentzler, editors. *Translation and Power*. Amhest: U Massachusetts P, 2002.

Urquhart, Jane. “Poetry: *Lords of Winter and Love*.” Rev. of *Lords of Winter and Love*, edited by Barry Callaghan. *Quill & Quire*, vol. 50, no. 6, 1984, p. 46.

Vendler, Helen. “Poetical Correctness.” Rev. of *World Poetry: An Anthology of Verse from Antiquity to Our Time*, edited by Katherine Washburn et al. *New Republic*, vol. 218, no. 24, 1998, pp. 34–37.

Venuti, Lawrence. *The Translator’s Invisibility: A History of Translation*. London: Routledge, 1995.

——. “Translation, History, Narrative.” *Meta*, vol. 50, no. 3, 2005, pp. 800–15.

Voisin, Marcel. “Le dialogue auteur-traducteur au service de la poésie et de la culture.” *Cahiers Internationaux de Symbolisme*, no. 92–94, 1999, pp. 205–12.

Voldeng, Évelyne. “Literal Translation.” Rev. of *Anne Hébert: Selected Poems*, translated by Alfred Poulin Jr. *Canadian Literature*, no. 130, 1991, pp. 175–77.

——. *Lectures de l’imaginaire: Huit femmes poètes des deux cultures canadiennes (1940–1980)*. Orléans, ON: Éditions David, 2000.

Walker, David. “Exorcising Demons.” Rev. *Poems by Anne Hébert*, translated by Alan Brown. *Canadian Forum*, no. 56, 1976, pp. 38–39.

Washburn, Katherine, et al., editors. *World Poetry: An Anthology of Verse from Antiquity to Our Time*. New York: Norton/BOMC, 1998.

Watchel, Eleanor. “Rattle in Your Brain.” Rev. of *To Say the Least*, edited by P. K. Page. *The Vancouver Sun*, 22 Feb. 1980, p. 38L.

Watteyne, Natalie, editor. *Œuvres complètes d’Anne Hébert, Tome I—Poésie suivi de Dialogue sur la traduction à propos du Tombeau des rois*. Montreal: Presses Université de Montréal, 2013.

Weaver, Kathleen. “Magda Portal: Translation-in-Progress.” *Translation Review*, no. 32/33, 1990, p. 41–43.

Weaver, Robert and William Toye, editors. *The Oxford Anthology of Canadian Literature*. Toronto: Oxford UP, 1973.

Weir, Lorraine. "'Fauna of Mirrors': The Poetry of Hébert and Atwood." *Ariel*, vol. 10, no. 3, 1979, pp. 99–113.

Wells, Zachariah. "A Claptrap Canon: On the Modern Canadian Poets Anthology." *Contemporary Poetry Review*, 20 Apr. 2012. cprw.com.

"Where are the Modern Poets?" Rev. of *Poetry of Our Time*, edited by Louis Dudek. *The Ottawa Journal*, 12 Mar. 1966, p. 6.

Whiteman, Bruce. "Raymond Souster." *Canadian Writers and Their Works*. Poetry Series, no. 5, edited by Robert Lecker and Jack David. Toronto: ECW, 1983, pp. 237–54.

Wilss, Wolfram. *The Science of Translation: Problems and Methods*. Tubingen, Germany: Gunter Narr, 1982.

Wolfe, Morris. "The Anthology Game: Who's In, Who's Out." Rev. of *The Oxford Anthology of Canadian Literature*, edited by Robert Weaver and William Toye. *Saturday Night*, May 1973, pp. 39–40.

Wonham, Jonathan. "French Poetry by Women." *Connaissances*, 18 Mar. 2006.

Woodcock, George. "Robert Weaver." *The Oxford Companion to Canadian Literature*. Second edition. Edited by Eugene Benson and William Toye. Toronto: Oxford UP, 1997, p. 1172.

Woodcock, George, and Rosemary Sullivan. "P. K. Page." *The Oxford Companion to Canadian Literature*. Second edition. Edited by Eugene Benson and William Toye. Toronto: Oxford UP, 1997, pp. 898–900.

Woodsworth, Judith. "Writers and their Translators: the Case of Mavis Gallant." TTR, vol. 1, no. 2, 1988, pp. 47–57.

Woollatt, Richard, and Raymond Souster, editors. *Poems of a Snow-Eyed Country*. Don Mills, ON: Academic Press Canada, 1980.

"The Yale Anthology of Twentieth-Century French Poetry." *Yale Press Website*. http://yalebooks.com/book/9780300143188/yale-anthology-twentieth-century-french-poetry. Date accessed 6 June 2016.

Young, Vernon. "Modernism Rewritten." Rev. of *The Contemporary World Poets*, edited by Donald Junkins. *American Poetry Review*, no. 6, 1977, pp. 17–19.

Interviews and Personal Communications:

Bernard Pozier. E-mails to author, February 11, 2004.

Daniel Sloate. Interview in Montreal, February 19, 2003.

Evan Jones. E-mails to author, October 6, 2013.

Graham Dunstan Martin. Letters to author, February 23, 2004–April 20, 2005.

Janis L. Pallister. E-mails to author, June 14–16, 2004.

Jo-Anne Elder. Interview in Fredericton, July 20, 2004. E-mails to author, September 4, 2005.

John Robert Colombo. E-mails to author, March 17, 2005.

Leslie Monkman. E-mails to author, March 13, 2005.

Lola Lemire Tostevin. E-mails to author, February 5–6, 2004.

Morton Weinfeld. E-mails to author, February 17, 2005.

P. K. Page. E-mails to author, March 30, 2005.

Wanda Campbell. E-mails to author, October 4, 2013

William Toye. Letter to author, February 9, 2005.

Willis Barnstone. Interview in Bloomington, October 14, 2005.

Index

CANADIAN LITERATURE COLLECTION /
COLLECTION DE LITTÉRATURE CANADIENNE

Series Editor: Dean Irvine

The Canadian Literature Collection / Collection de la littérature canadienne (CLC) is a series of nineteenth- to mid-twentieth-century literary texts produced in critical editions. All texts selected for the series were either out of print or previously unpublished. Each text appears in a print edition with a basic apparatus (critical introduction, explanatory notes, textual notes, and a statement of editorial principles) together with an expanded web-based apparatus (which may include alternate versions, expanded textual notes, previous editions, correspondence, photographs, source materials, and other related texts by the author).

The Literary Studies sub-series of the CLC features monographs and edited collections that complement the historical focus of these critical editions.

Previous titles in this collection

Laurie Kruk, *Double-Voicing the Canadian Short Story*, 2016

Bart Vautour and Emily Robins Sharpe (editors), *Meet Me on the Barricades* by Charles Yale Harrison, 2016

Kailin Wright (editor), *The God of Gods: A Canadian Play* by Carroll Aikins, 2016

Miguel Mota and Paul Tiessen (editors), Chris Ackerley and David Large (annotations), *The 1940 Under the Volcano* by Malcolm Lowry, 2015

Robert D. Denham (author), *Northrop Frye and Others: Twelve Writers Who Helped Shape His Thinking*, 2015

Emily Robins Sharpe (editor), *Hugh Garner's Best Stories*, 2015

Bart Vautour (editor), *This Time a Better Earth* by Ted Allan, 2015

Patrick A. McCarthy (editor), Chris Ackerley (notes), and Vik Doyen (foreword), *In Ballast to the White Sea* by Malcolm Lowry, 2014

For a complete list of our titles in this collection, see:
https://press.uottawa.ca/series/french-and-canadian-studies/canadian-literature-collection.html